The Best Butter
in the World

J. Sainsbury

THE FIRM THAT SELLS THE
BEST BUTTER IN THE WORLD

Will Open their NEW BRANCH

48, TAVERN ST., IPSWICH

TELEPHONE 2129

On Friday, Oct. 10th

WITH A NUMBER OF

SPECIAL OFFERS

AND A

GRAND DISPLAY

IN ALL DEPARTMENTS

Groceries	Fresh Meat
Provisions	Poultry
Dairy Produce	Cooked Meats

J. SAINSBURY

THE WORKING MAN'S FRIEND

P.T.O.

The Best Butter in the World

A History of Sainsbury's

by

Bridget Williams

EBURY PRESS
LONDON

First published in 1994

Text and illustrations copyright (unless otherwise specified)
© J Sainsbury plc 1994

Published exclusively for J Sainsbury plc by
Ebury Press
Random House
20 Vauxhall Bridge Road
London SW1V 2SA

A CIP catalogue record for this book is available from the
British Library.

ISBN 009 1821371

Editor for J Sainsbury plc   Nicholas Salmon
Editor for Ebury Press   Alison Wormleighton
Design   Harry Green

Colour separations by Magnacraft, London
Printed and bound in Italy by New Interlitho Italia S.p.a., Milan

FRONTISPIECE   A handbill advertising the opening of Sainsbury's
branch at 48 Tavern Street, Ipswich, on 10th October 1930.

Contents

*T*he achievements of the past 125 years of our Company would not have been possible without the vision of the founders, their commitment to quality and their belief that they should provide their customers with unrivalled value. Each generation that has followed them has striven to fulfil those same objectives.

Our growth, from one small shop to being the nation's largest food retailer, is evidence of the soundness and success of such priorities.

However, that success has only been achieved because of the hard work, loyalty, and ability of our staff. It is right, therefore, that this history should be dedicated to all who have worked for Sainsbury's. What we have achieved is the sum of the personal achievement of all our staff who have striven so hard to fulfil the vision of the founders over these 125 fast-changing years.

LORD SAINSBURY OF PRESTON CANDOVER, KG

Foreword

The story of how my great-grandparents founded Sainsbury's, and how the business grew over the next 125 years, is one of both consistent values and continuous innovation. When the founders set up their tiny business in Drury Lane, an extremely poor part of London at that time, they wanted to give their customers 'the best butter in the world' at prices they could afford. This philosophy of giving customers the best value for money is a theme which runs through the whole history of the Company. The sign on the shopfront of the store we opened in Islington in 1882 read 'Quality Perfect, Prices Lower', and in recent years the same approach has been encapsulated in the slogan 'Good Food Costs Less at Sainsbury's'. A commitment to excellent customer service, an obsessive concern with food hygiene, and a belief that well-trained and highly motivated people are the key to successful food retailing, are also themes that occur throughout our history.

The values of the business have been consistent, but throughout the history of the Company there has been a 'passion to innovate', and as economic, social and technological changes have impacted food retailing, the Company has changed to take account of them. Whether it was new products, advances in food technology, changes in transport, the invention of the computer, or the development of self-service trading, the Company has always been in the lead in seeking new ways to serve the customer better.

The history of the Company is not only a story of consistent vision, but also one about the skill and enterprise of the thousands of people who invented modern food retailing. We hope it will be of interest not only to social historians, but also to all those interested in entrepreneurship, innovation and management skills. As a result of this process of continuous innovation, the tiny business set up in Drury Lane has grown into an international company which now serves over ten million customers each week and employs over 125,000 people.

Today, the forces of change in food retailing are as great as ever. A very discriminating customer is looking for high quality, authentic products from all over the world, and value for money. Food technology is advancing rapidly and information technology is opening up major new opportunities. Environmental issues are presenting new challenges, and the need to involve staff and give them high levels of training is as important as ever. In these circumstances, the Company will have to innovate as rapidly as it has done in the past whilst maintaining the essential values which are described in this history of its first 125 years.

DAVID SAINSBURY, *Chairman*

QUALITY PERFECT, PRICES LOWER

J. SAINSBURY FOR BEST PROVISIONS

KEEP THE SHOPS WELL LIT

*Chapel Street, Islington, c1895.
At the time this photograph was
taken, Sainsbury's had four
branches in the street.*

Quality perfect, prices lower

'Sainsbury, John, Dairyman.' This entry in the 1870 edition of *Kelly's Post Office Street Directory* recorded the existence of a new small business at 173 Drury Lane, Holborn, London. Sainsbury's beginnings were so modest that there is no record of the date on which the business was founded and no detailed description of the first shop. We do not even know much about the John Sainsbury who was named in the street directory entry; although he rose from poverty to considerable wealth in less than twenty years, he seldom spoke of his early life and left only circumstantial evidence of why his business prospered so spectacularly.

The date of Sainsbury's foundation is generally taken to be 20th April 1869. This was the day when John James Sainsbury married Mary Ann Staples at the parish church of St Giles-in-the-Fields, Holborn. It is probable that the Drury Lane shop opened earlier than this but the choice of the young couple's wedding day recognises the equal part played by Mary Ann in running the Drury Lane shop during its first few years. When they married, Mary Ann was nineteen and John James twenty-four.

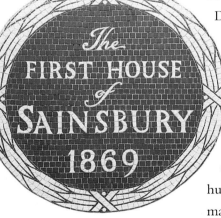

A mosaic plaque from Sainsbury's first shop at 173 Drury Lane.

John James and Mary Ann Sainsbury, the founders, pictured on the wedding day of their eldest son, John Benjamin, 6th January 1896.

The young John James Sainsbury

The story began nearly twenty-five years earlier, on 12th June 1844, when John James was born at 5 Oakley Street, Lambeth, London. His mother, Elizabeth, registered the birth just over three weeks later and, like many of her humble background, was unable to write her own name. Instead she made her mark under the watchful eye of the registrar. The new baby was the fourth and last child of Elizabeth and her husband John, who already had three daughters: Elizabeth Sarah, aged three and three-quarters, Eliza Jane, aged two and a half, and Margaret Maria, aged eighteen months.

John Sainsbury senior was a craftsman who was described on his children's birth certificates as an ornament and picture frame maker. No records survive of the family's circumstances except that they rented rooms in an impoverished part of Lambeth. It was in such rooms that tragedy struck in May 1846 when little Margaret Maria, aged three, died. A post-mortem revealed that the cause of death was 'phthisis' (probably pulmonary tuberculosis). This time it was the register of deaths which Elizabeth Sainsbury marked with her 'X'.

Young John James took his first job at the age of fourteen – with a grocer in the New Cut – within a few hundred yards of his birthplace. It is not clear whether he

A studio portrait of John James taken in the early 1870s at around the time he opened his second shop, at 159 Queen's Crescent, Kentish Town.

stayed at school until this time or whether he helped his father at home. The children of most poor families left school by the age of ten, as elementary education was neither free nor compulsory. It is possible that John James stayed on as a 'monitor', keeping order among the younger children. The New Cut grocer's business was probably busy, since the street market there was one of London's largest, but because of the poverty of the area it would have sold only a limited range of goods. It was therefore a step up when John James secured a job with Henry Jeans, an oil and colour merchant, at 4/5 Green's End, Woolwich.

In November 1862, John Sainsbury senior contracted bronchitis. Two months later this turned to pneumonia, and on 31st January 1863 he died, aged fifty-three. His death was a severe blow to his wife, Elizabeth, who by now was forty-five years old, his daughters – Elizabeth Sarah and Eliza Jane, aged twenty-two and twenty-one respectively – and John James, who was now eighteen years old. Added to the sorrow of bereavement must have been renewed anxiety about money. John James was probably not yet earning the wages of a grown man, and may even have lived in with Henry Jeans, in which case he would have had very little spare money to give to his mother. There is little doubt that the three women must all have had to earn their livings. Soon, however, Eliza Jane's health began to fail. She contracted tuberculosis, as her infant sister had done twenty years earlier, and died on Christmas Eve 1866.

Despite these sorrows, John James was making good progress. Henry Jeans's business was a substantial one, selling over two thousand articles: 'everything from chicory to gunpowder'. As the Jeans family had previously been butchers he may even have sold meat, although this was not usual in oil and colour shops. Traditionally the latter sold oils of all kinds – lamp oil, cooking oil, linseed oil and petroleum – together with gums and resins and blocks of solid colour from which paints could be ground and mixed.

It was also common for this type of shopkeeper to sell basic groceries like rice, dried fruits and dried meats, as well as household goods including soap, starch and candles. Serving these items involved weighing, measuring and packing each one. The exceptionally wide range of goods sold by Henry Jeans provided John James with valuable experience in handling and storing goods as well as business skills such as stocktaking and finance.

By the late 1860s young John James had moved jobs again, this time to 57 Strutton Ground, Victoria, where he worked for George Gillett, another oil and colour merchant. It was here that he met Mary Ann Staples, his future wife. She was employed by Tom Haile, who kept a dairy shop at 32 Strutton Ground.

Mary Ann's influence

Mary Ann Staples's background was similar to her husband's. She was born on 30th June 1849, the eldest child of Benjamin and Elizabeth Staples. Benjamin and his wife Elizabeth also had two sons, Francis and Edward, born in 1854 and 1859 respectively. Mary Ann's father, like John James's, had been a minor craftsman – a woodcarver. This had also been the trade of Mary Ann's grandfather, Edward Staples. Although Benjamin had originally followed his father into woodcarving, within a few years he had become a 'carman' (the term for anyone who made a living driving a horse and cart). In *c*1864 he made the transition into retailing when he set up a dairy shop at 87 Chalton Street, St Pancras. The family's dairy business prospered, and during the 1870s became a small chain of half a dozen shops, most of which were later to become branches of Sainsbury's. It was Mary Ann's experience in the dairy trade which led the young couple into this area of retailing.

Mary Ann had an important influence on the business in its formative years. Annie Deacock, who later became Mrs David Greig, had known Mary Ann from an early age, as her father, Sam Deacock, had been a partner of Tom Haile's when Mary Ann worked there. Annie recalled in her autobiography *My Life and Times* that the Drury Lane shop was opened before Mary Ann and John James's wedding: 'upon the success of this venture depended their prospects of an early marriage.

The certificate recording the marriage of John James Sainsbury and Mary Ann Staples on 20th April 1869.

John Sainsbury was under contract not to leave Gillett's without three months' notice, but when he had finished his day's work with them he went over to Drury Lane and scrubbed the counters and cleaned the scales and weights . . . The business prospered and John Sainsbury and Polly [Mary Ann] Staples were duly married.' Although we cannot be sure of the accuracy of this account, as Annie Deacock was a little girl at the time, this arrangement would have had the advantage of providing a small income while trade was built up in the Drury Lane shop.

John James and Mary Ann had few other resources upon which to draw. It is unlikely that Benjamin Staples would have been able to offer much financial support to his daughter and son-in-law. The – probably apocryphal – £100 savings which John James is said to have used to start his business, although worth at least £6,000 in today's money, would have been barely adequate. John Badcock, in *The Complete Book of Trades*, estimated in 1842 that this was the minimum sum needed to set up a 'butterman's' business. The annual rent for 173 Drury Lane was around £128 per annum, and the rates were a further nine guineas (£9.45). The shop's equipment would have included weights and scales together with churns and

DUC—DUK

DRURY LANE—*continued.*
168 Glover Brothers, wheelwrights
169 Martini Joseph, confectioner
170 Browning Mrs. Priscilla, grocer
171 Taylor Joseph, tobacconist
172 *Red Lion & Still,* Geo. Stanier
173 Sainsbury John, dairyman
174 Carter George, grocer
....*here is Charles street* ....
175 Knapp George, tripe seller
176 Bray Adam, oil & color man
177 *Victoria Wine Co. (branch of)*
178 Heins Hy. Rudolph, timber mer
178 Collins George, cheesemonger

An entry from Kelly's Post Office Street Directory of London, *1870, listing 'Sainsbury John, Dairyman'.*

measures for the milk and a block upon which to pat up butter. John James and Mary Ann risked everything they had in setting up in business together.

Life in Drury Lane

Drury Lane was described by a contemporary journalist as 'an honest, hard-working and thrifty thoroughfare . . . but between the churches of St Giles-in-the-Fields and St Clement Dane's an amazing amount of beggary, destitution, profligacy, vice and downright villainy hides its many-headed misery.' As late as 1884 the Reverend Rice-Jones was to express disapproval of the Lane's overcrowding and suggest that the pernicious influence of the playhouses had played a part both in the poverty of the area and in its failure to attract philanthropic support for housing improvements.

The premises at number 173 had previously been occupied by Thomas Skivens, described in different editions of *Kelly's Post Office Street Directory* as a 'butcher' or a 'greengrocer'. Skivens appears initially to have sublet the shop to John James. It was not until December 1874 that the latter signed a lease with the freeholder, the Reverend T H B Baker. Shops in Drury Lane which competed with Sainsbury's included two dairies, five cheesemongers, two cowkeepers – who would have sold milk from cows kept on the premises – and an egg salesman.

The house had five floors which included the shop, an attic and a basement. The Sainsbury family's living conditions must have been cramped as the 1871 census records that they shared the premises with three other families. These were a gold and silver refiner and his mother; a maker of inks, his wife and their two small

Tiles used to decorate the walls of the first shop at 173 Drury Lane.

children; and a police constable, his wife and two year old daughter. Each family probably occupied only a couple of rooms.

Mary Ann continued to work in the shop even after her husband left Gillett's. The couple's declared aim was 'to have the best butter in London'. The principal trade was in butter and eggs, although milk was also sold. Sarah Pullen, one of the first employees, later recalled how 'it was Mrs Sainsbury who made the shop famous for the quality of its butter. She was always up very early in the morning and took great pride in the cleanliness of the shop.'

The couple's first child, named Mary Ann after her mother, was born on 29th December 1869. She lived for just five months, dying at her grandmother's house in Wandsworth Road of 'diarrhoea, dysentery and convulsions' on 30th May 1870. Such tragedies were common at the time – one in six babies born in 1869 died before their first birthday. Crude infant mortality figures, however, disguise the grief of bereavement. The strain of working long hours in the shop and of losing her daughter told on the young mother's health. Mary Ann was informed by her doctor that she would be unwise to have further children. It was, however, already too late to take this advice. Eight months later, on 8th January 1871, a son was born in a room above the Drury Lane shop. He was named John Benjamin, after his father and his maternal grandfather.

173 Drury Lane pictured shortly after the end of the First World War.

John James and Mary Ann made a shrewd decision when they decided to emulate Benjamin Staples in opening a dairy shop. This was a line of business which was steadily gaining in importance. The capital's growing population and a slowly rising general standard of living meant that there was an increasing demand for food. Milk, eggs and butter were all gaining in popularity. The habit of drinking strong sweet tea instead of the traditional ale also helped to promote the demand for milk. The excise duty on both tea and sugar fell dramatically: tea duty was reduced from 1s 10d per pound in 1853 to 6d in 1865 and 4d in 1890. This transformed it from an expensive luxury into a cheap drink for everyone.

Equally important were changes in the way in which milk was supplied to the capital. Milk and

An atmospheric view of Drury Lane, taken in 1904.

dairy produce brought in from outside London were beginning to replace the keeping of cows in filthy backyards, in basements or on any patch of scrub land. Cheap railway transport made it possible for milk to come from as far away as Devon, Dorset and East Anglia. A prolonged and deep depression in the prices of crops like wheat and barley gave farmers an added incentive to produce milk, for which prices were less volatile. Nevertheless, milk was often contaminated. It was sold straight from the churn or bucket into customers' jugs and so became polluted with the smuts of London's smog-laden atmosphere and soured by dirty churns and measures. The addition of water was so common that the local pump was ironically referred to as 'the cow with an iron tail'. Yellow colouring was also added to counteract the bluish tinge of diluted milk and to make it look creamier. It was hardly surprising that contemporaries like Sarah Pullen were impressed by Mary Ann's passion for cleanliness.

The next step: Kentish Town

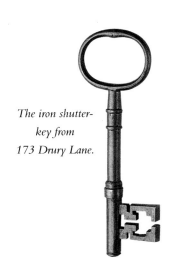

The iron shutter-key from 173 Drury Lane.

Domestic concerns were, however, beginning to occupy more of Mary Ann's time. In October 1872 she gave birth to another son, George. About a year later, the young family moved to 159 Queen's Crescent, Kentish Town, North-west London, leaving a manager to look after the original shop. Over the next seventeen years nine more children were born: Alice, Frank, Louise, Lillian, Arthur, Alfred, Elsie, Dorothy Maud and Paul James. As her family grew, Mary Ann was forced to relinquish her active role in the business. Nevertheless, in later life John Benjamin (known in the firm as Mr John) recalled as a small child working beside both his parents wearing a little white apron which his mother had made for him. His first job was to serve eggs, but as he grew older, he was allowed to help drive his father's first single-horse van.

The move to Kentish Town was an important step forward. It was a remarkable achievement to have opened a second shop after only four years in business. In 1873 John James was still only twenty-nine years old, while Mary Ann was twenty-four. The premises into which the young family moved were a great improvement over the tenements of Drury Lane.

Kentish Town had developed rapidly during the third quarter of the nineteenth century. At the time of John James's birth it had been a suburban village surrounded by fields. By the time the Sainsbury family moved there from Drury Lane it was part of London's metropolitan sprawl. Central London was heavily overpopulated and had, some believed, too many shops. W Glenny, for example, wrote in 1876 that in the East End of London, 'the number of shopkeepers is greatly in excess of what is necessary for safe competition in the sale of food generally'. Kentish Town, by contrast, was on the edge of an area of new suburban development where the number of houses outstripped the provision of shopping facilities. At Queen's Crescent customers came quite a distance to do their shopping. Mr John later recalled how the market 'served a big district as far out as Hendon. These customers travelled by the Midland line to Allcroft Road station.'

Kentish Town was less impoverished than Drury Lane. Employment was available on the expanding railway system, and in piano factories such as Brinsmead's, Collard & Collard and Salter & Sons. Some even alleged that the relative prosperity of the Kentish Town workmen enabled them to spend excessive sums on drinking in the area's many public houses.

The new shop did well, and in 1875 the young couple decided to open another branch in Queen's Crescent, four doors away at 151. Imported Irish bacon was added to the range of goods on sale. The trade continued to grow, and six years later a third branch was added to the Queen's Crescent chain, this time at number 94. In 1885 the branch at 94 was replaced by another at number 98.

Sainsbury's did not own the freehold of 173 Drury Lane until 1920, when it was purchased by Mr John. John James chided his son for making a business decision for sentimental reasons.

The logic of trading from three small branches rather than a single larger one reflected both the modest size of the premises in Queen's Crescent and the importance of the market stall which was set up outside each shop. Here, as in Drury Lane, Sainsbury's traded both from the open windows of the shops, and from trestle tables outside in the market itself. These formed an adjunct to the shop and added as much as 50 per cent to the sales area. The market stalls influenced the trading methods of the day. Salesmen stood outside the shops shouting out the good value and quality of their wares – a practice known as 'barking' – and enticed customers inside the shops to sample the wider range of goods available.

The average size of each shop was very small: probably under 500 square feet. Having three branches in the same street was therefore the best way to serve more customers. There was rivalry between the branches for trade, which kept the staff on their toes. This even extended to competition between salesmen in the same shop. Mr John recalled how at 151 Queen's Crescent on Fridays and Saturdays he competed with the regular bacon hand to achieve record sales of bacon. George sold Irish and Danish bacon from his pitch at the left-hand window, while Mr John sold Canadian Beaver Brand, a new type of bacon, from the right-hand window. 'If I remember rightly,' recalled Mr John with great satisfaction, 'my best sale was sixteen sides.'

A customer remembered how her family referred to the three Queen's Crescent branches as 'upper Sains', 'middle Sains' and 'lower Sains'. At 'middle Sains' (159)

Hetty Scott's stall outside 159 Queen's Crescent, Kentish Town. Her daughter, Sophie, was regularly sent to Sainsbury's to buy a farthing's worth of milk for her mother's tea.

there was a 'mechanical cow': a slot machine into which you could put a copper, draw down a lever like a beer-pump handle, and collect a jugful of milk when the shop was closed. 'Many is the clip I received from my mother,' she admitted rue-fully, 'for pouring a little of the milk on to a neighbour's doorstep for the cat.'

Growth of the trading area

In 1881 John James took over a cheesemonger's shop at 68 Watney Street, Stepney, which had been run by his brother-in-law, Edward Staples. This shop served the East End dockers and lightermen with cheese and salt bacon. Over the next few years he also acquired two Staples's branches at Hoxton in North-east London, and

Benjamin Staples's original shop at 87 Chalton Street, St Pancras. These localities were closer in character to Drury Lane than to Kentish Town.

Understandably, newcomers were frequently unwelcome in areas where competition was intense. When John James took over Edward Staples's Watney Street branch, he incurred the wrath of a trader who, although he had set up shop there only four years earlier, had already come to dominate the local dairy business. Mr

John recalled that 'Mike Drummond [was] . . . a very popular Irishman . . . who fought relentlessly all newcomers to the trade. He was a bachelor and very charitable, and since the district was mostly populated by Irish emigrants you can imagine he was a tough competitor.' To compete with the Irishman's gift of the gab, John James engaged a man by the name of Husk to chat to passers-by and encourage them to try his wares. This was highly successful but he then found that he needed to conceal from Mike Drummond how much his trade had grown. He did this by buying a private house behind the shop so that he could avoid delivering goods to the front entrance. Eventually, after Mike Drummond retired (c1894), his nephew sold out to Sainsbury's.

Moving into premises previously occupied by his wife's family may have helped John James to win acceptance from the locals. It also saved some of the expense of buying equipment for the shop. By increasing the number of branches he could buy goods in greater quantities and negotiate advantageous prices with his suppliers.

A detail from a hand-painted wall panel used to decorate the shop at 159 Queen's Crescent.

In 1882 he acquired his first branch in Chapel Street, Islington, another of London's busiest market streets. The previous occupant was Edward Deacock, whose brother Sam Deacock, like Mary Ann, had worked with Tom Haile in his dairy at 32 Strutton Ground, Victoria, in the 1860s.

The shop at 48 Chapel Street was the first of many acquisitions from members of a 'pact' set up between several food retailers with small chains of shops in London. The purpose of this was threefold. Members agreed to combine their buying activities to gain additional discounts, not to open shops in direct competition and to help each other gain a foothold in new trading areas by offering first refusal to other members of the group before selling up.

Most of the pact members were either related or had been close business associates for many years. Apart from Sainsbury's, Staples's, and Mary Ann's former employer Tom Haile, the other members were the Deacocks and the Peppers

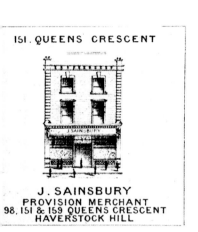

151. QUEENS CRESCENT

J. SAINSBURY
PROVISION MERCHANT
98, 151 & 159 QUEENS CRESCENT
HAVERSTOCK HILL

Sainsbury's second shop in Queen's Crescent, which opened in 1875. This engraving dates from 1890.

John Hedges, manager of 48 Chapel Street, Islington, pictured with his staff in c 1900.

(both related by marriage to the Hailes); David Greig, whose wife Annie was a Deacock; Alfred Banton, who had been one of Sainsbury's earliest employees; and the Frosts and Coppens, who were probably known to the other pact members through the Staples family.

The agreement by pact members not to open shops in close competition with each other continued to be observed by Mr John and David Greig until the inter-war years. Mr Alan, Mr John's eldest son, recalled how it was brought to an end when his father discovered that Greig's were erecting billboards advertising their imminent arrival in localities where they had not even acquired a site. His father sent him round to see Ross Greig at his office in Waterloo Road, to tell him that Sainsbury's would no longer observe the agreement. Ross Greig was furious. 'I'll drive you into the ground!' he spluttered.

79 Angel Lane, Stratford, East London, c1905. This was one of several shops taken over from Alfred Banton.

Harry Goshawk, manager of 18 Walthamstow High Street.

By 1890, this group of pact members had between seventy and eighty shops and exercised considerable joint buying power. For Sainsbury's the most important aspect of the pact was in helping to expand its trading area, as the acquisition of pact members' shops provided opportunities to trade in new locations. In 1895, for example, four shops were acquired from Tom Deacock in the fashionable sub-urb of Holloway. Six years later Deacock's flagship store at 422/4 Tottenham High Road was added to John James's growing chain. Alfred Banton's shops were mainly in East London, and branches at Walthamstow, Hackney, Leytonstone and Strat-ford were taken over by Sainsbury's between 1900 and 1906.

Despite the gradual growth of the trading area the branches in the market streets remained important to Sainsbury's. The shop at 48 Chapel Street, Islington, for example, was the first of four shops to open in that busy thoroughfare. Its fas-cia board proudly proclaimed that 'J. Sainsbury's Shilling Butter is the Best Value in the World'. Mr John later recalled how this shop developed a prodigious trade. One Friday it achieved record sales of £400 for a day's takings. 'It was an achieve-ment of exceptional merit for all those engaged of which I was one (excuse me). The occasion stands out clearly in my mind. W Elderton was manager, Hardy the cheese hand and Seal the first butterman.' As with the other branches in market streets, 'we did a great deal of business from the open windows and the stalls, cheese in the left window, bacon the right, eggs on the left stall and Ostend rabbits and pickled pork on the right'. The other shops in the Chapel Street chain were a second provisions shop at number 76, a branch specialising in game at number 51, and a dairy taken over from a competitor, George Jackson, at number 44½.

Some of the attractive blue and white tiles used to decorate the walls at 79 Angel Lane, Stratford.

Open all hours

The hours of trading in market streets were long. In Watney Street the police would blow a whistle at 6am as a signal for business to commence. There would be a great rush to set up the stalls, in which the shopkeepers had the advantage that they need only step across the kerb with their trestles and tables. It was not, however, the early morning trade which most preoccupied contemporaries, but the pressure to work late into the night and even on Sundays. W Glenny remarked in 1876 that 'the working class . . . demand terms of labour from the shopkeeper that not one of them would accord to the capitalist'. Shopkeepers and their staff commonly worked over eighty hours a week and even up to a hundred hours when their customers demanded it.

There were two reasons for this. Firstly, the tradition of family ownership in retailing, in which the shopkeeper lived on the premises, meant that there was someone available to serve customers at almost any hour of the day or night. As this tradition was gradually eroded, it was replaced by the system of 'living-in' staff, who were expected to maintain similar hours. Secondly, intense competition

23

meant that the shopkeeper had to respond to the demands of his customers at whatever hour they cared to shop. This problem was exacerbated by the custom of paying wage earners on Saturday night after their own long week's work. Saturday evening was therefore the busiest time of all, with shops remaining open into the early hours of Sunday morning. George Dodd, writing in 1850, described how 'as the hour approaches when the artisans receive their money, so do the itinerant dealers take their stand' and how, despite occasional disputes about trading 'pitches', the streets would suddenly fill with people. Late at night, by flickering gaslight, 'the influx of customers is so vast that there is trade for all.'

Serving in such an environment could involve extra duties for shop staff. The first port of call for many people was the public house, and customers would arrive at Sainsbury's still clutching their beer mugs. One of H F Jones's duties at Somers Town was to clear up the tankards and take them back after the shop closed. It was a serious offence, however, for Sainsbury's staff to partake themselves. George Hoare recalled a severe telling-off for going across the road for a pint at half-past twelve one Sunday morning.

Although the shutters were pulled down before midnight to protect the stock, trading continued as long as there were customers to serve. Pilfering was common. 'One old girl,' said Mr T C Topp, 'was spotted lifting a pound of tea late one Saturday, and the manager tackled her about it, but she tucked it up her skirts and defied him to get it back. So we were a pound of tea down on that day's trading.' 'Little' A McCarthy was employed as a shop boy at 159 Queen's Crescent to keep an eye out for shoplifters. He was so small that he had to stand on a box. When he spotted someone pilfering, he would call out in back slang – a code in which each word was spelt backwards – to attract the attention of those serving.

After the last customer left, the shop would be scrubbed down from top to bottom ready for Monday morning. This was particularly hard work in the few branches which had wooden counters and floors, rather than the more hygienic tiled surfaces of other Sainsbury's shops. While the most junior staff cleaned the shop, the other staff would be counting the takings. T C Topp recalled that 'the manager counted the gold, the first and second hands counted the silver, and anyone counted the copper. I did the sales sheets.' After this, the staff would be free to go. For these long hours a junior would receive eight to ten shillings a week.

Even these conditions, however, were better than those of many shopworkers. The half day off given to Sainsbury's staff in the early part of the week did not become a statutory right until the 1911 Shops Act enforced a weekly early closing day. Despite repeated efforts by MPs, the Grocers' Federation and the National Association of Shopworkers to regulate opening hours, it took many years for even the most basic protection to be afforded to shop staff. Late night trading was not

Harry Byford, manager, with his staff at 87 Chalton Street, Somers Town, c1904. This shop belonged to the Staples family from c1864 until 1882, when it became a Sainsbury's branch.

regulated until the First World War, when opening hours were restricted under the Defence of the Realm Act of 1914. The situation with regard to Sunday trading was confused. Some types of retailing – for example, the sale of fresh meats – were definitely prohibited. However, most products could be legally sold on the sabbath. The 1904 Shops Act gave local authorities the power to make orders fixing hours of closing within their area. It was not until the Shops (Sunday Trading Restrictions) Act of 1936 that Sunday trading became more generally regulated. The long hours and low returns of Victorian shopkeeping were familiar to Sainsbury's founders well before they set up in business. Both had grown up in areas where they had seen at first hand the struggle for survival of those who traded in London's market streets.

John James and Mary Ann's greatest achievement was to recognise that price competitiveness need not be achieved by compromising the quality of the goods they sold. The sign on the shopfront of the first branch in Chapel Street, Islington, which read 'Quality Perfect, Prices Lower', summed up the fundamental trading precept that directed Sainsbury's activities from the very beginning.

J. Sainsbury for best provisions

The census entry for the night of Sunday, 3rd April 1881 described the three Queen's Crescent branches and their inhabitants: 'John Sainsbury, Head, Married, age 36, Provision Merchant. 3 shops, 159, 151 & 94. Master and 5 men.' It appears that the accommodation above 94 Queen's Crescent was used as a hostel for the young men who worked at the other two branches, as the residents were six boys aged between fourteen and eighteen years, each of whom was described as a 'shopman'. The census reveals that most of them had been recruited locally. At 151 Queen's Crescent, as at the original shop at 173 Drury Lane, a married manager lived in. The Drury Lane shop was managed by James Pullen, whose wife Sarah had been John Benjamin's nursemaid and is said to have been the firm's earliest employee. The youngest member of staff recorded in the census was Thomas Badger, a ten year old 'cheesemonger's boy', who lived in at Drury Lane. Although the census described John James as a 'provision merchant', he now appeared in *Kelly's Post Office Street Directory* as a 'cheesemonger' rather than a 'dairyman'. Contemporary advertisements also described him as a wholesaler but this was never an important part of his business.

The young Sainsbury family had also grown. At the time of the 1881 census Mary Ann was thirty-one. She now had six children: four sons and two daughters, ranging in age from John Benjamin, who was ten, to Arthur, a baby of eleven months. It seems likely that even the Kentish Town premises were becoming cramped. There was no room for Ellen Simmons, their domestic servant, to live in with the Sainsbury family as one might have expected. Instead she lodged with the family of the manager at 151 Queen's Crescent.

A wholesale price list for Sainsbury's 'Peat Smoked' bacon, c1882.

The first depot

The acquisition of new branches made it necessary for John James to provide warehousing facilities. While a retailer with only one or two outlets could rely on buying small quantities at bargain prices on the wholesale markets, this was not satisfactory for a larger business. Competitiveness depended upon the judicious buying of greater quantities at prices which had been carefully negotiated with suppliers. This made it necessary to have a warehouse in which goods could be received from wholesalers, and where consignments could be made ready for distribution to the branches. In September 1882, therefore, John James set up his first 'depot', at 90 Allcroft Road, near his three Kentish Town shops.

The new premises consisted of a private house, four sets of stables with rooms above, and a mews that was three hundred feet long. Three of the stables were cleared of their fittings and used as warehouses for butter, cheese and eggs. None of these had any refrigeration. The ground floor of the house was turned into an office while the first floor provided accommodation for a resident foreman called William Goodwin.

A price card (c1885), advertising the extension to Sainsbury's Allcroft Road depot, which had been established three years earlier.

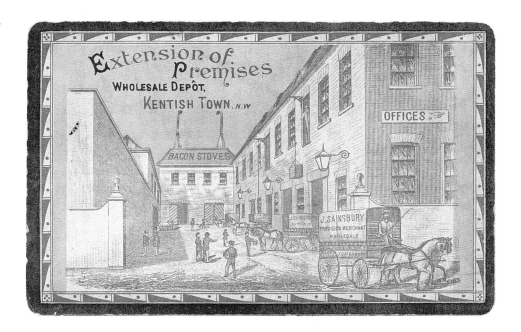

John James also made his first excursion into production when he built two bacon-smoking stoves on the site. Bacon smoked in Sainsbury's own stoves was soon to be described as 'Sainsbury brand' – probably because it actually carried the mark of a fire brand.

Croydon: the model shop

At the same time as he was developing the Allcroft Road site John James acquired a new shop at 6 (later 11) London Road, Croydon. This was the first Sainsbury's shop to open outside London. John James was attracted to Croydon by its rapid expansion. The town's population had increased from about 6,000 in 1801 to 20,355 in 1851 and 78,947 in 1881, making it into the largest suburban town in the neighbourhood of London. In 1883 Edward Walford attributed this phenomenal growth to 'the great facilities afforded by railway communication'. From Croydon's eleven railway stations some 400 trains – operated by four different companies – ran daily to and from London. Sainsbury's new shop was opposite West Croydon station, one of the most important in the town. John James felt that the prosperity of the area offset the problems of supplying the new shop by horse and cart from his depot north of the Thames.

During the autumn of 1882 John James converted his shop in London Road into a model branch. Mr John later recalled the great care his father gave to the

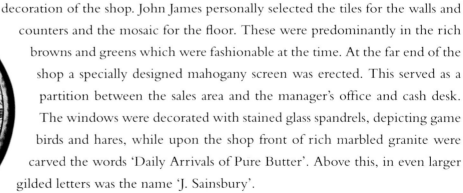

John James's flagship branch at 11 London Road, Croydon. This photograph pre-dates the branch's extension in 1896.

A pheasant which formed part of a stained glass window spandrel dating from 1888.

decoration of the shop. John James personally selected the tiles for the walls and counters and the mosaic for the floor. These were predominantly in the rich browns and greens which were fashionable at the time. At the far end of the shop a specially designed mahogany screen was erected. This served as a partition between the sales area and the manager's office and cash desk. The windows were decorated with stained glass spandrels, depicting game birds and hares, while upon the shop front of rich marbled granite were carved the words 'Daily Arrivals of Pure Butter'. Above this, in even larger gilded letters was the name 'J. Sainsbury'.

Many contemporaries thought John James had been far too lavish in fitting out the new shop. Mr John later recalled that 'failure was predicted for such extravagance' by others in the trade. Although no figures have survived of the sums expended on the Croydon branch, fitting expenses for similar Sainsbury's shops that opened in the late 1880s suggest that John James's rivals had good grounds for their criticisms. At Lewisham, for example, the total works – including counter equipment such as scales and butter blocks – amounted to £1,431 10s 11d. A

The Christmas display at the first Croydon branch in c1900. A contemporary advertisement described the premises as being 'well lighted and elegantly fitted with mahogany, the walls being lined with tessellated tiles, whilst marble slabs and counters give to the whole an inviting air of coolness and cleanliness at the hottest season'.

further £94 14s 8d was spent on marble for the counters and shelves, and £50 on decorative glass.

The internal decorations not only were highly attractive but also fulfilled a more practical function. As Mr John recalled, 'the critics missed the point my father had in mind, and that was to produce a shop to ensure perfect cleanliness and freedom from the menace of all food shops in those days – mice and rats. For all time my father must stand as the founder of the modern provision trade.'

At Croydon, customers could choose from a far greater range of products than in any previous Sainsbury's shop. An 1894 advertisement described the goods on offer: 'The choicest butters of absolute purity, obtained direct from the farms of Brittany, Dorset and Aylesbury; new laid eggs; Wiltshire and Irish bacon; York, Cumberland and Irish hams . . . ox tongues in tins, fresh and salt dairy-fed pork, and all descriptions of poultry and game in season.' Among the cheeses available were Stiltons, 'rich, ripe and blue', Gorgonzolas 'of the finest quality', 'gold medal' Gruyère, 'specially imported' Canadian Cheddar and American Cheshire ('pale and coloured'), Camembert, Neufchatel, Roquefort and 'Port du Salut'.

*Oswald Beaumont Carpenter,
manager, pictured with his staff
at 65 South End, Croydon,
c1899.*

*This paper bag is the oldest
known surviving example of
Sainsbury's packaging. It dates
from c1887.*

Sainsbury's claimed to be 'the only house in Surrey' to stock so many cream cheeses, including Bondons, York Creams and Alpine Creams. Contemporary price lists offered 'Sainsbury pork pies', brawn and Bath chaps, which were probably made in the firm's own 'kitchens'. The poultry range was stupendous, including not only familiar lines such as grouse and pheasant but pintail, widgeon, hares, Egyptian quails, ortolans (a European bunting), Bordeaux pigeons, jellinots and larks (by the dozen).

The new store confounded the critics and proved immensely

*Tiles from 44/46 High Street,
Lewisham, 1888. Similar ones
were used on counter-fronts at
Croydon, Balham and
Brondesbury.*

successful. John James exploited this by opening further branches in Croydon. Some were specialist stores with a more restricted range than the first shop. In 1884 a branch was opened at 18 London Road (later renumbered 35 London Road) that was a pork butcher's shop. This was the first branch to sell Sainsbury's own sausages which were manufactured on the premises using a hand-operated sausage-making machine. These proved so popular that Mr Hancock, the employee responsible for their manufacture, was soon making them for other Sainsbury's shops. A third branch in London Road, which opened in *c*1888, specialised in game and poultry. Another 'auxiliary' branch for the sale of provisions was opened in November 1889 at 122 (later 134) North End Road. In 1896 the original shop was extended by the purchase of the adjoining premises. By this time the street had been renumbered and the enlarged shop became 9/11 London Road.

A wider market and product range

Brass advertising tokens. Several designs were issued between 1882 and 1913, usually to mark the opening of new branches. Most were copies of George III spade guineas and dated '1798'.

The success of the first Croydon branch was important in determining the long-term progress of the business. No contemporary records survive of its profitability, but it is beyond doubt that the luxury goods it sold, although cheaper than other retailers', attracted higher profit margins than those on basic foods. By broadening both his range of goods and the markets in which he offered them John James set his business apart from rivals such as Lipton, Home & Colonial and Maypole Dairies, which sold only a limited range of products and whose shops were intended to appeal primarily to the working classes.

It was not until 1888 that similar branches to Croydon were established in other middle class areas. In this year John James opened shops in Balham, Brondesbury and Lewisham. These carried a range of goods comparable to those offered at Croydon. Lewis J King, who began work at the Balham branch in 1895, was impressed by the astonishing variety of eggs it sold. 'You could tell where an egg came from by the colour of its yolk. The Austrian egg was small, but had a golden yolk which would always maintain its spherical shape. The Italian was a little larger with a fine reddish brick-coloured yolk. Both Dutch and Danish had pale yellow yolks, and eggs from Brittany scintillating globules of rich gold.'

The opening of these 'high class' branches led to an increase in the range of goods sold in less prosperous neighbourhoods. One example was the opening of a specialist branch for the sale of game and poultry at 51 Chapel Street, Islington, in 1888. John James seems to have used the shop to sell off supplies of game which were surplus to the requirements of his up-market branches. This was to the advantage of the local residents, who were able to buy luxury items at very competitive prices.

The expansion of Sainsbury's business in the late nineteenth century coincided with major changes in the food industry. Technological improvements in transport and production methods had greatly reduced the price of many agricultural goods.

The national railway networks of North America, Argentina and Russia opened up vast tracts of land where food could be produced far more economically than in Britain. New canning, processing and refrigeration techniques meant that this produce could be transported by land and sea at minimal cost. In Denmark and Holland farming practices had been revolutionised by the application of modern methods, enabling dairy and meat products to be mass-produced to a standard rarely achieved by British farmers.

New products had also been introduced. These included items such as condensed milk, corned beef and margarine. Some of these evolved as a result of the many wars in Europe. Margarine, for example, was invented in 1869 by Mège-Mouriès as a cheap butter substitute to feed the French army during its foreign campaigns. By the late nineteenth century, mechanised production lines had made these into cheap products which soon became an important part of working people's diets.

The fact that Britain had pursued a free trade policy since the repeal of the Corn Laws in 1846 meant that few imported products carried any duty. This made them highly competitive compared with home-produced goods and contributed to the British agricultural depression of the 1880s and 1890s. Many contemporary observers were aware of the important role which food imports had played in improving the British diet. Even a relatively obscure newspaper like the *Journal and Weekly Directory for Hove* carried a story in July 1880 praising the import of 'American beef and American mutton, Chicago bacon and Californian cheeses, preserved fish and canned fruit'.

Sainsbury's branch at 18/19 The Exchange, Balham, which opened in 1888. The shop's imposing fascia is accentuated by the exaggerated perspective of this advertisement.

Cutting out the middleman

The growth of the imported provisions trade in the early 1880s transformed the wholesaling activities along the south bank of the Thames. To the consternation of the old, established companies, much of this new trade was unregulated. It soon outgrew the markets at Tooley Street, Smithfield and Lower Thames Street and began to occupy an area that stretched from the Pool of London almost to Waterloo Bridge. Owing to the shortage of wholesale market space – and in an attempt

These colourful tiles depicting birds and fruits were used at the Brondesbury branch, Kilburn, which opened in 1888.

to reduce costs – many multiple retailers began to cut out the middleman and buy direct from foreign suppliers or at the wharves from shipping merchants.

This threatened the livelihood of many London wholesale merchants. In 1887 a group of their leaders formed the Home and Foreign Produce Exchange Limited with the intention of regulating the provisions business by ensuring that only its own members were allowed to trade on the wholesale markets. Three years later they attempted to extend this restriction by recommending members to deal only with the newly formed Produce Agents Association (PAA), an alliance of importers and sellers. John James, who in his wholesaling capacity had become a member of the Home and Foreign Produce Exchange, received a visit from Jonathan Copeman (the chairman of the Exchange) in 1891. Copeman tried to persuade him to confine his bacon-buying activities to PAA members. John James refused to give any such undertaking, declaring that 'it would not be convenient for the firm on occasions to be confined to PAA members'.

The founder's lunch box which he used when out visiting his shops.

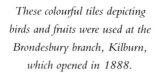

In fact, John James was being somewhat disingenuous in his reply. The truth was that he had already begun to exploit the price and quality advantages to be gained from buying direct from the producer. In 1886 he discovered

Fred Leach, an early employee of Lloyd Maunder, with his daily consignment of goods for Sainsbury's, c1910. Poultry, butter, eggs, rabbits and pigmeat were despatched by rail from Lapford station to Sainsbury's London depot.

that the importers from whom he had been buying Dutch butter had been storing it in ice caves in order to sell it when the market price was high. As a result the product was rarely fresh. He therefore appointed the Royal Buisman Dairy Exchange of Leeuwarden to act as his agents in the Friesland markets. Henceforth consignments of butter were sent direct to Sainsbury's from Buisman's twice a week. R Buisman recalled how John James would personally inspect every delivery of butter when it arrived at his warehouse. Any butter John James rejected was sent to be sold at the Tooley Street provisions market. He also insisted that every case of butter be stamped with the date of its production. This was an innovation at the time but was later made compulsory by the Dutch government.

As the century drew to a close, Sainsbury's established further contacts with producers. These sometimes came about purely by chance. In 1898, for example, a miller at Witheridge in North Devon received a letter from John James informing him that henceforth the firm would only accept parcels of twenty to twenty-five chickens. The miller considered it impossible to meet this demand as his poultry breeding was only a sideline. Instead he passed the letter on to a local farmer's son called Lloyd Maunder. He immediately recognised that the metropolis could be an important new market for the depressed West Country farming industry and travelled up to London to meet Mr Arthur Sainsbury, the founders' fourth son, who was responsible for pork buying. The two men came to an agreement whereby Lloyd Maunder would send Sainsbury's a regular supply of quality poultry, butter, eggs, rabbits and pigmeat.

Lloyd Maunder's contract with Sainsbury's was so significant that he referred to the firm as 'A1', so that his rivals would not discover the secret of his success. In 1912 he established an abattoir adjacent to the railway at Willand, near Tiverton, in response to the growing demand from his most important customer. The goods, which in later years included beef and mutton, supplied by Lloyd Maunder were referred to by Sainsbury's as products 'from our own farms', even though the company never had a direct interest in Lloyd Maunder's business.

Origins of the firm's own farms

Mr Arthur, c1900.

It may have been the success of this close link with a producer which prompted John James to purchase his own farm at Blunt's Hall, Little Wratting, near Haverhill in Suffolk. John James's third son, Frank, was appointed as its manager.

It is said that Mr Frank had always wanted to be a farmer but had been persuaded against his will to enter the family business like his brothers. Although he progressed far enough to be appointed manager of the branch at 18/20 Seven Sisters Road, Holloway, his heart was never really in the business. Tales of his hasty temper became well known within the firm. On one occasion he caused chaos in his shop when he pushed an employee into an elaborate egg display!

Things came to a head, however, when John James paid a surprise visit to Mr Frank's branch. On entering the shop he found his son giving orders to the staff while weaving in between the customers on a bicycle. John James immediately told him to hand in his keys. When Frank arrived to collect them the next morning, his father told him politely but firmly that he had been dismissed. Luckily Mary Ann intervened on her son's behalf and persuaded her husband to send Frank to work for a trial period on the farm of a family friend, Mr Mitchell, at Withersfield Hall in Suffolk. This proved so successful that John James eventually established Frank on his own farm.

Mr Frank, c1900.

As new branches were opened it became necessary to ensure a regular supply of good quality fresh eggs at a competitive price. Home-produced eggs had a poor reputation among shoppers because farmers took little trouble to ensure their freshness. The *Grocer's Manual* in 1896, for example, complained that 'English and Irish eggs are carried to the markets only once a week or fortnight, and are liable to be two, three or four weeks old before they are actually eaten'.

French eggs had a much better reputation, due to the existence of egg-collection schemes which ensured the freshness of the product. One of the earliest of these had been started in 1810 by Paul Augustus Nurdin who later founded the wholesale company Nurdin & Peacock. Eggs were collected from farmers in the Cherbourg area and then graded and packed ready for despatch to England. Often

Frank Sainsbury's Staff
(Egg Department)
July 18th 1927

The staff of Mr Frank's egg department at Haverhill, Suffolk. Mr Frank is seated in the centre of the second row from the bottom of the photograph, with his nephew Mr Alan on his right.

these came onto the market within three days of being laid. They soon established an excellent reputation which enabled them to be sold at prices well above those for home-produced eggs.

The popularity of eggs sent to Sainsbury's shops from Mr Frank's farm demonstrated that customers could be persuaded that Sainsbury's home-produced eggs were as good as those from the farms of Brittany, while also being cheaper. Demand for Mr Frank's eggs far outstripped supply, so in 1912 he established his own egg-collection scheme in East Anglia. The eggs were collected fresh from the local farms and taken to a centre at Little Wratting. Here they were candled – held up against a light to check for defects – and packed for despatch to Sainsbury's.

The link between Mr Frank's activities and the main retailing business appears to have been rather haphazard and to have caused the firm's auditors, Clark Battams, some disquiet. On 3rd February 1919, for example, they warned that 'several questions have arisen in connection with the relationship between your firm and the business of Mr Frank Sainsbury at Haverhill. We suggest that the time has arrived when these points should be settled.'

The egg-collection scheme was not the only way in which Sainsbury's buying activities influenced East Anglian agriculture. In collaboration with his father, Mr Frank also attempted to improve the quality of pigmeat. A pig-house was built on the farm for a dozen pedigree boars. Local farmers were encouraged to bring their sows to be serviced to improve the local stock. A slaughterhouse was also built and pigs purchased by Mr Frank were sold in his father's shops. During the period before the First World War the costs of the abattoir were supported by the main retail business. Nevertheless, it provided the meat for the sausages and cooked pork products which became an important part of Sainsbury's business in the 1890s. The quality of Sainsbury's pork also served as a useful yardstick by which to judge stocks purchased from other suppliers.

A poster for Sainsbury's pies and sausages. 'Dairy-fed' pork was regarded as the premium quality.

New lines and new links

Direct contact between producers and retailers was particularly important when introducing new lines. Among the businesses which were most active at promoting their products direct to retailers were the margarine companies, Van den Berghs and Jurgens. Jacob Van den Bergh and his younger brother Henry had come to London in 1879 to establish a London office for the Dutch parent company, and by the 1890s had been successful in taking the lead in the British market over their arch rivals Jurgens.

Margarine was originally marketed in Britain as 'butterine', a cheap substitute for butter which became popular with the working classes. The misleading term 'butterine' was banned by the Margarine Act of 1887. Over the course of the 1880s and 1890s the quality of the product improved immensely from its earlier unappetising character – one of the original ingredients had been minced cow's udder – and the better types of margarine compared favourably with cheap butter. Sainsbury's premium margarine was originally called 'Cremos', but this had to be changed under the terms of a further Margarine Act in 1907 which made it illegal to use brand names that might cause confusion with true dairy produce. It was renamed 'Crelos'. Margarine was never as important to Sainsbury's business as it was to other retailers, mainly because the company's emphasis on quality led it to have a bigger interest in butter. By 1914, however, margarine accounted for 75 per cent of the sales of Maypole Dairies. Van den Bergh's and Jurgens were eventually to buy out multiple retailers

Margarine advertisement c1915. 'Double weight' offers gave customers twice as much for the normal price.

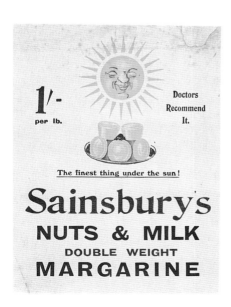

1/- per lb.

Doctors Recommend It.

The finest thing under the sun!

Sainsbury's NUTS & MILK DOUBLE WEIGHT MARGARINE

*18/20 Seven Sisters Road,
Holloway, c1900. This branch
was acquired from Tom Deacock
in 1895 and was subsequently
managed by Mr Frank.*

like Lipton's, Home & Colonial and Maypole Dairies. These formed the nucleus
of the retailing arm of Unilever and ultimately of Allied Suppliers. Van den Bergh's
never acquired a financial interest in Sainsbury's.

Shunning sharp practices

John James was determined to establish the highest standards of quality control.
This had been a central tenet of his trading policy from the earliest days. In the
context of the mid-nineteenth century this was a brave decision. As some of the
early co-operative societies found, many poorer customers were unaware of how

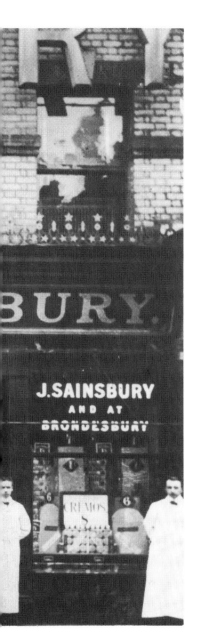

*A jar which contained
bloater paste manufactured in
Sainsbury's factory, c1890.*

badly they were being served, and frequently distrusted pure food because it looked and tasted different from the adulterated goods with which they were familiar. There were few statutory controls on retailing, which meant that adulteration and the giving of short weight were endemic, especially among shopkeepers who found it difficult to make a profit except by cheating their customers.

Legislation in 1860 and 1872 had gone some way towards curbing the worst forms of adulteration. A Select Committee report of 1874 was able to claim that people were 'now cheated rather than poisoned'. However, sharp practices still remained a serious problem. Cheating on weights was extremely common, with some retailers even having two sets of weights – one false and one fair – so that the latter could be offered to the inspector of weights and measures should the need arise. Robert Roberts, who was the son of a Salford shopkeeper, recalled in his autobiography, *The Classic Slum*, how as a child at the turn of the century one of his jobs was to dive beneath the counter if the weights and measures inspector appeared and dislodge the lump of bacon fat attached to the bottom of the scale.

Sainsbury's scales were specially made by Herbert & Sons of Smithfield. Herbert's scales were advertised as having 'a quick movement and a long drop' so the customer could see that she was getting a fair weight. They were also accurate to $\frac{1}{32}$ of an ounce. Sainsbury's staff could be sacked on the spot for giving short weight. Some customers took care to exploit the tiny margin of error which was given in their favour. Mr A W L Downes recalled how his grandmother regularly requested eight pounds of sugar, all in separate bags, so that on all eight she received the 'turn' on the scale when the loaded pan dipped.

Ironically, the multiple food retailing companies were both the cause of and the cure for such problems. Many independent retailers felt that they had to cheat to compete with the multiples' low prices, while the stiff penalties faced by large food companies for being caught cheating were an effective deterrent against their using such dubious practices. As a result, multiple retailers – whether national in scope like Lipton's and Home & Colonial or regional like Sainsbury's – were in the vanguard of providing pure food for the nation.

Keep the shops well lit

*I*n 1890 Home & Colonial opened a branch in Queen's Crescent, Kentish Town. Mr John recalled that this was a milestone in Sainsbury's development, for his father realised that in order to compete with the multiples, it was necessary to step up the rate of the firm's growth. 'Otherwise,' said John James, 'we shall be beaten in our position as buyers in the sources of production.' Although John James was no stranger to competition, it had mainly been from small-scale traders in the market streets of North and East London. John James had succeeded in matching the cut-throat prices of these retailers while also offering better quality goods. However, in comparison with companies such as Home & Colonial, Lipton's and the International Tea Company, Sainsbury's growth had been modest. In twenty-one years it had opened only sixteen shops, all of which were located in the London area. By 1890 Home & Colonial, although founded only five years earlier, had over a hundred shops in towns and cities throughout Britain. Thomas Lipton – who had started his business in Glasgow in 1871 – had a similar number. The International Tea Company had over two hundred shops.

OPPOSITE *In c1886 the Sainsbury family moved to the fashionable suburb of Highgate. John James and Mary Ann are pictured in their new conservatory, c1895. In the centre are Mr John, and his fiancée Mabel, daughter of Jacob Van den Bergh.*

The national multiples had been spectacularly successful in matching the growing supply of cheap provisions to the rapidly expanding working class markets of Britain's major cities. Their profitability was a result of a rapid turnover at profit margins of between a half and a third those of small retailers. W N Hancock, in his book *Competition Between Large and Small Shops*, had drawn a parallel between the efficiency of modern retailing methods and the methods of manufacturers who had made the production of cheap consumer goods – and foodstuffs – possible: 'the substitution of quick for slow sales is precisely like an improvement in machinery which cheapens the cost of production.'

The scale of the national multiples' operations gave them tremendous buying power and enabled them to negotiate the lowest possible prices from producers. They also controlled their own wholesale arrangements, thereby further cutting costs. As Thomas Lipton remarked in his autobiography, *Leaves from the Lipton Log*, 'If I paid the middleman's prices for the goods I required I would be no better off than any man trying to make a living by selling the goods in which I specialised.'

Specialisation was another feature of the multiples' operations. In 1890 Maypole Dairies, for example, stocked just five commodities: eggs, condensed milk, tea, margarine and butter. Thomas Lipton's main lines were tea, ham, cheese, butter, and bacon, although his product range had broadened slightly by 1914.

Although John James had no ambition to convert his small chain into a national enterprise, he recognised that the challenge posed by the multiples in areas like Kentish Town necessitated swift action. To compete with their prices it was essential for him to be able to buy goods on equally favourable terms. This meant buying in larger quantities and increasing the rate at which he opened branches. It was necessary to improve his depot facilities to supply these new shops.

Although the Allcroft Road depot had served the business well, by 1890 it had

become outdated and inconvenient. All the goods purchased in the wholesale markets or arriving at the docks had to be transported the five miles to Kentish Town and then assembled for delivery to the branches. This became an increasingly time-consuming arrangement due to traffic congestion in central London. In 1891 the architect Arthur Cawston estimated that every one of the 92,372 horse-drawn vehicles passing through the city of London and its approaches was delayed on average by half an hour. The old depot was also no longer close to the Sainsbury family's home. In c1886 they had purchased a house in the fashionable suburb of Highgate, a move which reflected their rapidly advancing social status.

On 22nd July 1890 John James took a seventy-eight year lease on 11 Stamford Street, Blackfriars, and the adjoining building at 10–13 Bennett Street. The premises consisted of three sets of stables, a carriage room, a covered ride with an imposing arched gateway, a granary, outbuildings and offices. The location was perfect. It was within a few hundred yards of the Thames and easily accessible to its busy wharves. It was also close to the wholesale markets at Smithfield, Leadenhall and Tooley Street and convenient for Blackfriars Bridge station and for the railway termini at Liverpool Street, London Bridge and Waterloo. Most important of all, by locating his head office at the eastern end of Stamford Street, John James placed his business alongside 'London's Larder': the area on the South Bank where all the most important firms in the nation's imported provisions trade were based. In recognition of his new status the entry in the 1893 *Post Office Street Directory* read: 'Sainsbury, John, provision merchant and agent, bacon drier and pork butcher etc., 11 Stamford Street SE and retail cheesemonger . . . game dealer . . . and dairy.'

The Blackfriars depot in 1894.

Once the Blackfriars depot was established, Sainsbury's growth rate increased dramatically. Between 1890 and 1900 the number of branches trebled to forty-eight. Many of these were located on the main thoroughfares out of London to the south and east, for example at Sutton, Streatham, Walthamstow and Leytonstone. These were far more accessible from central London than from the Kentish Town depot. By 1900 Sainsbury's trading area extended to Redhill, Ilford, Enfield, Ealing, Harrow and Watford. Even so, it remained small by comparison with the national multiples.

Sainsbury's slower rate of growth was a corollary of its more complex business. Its wider product range and more elaborately decorated shops required greater investment than the national multiples' branches. However, Sainsbury's profit margins were far lower than those of the 'high class' provision merchants who offered these features, and compared favourably with those of the national multiples. By the turn of the century Sainsbury's was large enough to exert considerable buying power. It appears to have had few problems in competing as an equal in the many markets in which it traded alongside branches of these 'company shops'.

BACON & HAM CURING DEPÔT, NEW WAREHOUSES, GRAVEL LANE, S.E.

The Union Street bacon stoves, c1900.

The emerging 'house style'

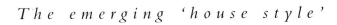

From the 1890s onwards, Sainsbury's new shops shared a common 'house style' – the few exceptions occurred when the firm took over shops which were already fitted out to John James's high standards. The model for Sainsbury's house style was the original Croydon shop, with its long shape, tiled walls and marble-topped counters. Sites were carefully chosen, with a central position in a parade selected in preference to a corner shop. 'Corners,' pronounced John James, 'are for banks.'

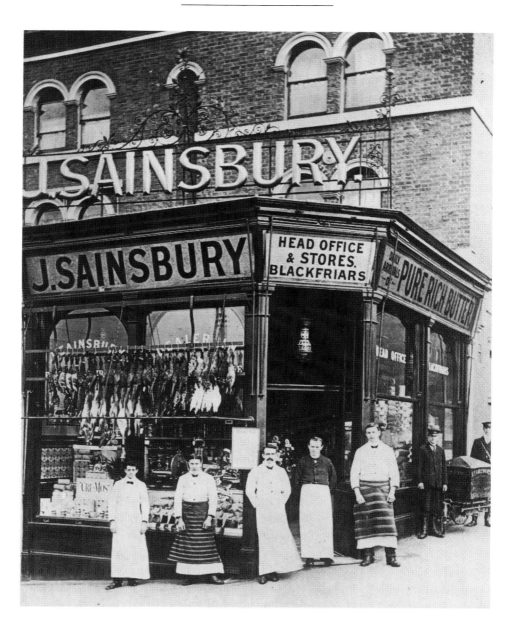

Staff pictured outside 13 Blackheath Village, c1902. This branch, which opened in 1896, was unusual in its corner location.

Shops located within a parade offered the maximum amount of counter space from which to serve customers and to display goods. The shop layout preferred by Sainsbury's had little window space relative to its depth. This made it easier to keep goods cool than in a shop with windows on two sides – an important considera-tion at a time when the only refrigeration was an ice-box in the basement. The lat-ter was refilled twice a week by the North Pole Ice Company. Shops in the centre of a parade were also easier to keep clean than corner shops, which collected dust and dirt thrown up by horse-drawn vehicles. If the trade warranted it, the shops on either side of a branch in a parade might offer room for expansion.

The tiling and other decoration used in Sainsbury's branches were standardised. Highly glazed ceramic tiles were produced specially for Sainsbury's by Minton

Hollins. The pattern was complex. On the walls the central motif was of stylised crown imperials in cream relief. This was surrounded by a rectangular pattern of chrysanthemums in white on a blue and brown background which stretched from just above the top shelf behind the counter almost to ceiling level. Just below the ceiling there was a border of celadon green tiles which depicted stylised dolphins and fleurs-de-lys. From dado level to the floor behind the counters, a pattern of relief tiles in yellow, brown and white was used. The tiles on the counter fronts were glazed in what Minton's termed 'Sainsbury's teapot brown'. The counter tops and shelves were of white Sicilian marble and the floor was of ceramic mosaic in

143 Guildford High Street on opening day, 6th November 1906. This shop exemplified the 'house style' used by Sainsbury's from the 1890s until after the Second World War.

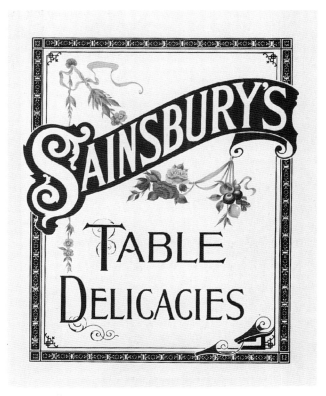

A glass advertisement panel used at the Kingsland branch, Dalston, East London, c1905.

Details of tiles and mosaic made for Sainsbury's by Minton's of Stoke-on-Trent.

45

subtle shades of grey, blue, green, white and brown. The latter were also made and laid by Minton's, who employed Italian craftsmen to construct them.

Great attention was paid to the artificial lighting used in the shops. To begin with, gaslights were installed both inside and out, providing a bright light which showed off the merchandise to good effect and acted like a beacon in the dark winter streets. John James even used expensive 'recuperative' gas lights in many of his branches. These were said to economise on gas consumption as they pre-heated the gas by circulating it around the burner before it was ignited. Electric lighting – installed in new branches from c1905 – initially took the form of a simple row of naked forty-watt light bulbs suspended over each counter. By 1914 most older branches had been converted to electricity, although external gas lamps continued to be used for forecourt and window trading well into the interwar years. More powerful and sophisticated electric lamps were introduced once they became available. John James regarded the proper illumination of his merchandise as so important that, from his deathbed in 1928, he is said to have exhorted his successors to 'keep the shops well lit'.

Contemporaries were impressed by Sainsbury's house style. A reporter from the *Finsbury Press* who visited the East Finchley branch in 1912 wrote: 'it [is] impossible to go along the High-road without noticing this new addition to the shopping facilities of East Finchley . . . the shop appeals very strongly to the public confidence.' Two years later, the *Eastbourne Gazette*

Mosaics such as the one above were standard features in branch doorways.

Christmas poultry at 8 London Road, Forest Hill, c1910. This picture illustrates the impressive scale of Sainsbury's shop fascias of this period. The large external lanterns attracted late night shoppers and provided illumination for outdoor trading.

reported on the opening of the branch at Cornfield Road, Eastbourne: 'One cannot fail to be impressed by its dignified proportions, its lofty ceiling, and the ample floor space between the two counters.'

The exteriors of Sainsbury's shops were even more striking than their interiors. Into a frontage of highly polished red Norwegian and grey Swedish granite were set tall sash windows framed with polished teak. On the top sash appeared slogans such as 'Dealer in Poultry and Game' and 'Purveyor of High Class Provisions'. Between the windows was the doorway, with an entrance mosaic upon which 'J. Sainsbury' was picked out in coloured lettering. The doorway was closed at night by means of a heavy wooden shutter. A black glass fascia panel stretched over the whole width of the shop, with 'J. Sainsbury' painted upon it in gold leaf. Above this was an ornate wrought-iron structure decorated with matt green paint so dark as to look black. Upon this were mounted huge wooden letters, decorated in gold leaf, which again spelt the name 'J. Sainsbury'. Sainsbury's shop fascias were so tall

J. SAINSBURY
BRITISH BIRDS
SAINSBURY'S
BRITISH BIRDS
J. SAINSBURY.
BLACKFRIARS
TURKEYS.
TURKEYS.
BRITISH BIRDS
BRITISH BIRDS
YOU ARE INVITED
INSPECT
DISPLAY.

that they were clearly visible from the other end of the street or above the tallest tram or horse bus.

The powerful image of quality and reliability inspired by these shopfronts was particularly important in areas where Sainsbury's name was not familiar to shoppers. The firm also selected sites where the neighbouring traders would help to attract custom. The branch which opened at 5 The Parade, Watford, in October 1898 – the most distant from head office at that date – was next door to the newly opened Clement's department store. Together, these two shops transformed the top end of Watford High Street from a residential district into a busy commercial area.

At Lewisham the desire to ensure that a neighbouring shop matched up to Sainsbury's standards led to the acquisition in 1902 of a draper's business. The owner, W A Matthews, had found himself in financial difficulites. It was unthinkable to John James to have a large, unoccupied shop next door to his prestigious branch at Obelisk Buildings. The extent of his liability, however, only became clear when the shop burned down soon after he had taken it over. To his dismay he discovered he was not insured. He consulted William Meredith Browne, manager of the Westminster Fire Office, with whom all his other shops were insured. 'What would you have done, Mr Sainsbury, had you known that you were not insured?' asked Mr Browne. 'Why, I should have insured it with the Westminster,' replied John James. 'Very well then,' said Mr Browne, 'we will issue a policy dating from the time of the purchase and we will meet your claim.' Mr John, who accompanied his father to the Westminster Fire Office, recalled that as they left, his father turned to him and remarked, 'That, my boy, is the way that gentlemen do business.' Mr Browne's generosity was matched by his shrewdness. To this day his company, now part of the Sun Alliance group, handles much of Sainsbury's insurance.

J. Sainsbury's pure teas

Among the shops John James purchased from Tom Deacock in 1903 were three adjacent branches at 12, 14 and 16 Kingsland High Street, Dalston. The shop at number 12 was a grocery store which stocked tea, sugar, coffee, cocoa, canned fruit and canned fish – all products unavailable at Sainsbury's other branches. John James decided to add them to his steadily growing product range.

Traditionally the grocer sold dry goods, many of which were imported from Britain's colonies by specialist shippers and merchants. The retail grocer's role was to prepare the goods for sale, blending teas and spices and roasting and grinding coffees, often to closely guarded recipes. The word 'grocer' was derived from the French 'grocier', meaning someone who purchased goods in bulk and repackaged

Sainsbury's Red Label tea, c1918.

An impressive window display of Sainsbury's tea at 639 Christchurch Road, Boscombe.

them, although this hardly did justice to the mystique which surrounded the skilled 'high class' grocer.

By the late nineteenth century this exclusive image had begun to change. The abolition of import duties had made groceries, particularly tea and sugar, affordable by many more people. Thomas Lipton's introduction of cheap ready-packed tea into his shops in 1889 had helped to break down the historic boundaries between the provision merchant's trade and that of the grocer. As it was impractical for John James to establish direct contact with the producers of his teas, he enlisted the help of George Payne, a tea merchant based near Tower Bridge.

The introduction of tea was particularly successful. Together, John James and George Payne selected a series of Sainsbury brand teas. Each blend was named after the colour of the seal on its packet. Blue Label tea was sold at 1s 2d a pound, Green Label at 1s 4d and Red Label at 1s 6d. The launch of these teas coincided with the opening of a new branch of Sainsbury's at 130 Uxbridge Road, Ealing, in March 1903. Mr P Wigley, who worked at the shop, recalled the excitement the staff felt at the launch of the new product and their satisfaction as all the customers 'went out with a packet of Sainsbury's tea'. He went on to add, 'We built a very good trade and by the end of July the sales were well over 900 lbs a week.' For this achievement the Ealing branch won a prize of £20 for the highest sales of any Sainsbury's shop. In 1904 the range was extended by the introduction of two further blends: Yellow Label at 1s 0d a pound and Brown Label at 1s 8d a pound.

Mr Alfred, c 1900.

It soon became apparent to John James that grocery buying required different skills from those needed for the purchase of perishable goods. He therefore sent his fifth son, Alfred, to serve an apprenticeship with George Payne to prepare him to be Sainsbury's grocery buyer. Alfred's apprenticeship was completed in 1906, by which time he was twenty-two years old. He then began work at Sainsbury's head office, receiving a curt note from his father instructing him to 'commence from April 30th . . . Time to be here 8 O'ck. Your half day Thursday.'

Although groceries became an integral part of Sainsbury's business, little attempt was made to increase the range of fresh meats. Tom Deacock's shop at 16 Kingsland High Street had been a butcher's shop, but its acquisition did not lead to a general extension of the range of fresh meats in Sainsbury's other branches. Fresh pork and poultry had long been sold by Sainsbury's, but these were regarded as a separate line of business from butchery proper. Instead, as well as continuing its previous retail business, 16 Kingsland High Street supplied Sunday joints for Sainsbury's live-in staff at other branches. It was not until *c*1910 that frozen New Zealand lamb was added to the range while fresh lamb, mutton and beef were not generally available at Sainsbury's until the First World War.

Many of the goods sold by Sainsbury's were seasonal. The supply of game was dictated by the statutory regulation of the shooting season. Pork was considered to be at its best when there was an 'r' in the month – from September to April – when young, fat pigs were available. Sainsbury's advertisements drew attention to the special virtues of the firm's 'dairy-fed pork' during the autumn and winter. Eggs were at their best from April until June, although the season was extended by imports and by selective breeding. During the winter months the supply was supplemented by cheap preserved eggs which had been stored in waterglass or 'pickled' raw in lime. The abundance of milk during the spring and summer months meant that this was when the best quality 'new grass' butter was available and prices were at their lowest. Sainsbury's only imported Dutch butter in the summer, from the beginning of May until September. 'It was with relief,' wrote Mr R Buisman, 'that [we] saw the first leaves of the beech as this was the sure sign that a telegram [from Sainsbury's] would arrive.'

Although it was legal to sell tea by gross weight until 1926, Sainsbury's sold it net, as this 1911 advertisement shows.

Into the suburbs and the 'country'

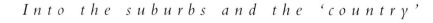

Between 1861 and 1911 the population of Greater London more than doubled. Areas such as Hampstead and Finchley to the north of London and Streatham and Blackheath to the south, which in the mid-nineteenth century had been villages, were absorbed into the capital's suburban sprawl. Sainsbury's opened branches in each of these locations, often recognising their potential before their markets had fully developed.

By the turn of the century Sainsbury's had begun to develop its own sites further afield. In June 1899 the 'market field' at Redhill was acquired at a quarterly ground rent of £18. The shop which was built there was the first to be classified by Sainsbury's as a 'country' branch, marking the beginning of a new phase. During the first decade of the twentieth century Sainsbury's opened 'country' branches in provincial towns such as Brighton, Hove, Eastbourne, Bournemouth, Folkestone, Guildford, Ipswich, Tunbridge Wells and Oxford as well as continuing its expansion in London and its suburbs. As far as possible, new branches were on freehold sites, thus building up a substantial portfolio of property. Few figures survive relating to the value of the firm's capital assets, but at its incorporation in 1922 the new private company was valued at £1,300,000.

Transport innovations

The opening of the 'country' branches necessitated new transport arrangements. When the new depot at Blackfriars was acquired in 1890, Sainsbury's transport fleet had consisted of just eight vehicles: three two-horse vans and five single-horse

A two-horse bulk delivery van, 1909. Each 'carman' was responsible for grooming and harnessing his own horses.

vans. There was also a pony and cart that was used to collect the week's takings from each branch. In 1907 the company decided this was insufficient so it purchased two Foden steam wagons for longer journeys. Although the Fodens ran on cheap coke, this was partly offset by the expense of employing a driver and a stoker, both of whom were too dirty to handle foodstuffs when they reached their destination. A further expense was that the steam wagons required a separate garage at Blackfriars because of the smoke and dirt they generated when they were fired up in the mornings. They were also unreliable and their size caused problems at some shops.

Despite their faults the steamers were the most efficient transport available until shortly before the First World War. In 1911 Mr Arthur proposed that the firm should purchase a 1½–2 ton Milne Daimler lorry, which he thought would

Carmen, Freddy Goodwin and Benjamin Lunn, with a Milne Daimler 5-ton van, c1912.

One of Sainsbury's Sentinel steam wagons and its crew, c1921.

provide a faster and more reliable service to Watford than the steamers. Mr John was sceptical, asserting that 'the bad character of the roads and the hill to Harrow' would defeat the lorry. Eventually it was agreed that 'Mr A S obtain one motor of 1½ to 2 tons from the makers free of cost for demonstration for a few weeks. Mr J B S submitted that the test must be a fair one – with ordinary not special loads – and hoped it would be after Christmas.' Seven petrol vehicles were eventually purchased.

Even these, however, were not suitable for deliveries to the most distant branches, which continued to receive supplies by rail even though there were frequent complaints about the unreliability of the service. On 16th July 1915 Mr John wrote to one of his managers complaining that 'those branches solely dependent on the railways never know within 48 hours when the goods will arrive: goods sent to Folkestone last Thursday for delivery there Friday morning were not discovered until Monday morning, and unfortunately there were a lot of perishables.' It was as a result of such mishaps that sausages were sent by passenger train, rather than by goods train, arriving on the evening that they were made instead of the following morning. The Norwich branch, which opened in 1913, was supplied by means of an arrangement with the city's chocolate manufacturer, Caley's, whose vehicles made regular trips to London and returned filled with Sainsbury's provisions.

George Hoare (third from left), manager of the Oxford branch, celebrating the first anniversary of its opening with his staff at a Sunday picnic in May 1911.

Promotional activities

Not every new branch was an immediate success. Mr John spent successive week-ends at the Guildford store after it opened on 16th November 1906 in an effort to achieve weekly takings of over £40. The firm had to work hard at promoting itself in localities where Sainsbury's name was not yet familiar. The residents of Moor-town and Winton were offered the refund of their fares if they purchased a 'general parcel' from Sainsbury's new Bournemouth branch after 2pm on Satur-days. Even in the established trading area business could be slow to develop. The branch which opened at Belsize Park, Haverstock Hill, North London, in 1903 was managed by Mr S E Smith. In an attempt to increase trade Mr John and Mr Smith worked late into the night searching the street directories for names of local residents who had not yet opened an account.

The anniversaries of branch openings were marked by special promotions and free gifts, such as crayons and colouring books for children and offers of tea sets, cutlery and table linen, for which customers had to save coupons printed on the wrapping paper of Sainsbury brand products. One of the most spectacular events was staged in May 1911 to mark the Oxford branch's first 'birthday'. The manager, George Hoare, recalled how the branch was decorated with garlands of flowers:

> Fifty boxes of roses, smilax and other blooms were sent down from Covent Garden and with the aid of some locally grown plants, rockeries were laid out down the centre of the shop and festoons were hung from all the lighting points. The staff worked overnight to complete the picture. From Blackfriars next morning came two tons of fresh goods, decorated cooked meats and poultry, arriving at 7.00am. By 10.00am when Mr John walked in, the whole branch was in perfect order, every man in a clean coat and apron . . . As he led me up the shop . . . [he] told me to take another 10s on my salary.

Despite Sainsbury's efforts to tailor its advertising to the communities it served, it did occasionally encounter hostility from local traders. One of the most important claims made by the firm was that it offered 'London's lowest prices'. The intention was to reassure customers that 'the charges at all the numerous branches are precisely the same'. Such claims were, however, capable of misinterpretation. At Norwich a competitor launched a public attack on Sainsbury's, suggesting that it was undesirable to 'spend money with branch shops of a London House' and called upon residents to support local enterprise. John James immediately published a rejoinder:

> I must take exception to this, for I am personally a resident in the Eastern Counties and moreover pay tens of thousands of pounds sterling every year in exchange for local produce for the supply of my numerous shops. Then again the manager of my Norwich branch, Mr Adye, is in every way a local tradesman, with full power to interest himself in all city matters . . . all the assistants are local men, and . . . the advent of my business has improved the position of a large number of shop assistants in the city.

Sainsbury's rarely resorted to the brash advertising techniques for which Thomas Lipton became famous. Lipton used every possible advertising medium, from hot air balloons which dropped 'air telegrams' over the streets of Glasgow to monster cheeses which arrived at his branches pulled by elephants. Although extravagant publicity was not John James's style, he was goaded on one occasion into making a direct response. When Thomas Lipton was awarded a Royal

The first prize-winner at Watford roller skating carnival, 1911. This unnamed employee dressed up as the Crelos milkmaid depicted on the advertising postcard pinned to her apron.

Warrant, he erected signs over his shop fascias proclaiming, 'We serve the King.' Where Sainsbury's had branches directly opposite Lipton's, banners were erected which read 'God save the Queen!'

More typical of Sainsbury's advertising techniques were its 'fairy story tea cards'. These certainly succeeded in encouraging customers to shop regularly with the firm. Mrs F G Nice recalled how 'each Friday afternoon my mother would meet me from school, from where we went to the Redhill branch of Sainsbury's to buy the weekly groceries. For me the most important item was the

LITTLE RED RIDING HOOD.

V.

"AND what great arms you have," said Red Riding Hood, "all the better to hug you, my dear," said the Wolf. "And, what a great mouth you have," queried Red Riding Hood; "all the better to drink SAINSBURY'S Pure Tea," returned the Wolf. "And what large teeth you have," said the little girl, "all the better to eat you with," roared the Wolf, jumping out of bed and springing upon Red Riding Hood. He was about to devour her when in rushed a woodcutter, and with one blow of his axe he severed the wolf's head from its body, and thus saved the little girl's life.

"Red Riding Hood meets the wolf."

'And what a great mouth…' Red Riding Hood's errand was to deliver Sainsbury's tea to her grandmother.

packet of tea containing an instalment of a fairy story. I would wait in an agony of suspense until we opened the packet on leaving the shop.' These were fairy stories with a difference, for each tale included an important message about the qualities of Sainsbury's tea. Thus Sainsbury's tea was the drink which sent Goldilocks to sleep; it cured Jack of nervous exhaustion after he had climbed the beanstalk, and refreshed the guests between dances at Cinderella's ball.

The national multiples

The spectacular advertising and well-publicised price cuts of the national multiples such as Home & Colonial were a serious threat to independent retailers.

Many people predicted the demise of the small grocer in the face of what an editorial in *The Times* of 18th August 1902 termed 'the internecine strife known as "cutting".' The national multiples were perceived to be faceless. According to *The Times* they were 'nearly all conducted upon the same impersonal iron routine system with automatic managers and still more automatic assistants, the brains being supplied from headquarters with the consignments of goods'. The chief objective of the 'company shops' was said to be to make profits for their shareholders, even at the expense of customer service.

An impressive display of Sainsbury's sausages at the Watford branch in 1911.

Many of the criticisms levelled at the national multiples were scarcely logical. Far from reaching saturation point as *The Times* also alleged, the market for food was growing steadily. The population of the County of London had grown from 3,223,000 in 1861 to 7,251,000 in 1911. Improvements in purchasing power – particularly among the urban working classes, who formed the major part of the multiples' customers – also led to increased expenditure on food. Another criticism, that the multiples had caused a decline in ancillary customer services, was specious. While it was true that the 'company shops' did not provide retail delivery and credit, shops in working class areas had seldom delivered anyway and the offering of goods on 'tick' had long been criticised as encouraging fecklessness. Even the accusation that centralisation led to a lack of initiative among staff could be countered with the argument that it allowed standards to be set and maintained.

Setting standards

Sainsbury's combined the price competitiveness of the large multiples with the services offered by the high class independent retailers. Staff learnt the arts of salesmanship in order to handle the wide range of foods the stores stocked. Standardised working practices were introduced for staff and maintained by a small team of inspectors. Sainsbury's first inspectors were appointed in *c*1903. They later became known as district supervisors.

All the branches received regular visits from the inspectors. George Younger, who was responsible for the southern shops, distinguished between the 'senior' shops – the larger and more profitable branches – and the smaller, 'junior' shops. The 'senior' shops appear to have taken up most of Mr Younger's time. Each inspector was also required to report back in person on his branches' performance to Mr John at least once a week.

Inspectors came to know their managers well and looked after their welfare. Career ambitions, the problems of finding accommodation, and illness, all fell within the inspectors' remit. Despite this personal contact even well respected managers were criticised if they fell short of the firm's high standards. Edward Tupman received a severe dressing down from Mr John as a result of an inspector's visit: 'It was evident that you had not given any attention to your butter department, and that you had left "Smith" the bacon hand to use his own discretion in cutting up the bacon, and again the goods in the cooked meat department were heaped together, instead of being set out in an attractive manner.' However, on this occasion he got off lightly, as Mr John wrote: 'I cannot help thinking that you were not yourself yesterday, and in

The staff at 14 Cranbrook Road, Ilford, photographed in the yard behind the branch in c1910.

consequence I shall not enter in my private book the fact of your having a large number of packets weighed up for customers the majority of which were either over or under weight.'

As the business grew increasingly complex, it became necessary to set out the firm's rules and regulations in printed form. This was partly to ensure that standards were maintained but also because communication between head office and the branches was becoming more formal. The first proposal for a branch rule book was made by John James at one of the earliest recorded board meetings. At that time the idea was dropped as it was considered too risky due to 'the danger of these falling into outside hands'. It was not until January 1914 that the first rule book for managers was published. Its objectives were to bring about 'a universal form of management' and make it 'easier to continue our style and procedure when transferred from one branch to another'.

Each copy of the rule book was personally addressed by the branch management department to the manager who was to receive it. Particular attention was drawn to the importance of staff relations: 'The knowledge of how to handle men is one of the most important of business assets . . . a word of appreciation for work well done, a word of caution for unseen danger – a word of helpful criticism for faulty work – a word of advice in time of uncertainty – a word of encouragement when the spirit is low – these are important points in dealing with men.' Allied to this was the emphasis placed on training employees to fit them for more responsible positions. Until the First World War all Sainsbury's training was in the form of 'on the job' instruction and was therefore entirely the responsibility of the branch manager. The rule book contained the following reminder: 'Successful management can only be obtained with the aid of a properly trained staff, and however hard a manager may work personally, he is sure to be disappointed with the result if he neglects to instruct his men.'

A family business

The influence of the Sainsbury family ensured that the firm retained its independent character. Even when the business was registered as a joint stock company in 1922, John James refused to dilute its ownership. The Articles of Association stipulated that only family members could become shareholders. This was in marked contrast to Thomas Lipton. At his company's flotation in 1898, Lipton, a lifelong bachelor, retained only a one-third share in the company, which was valued at £2½ million. Thereafter he devoted less and less time to running the business in favour of yachting, racehorses and the patronage of charitable ventures.

John James had been carefully grooming the next generation to follow in his footsteps. In November 1911, at the earliest recorded board meeting, the first subject of discussion was how to divide up the responsibilities of running the business between the members of the younger generation. Mr John, the eldest, was now a mature man of forty years at the height of his powers. Born over the first shop, he had been schooled by his father in every aspect of the business. He was the keenest and most energetic of the brothers. Not surprisingly, he took on the most onerous duties: the bacon and ham departments; the buying of lamb and Ostend rabbits; 'works' (by which was meant both new store development and the maintenance of existing shops); engaging staff; vehicles and stables. George, aged thirty-nine, was allocated supervision of the 'office and counting house', together with butter and cheese, cold storage poultry and game and 'despatch' (distribution). The thirty-one

Harry Webb, a delivery lad, c1913. Delivery lads were expected to clean their machines daily before breakfast.

year old Arthur was assigned the management of the cooked meats factory, together with pork, eggs and statements (customer accounts), while Alfred, at twenty-seven the youngest brother present, became responsible for the management of the embryonic grocery department.

At this first board meeting Mr John expressed the view that one of his brothers should be qualified to take over the supervision of the branches 'in case of necessity'. It was important that whoever was chosen as his deputy should be the brother most easily spared from his buying and administrative duties. At a second meeting it was decided that young Alfred should fill this role. However, with hindsight it is clear that Mr John had no intention of allowing his brother to perform this task for long. It was Mr John's own eldest son, Mr Alan, who was destined to become his successor.

*George Huddle, manager at
143 High Street, Guildford,
with his fleet of Morris delivery
vans and their drivers, 1929.*

SBURY
NATIONAL PROVINCIAL BANK
LIBERAL
CLUB
PROVISIONS
J. SAINSBURY.

D o n ' t   p a r t   w i t h   y o u r   g o l d

'*D*on't let the eternal food question spoil your holiday this year. Sainsbury's have a wonderful selection of luncheon delicacies ready for the table.' Less than a fortnight before the beginning of the Great War holiday-makers in Eastbourne and Norfolk could escape from all thoughts of the impending conflict with a delicious spread of Sainsbury's piekins, cooked meats and pickles. Soon, however, the 'food question' was to refer to an altogether different problem. Britain's heavy reliance on imported foodstuffs now became a matter of considerable concern. Well before the outbreak of war some commentators had seriously questioned the nation's ability to avert starvation if faced with an enemy blockade. Over 75 per cent of the butter, cheese, eggs and bacon consumed in Britain was imported – from Ireland, Denmark, Holland and the United States – while grain from the North American prairies, beef from Argentina and lamb from New Zealand were also important elements of the nation's diet. Once hostilities commenced, the most pressing needs were to cut down on imports to save foreign currency and to requisition merchant ships for the war effort.

Important Notice

Usual quantities can only be served.
Give me time and I will do my best to keep all my regular Customers supplied.
J. SAINSBURY.

A handwritten inscription on the top of this poster reads: 'Beginning of Anglo-German War, August 1914'.

At the outbreak of the First World War John James was seventy years old. The firm he had founded forty-five years earlier was now a substantial business with 121 branches, 2,000 employees and a turnover of almost £2.7 million. John James, who had begun life in one of London's poorest areas and started his business with money saved from his job as a shop assistant, was now an extremely wealthy man. Although he still played an active part in the business, attending board meetings and supporting and encouraging his sons, the responsibility for Sainsbury's day-to-day management now lay with his eldest son, Mr John. In recognition of this, John James took his son into partnership on 27th March 1915.

P a n i c - b u y i n g   a n d   r i s i n g   p r i c e s

As soon as war was declared on 4th August 1914, notices were posted in the windows of all Sainsbury's branches stating that the firm would do its best to keep regular customers supplied, but warning against hoarding. Despite this appeal, queues formed outside shops as worried customers stocked up on basic foodstuffs. This

Undated portraits of the founder John James (LEFT) and his eldest son, Mr John.

panic-buying exacerbated an already serious situation. Faced with a massive increase in demand, wholesalers were forced to put up the prices of imported provisions. Retailers were then obliged to pass these price rises on to their customers. At Sainsbury's, instructions went out that butter was to be put up by 2d a pound.

Mr John predicted that sugar supplies would be the hardest to maintain. This was a shrewd assessment, for within a few days of going to war the price of granulated sugar had risen from 1¾d to 4½d a pound. Managers were instructed to reserve their stock for regular customers and not to sell more than two pounds to anyone. Customers hoping to bottle summer fruits and make jam must have been disappointed. The pre-war special offers on sugar became a thing of the past.

Although forced to increase prices for imported sugar, butter and bacon, Sainsbury's was able to influence the prices of home-produced food purchased directly from its own suppliers such as Mr Frank and Lloyd Maunder. The prices of cooked meats made in Sainsbury's own factory at Blackfriars were actually reduced in early September.

The speed at which prices increased did lead to problems. On 12th August 1914 Mr John complained to George Younger, 'I have personally visited one or two branches this morning, and found that the confusion caused last week by the many changes in prices has left several articles without tickets. It is . . . IMPORTANT that every article in the shop should be distinctly marked with the price. For instance, eggs are being sold in many Dairies at 2½d, whereas our price

Winifred, Edward and Arthur Skillen enjoying a picnic of Sainsbury's products, 1916.

An advertising postcard for Crelos margarine. Inflation during the early part of the war made it necessary to overprint the pre-war price.

today is only 1½d.' The lack of clear ticketing was an important omission in Mr John's eyes as it had long been Sainsbury's policy to mark clearly the prices of all its goods. This not only advertised their competitiveness but also reassured customers that everything possible was being done to ensure price stability.

Another reason for rising food prices was the purchasing activities of the military authorities. Most army provisions were bought on the wholesale markets. This increased demand and pushed up prices. Even when goods were bought retail, Sainsbury's quickly learned to be wary. Mr John instructed his managers that 'you must first make certain of the Regiment to which the goods are to be supplied, the destination of the barracks, and *do not part with anything* until you have an official order signed by the officer in charge.'

When troops were billeted in private lodgings, however, the extra mouths to feed could lead to an increase in trade. Mr Charles Phillips, manager of the newly opened Bournemouth store, reported enthusiastically on 21st September 1914 that '10,000 territorials are to be billeted here for six months, not under canvas but in the smaller boarding houses so we shall derive some benefit from this.'

Wartime changes

War brought many changes to working life in the branches. An initial request to postpone holidays became compulsory on 7th September 1914. Managers were authorised to close early if supplies ran short. The long-standing savings scheme for gifts of tea services, cutlery canteens and table linen was suspended. Orders by post were no longer to be accepted. Delivery services to some districts were also abandoned owing to the requisitioning of horses by the army. Customers were asked to carry home the smaller parcels for themselves and to pay their weekly accounts promptly. Mr John wrote to managers: 'I have to pay cash for all goods, and must ask my customers to do likewise.' Even changes to the currency caused problems. The paper notes that replaced the trusted gold sovereigns were regarded with suspicion by many people. Managers were instructed that they should accept the new notes, but told to preserve their gold and silver if £5 notes were tendered.

Wartime also brought shorter trading hours: opening time was now 9am rather than the pre-war 7.30am. In 1917 closing time was brought forward from 7pm to

6pm on Mondays to Thursdays. On Fridays and Saturdays the shops shut at 8pm. This replaced the pre-war convention of closing whenever the last customer left.

The appropriation of horses was a serious problem. One young lad, Albert Skinner, was promoted to roundsman when the usual delivery driver at the Tunbridge Wells branch joined up. Albert quickly became attached to 'Nobby', his horse, and hid him in side-streets when the army requisitioning authorities were about. For Albert, losing Nobby would have been a personal blow. For the business, the loss of horses meant the breakdown of deliveries of food to the shops. Branches whose supplies were disrupted were told to '*close at once* and post up a notice to the effect that, owing to difficulties of delivery, the shop is temporarily closed, awaiting fresh supplies'.

The most dramatic effect of the war concerned staffing levels. At Norwich the manager, Raymond Adye, and his deputy had to run the shop alone, when the whole of the rest of the staff enlisted at once. Almost every letter to branch managers mentioned staffing problems. The effects of voluntary enlistment were completely unpredictable. Mr John pleaded:

> Although I am anxious to afford every facility for the members of the staff to join the Colours, I must ask them to give me as long a notice as possible . . . five men at one of our branches . . . informed their Manager late on Thursday evening that they had joined the Colours and were starting first thing the following morning. . . Had they informed their recruiting Sergeant that they could not be released from their duties until Monday morning I feel sure that he would have been equally satisfied.

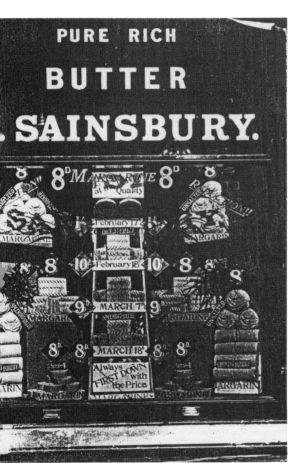

As the war progressed, prices began to stabilise. This window display, which probably dates from March 1915, charts the falling price of Crelos margarine.

Bulletins were circulated to branches insisting on at least six days' notice, and staff were reminded that the general welfare of the public was dependent upon the efficient distribution of food.

Staffing problems were made worse by Sainsbury's reliance on young men in the eighteen to twenty-five age group. These were the people most likely to answer the call to arms, yet they also played a crucial role in the running of the shops. By the age of eighteen a salesman was already skilled at his job and was responsible for training up the new recruits who worked alongside him. Branch staff who joined the Colours not only took with them their own skills and knowledge, but made it harder to ensure that those who remained kept up pre-war standards of expertise and service. These skills were hard to replace. Mr Goldup wrote

Mr John recognised the publicity potential of employing female shop assistants. This postcard shows six of the first recruits advertising Sainsbury's margarine at 9/11 London Road, Croydon.

from head office to the district supervisors at the end of August 1914 that 'there is little or nothing of any experience applying for situations'.

Recruiting women

Faced with a depleted male workforce, Sainsbury's began to recruit saleswomen. An advertisement for two hundred single young women elicited thousands of applications. The wages were £1 per week less 2s 3d deducted for tea and washing the white overalls provided by the firm. The female recruits were initially given simple tasks such as serving packaged groceries, dealing with customers' orders and 'making oneself generally useful'. Rings, jewellery and loose hair were forbidden. However, unlike their male counterparts, they were provided with chairs.

The women soon proved their worth and took on most of the jobs which had been performed by the men. To help new staff pick up the rudiments of food handling quickly, a training school was established at Blackfriars in 1915. This provided 'off the job' training. Here the new recruits spent a fortnight learning how to operate a bacon slicer, use scales and 'knock up' butter and margarine.

Despite the care taken to train the women, Mr John still saw the future of the business lying with the 'bright young fellows' who were too young to serve in the

WOMEN GROCERS.

GIRLS REPLACING SHOPMAN SOLDIERS.

The woman grocer's assistant is a product of the war, just as the woman guard has appeared on the Paris "Métro" railway, and as tramway and omnibus conductors in some of the French provincial cities.

A large firm of wholesale provision merchants, Messrs. Sainsbury, advertised for 200 single young women to replace a portion of the 500 of the firm's employees who have joined the colours. The salary offered was £1 a week.

Before noon, said Messrs. Sainsbury's general manager yesterday, several thousand applications had been received. The 200 women assistants are to be dressed in white, with white aprons, and will begin their duties this week.

At first they will only serve pounds of sugar, tea, and other commodities, but in a few weeks it is hoped they will have learnt how to cut up bacon and deal with the heavier goods of the grocer's store.

Messrs. Lipton, Ltd., 400 of whose assistants have joined the Army, are also filling as many posts as possible with women employees.

The employment of 'Women Grocers' caught the imagination of the press, as shown by this cutting from the Daily Mail *(8th September 1914).*

This still from a Pathé newsreel of 1915 is another example of the news value of female recruitment.

armed forces. He instructed his district supervisors to take a particular interest in their training and in 'pushing these young men forward'. Departing from the tradition of promoting from within the ranks of his own counter service staff, he even advertised for 'Practical Grocers and Provision Hands up to 40 years of age. Must have had experience in [the] first class cash trade.' Despite these measures staffing levels remained a problem. By Christmas 1914 a third of the workforce had left for the armed forces.

In September 1914, the branch management department interviewed the wives of all the married men who had enlisted during the first month of the war and made them an allowance to supplement the payments made by the Government. District supervisors were instructed to discover the extent to which the parents of single men joining the Colours were dependent upon their earnings. The firm was dismayed to realise that not everyone took it for granted that their jobs would be kept open for them: 'we thought the relationship between the Staff and Headquarters was such as to dispel any doubt on this point . . . Please convey to every member of the staff joining the Colours the Firm's high appreciation of their efforts and best wishes for their safe return to the old Firm.'

Time and again, Mr John emphasised that a manager could serve his country as well from behind the counter of his branch as on the battlefield. 'I must have a reasonable number of men, and those members of staff who are now working extra hard to keep things going are deserving of very great credit, and I shall not forget it.' He took great care to bolster the spirits of his store managers and sent personal letters of encouragement when visits became impossible. At Christmas 1915 he wrote to Edward Tupman, manager of the Watford branch: 'We are a good way yet from our goal and may be harder pressed before the war is over, but I am sure that you will manage somehow or other to successfully run your branch through this difficult period, and hope my message will cheer you on your way.'

The main reason staffing levels remained such a problem was the Government's reluctance to introduce conscription. Without conscription no plans could be made to fill essential jobs. Although the army's recruitment campaign, coupled with public opinion, placed men under enormous psychological pressure to join up, voluntary enlistment produced a haphazard response. Lord Derby's scheme, introduced

in the autumn of 1915, was intended to make the process of recruitment smoother by presenting volunteers with an armband in return for declaring their willingness to serve. This enabled them to stay in their normal jobs until they were needed and proved to the public that the men were not cowards. The scheme also introduced an appeals procedure for people in important war work. Mr John greeted these new arrangements with relief: 'When this has all been satisfactorily arranged, which I trust it will be in a very short time, those of us who are left in charge of the business will be able to settle down to work, which I quite realise is almost impossible now with the uncertainty of not knowing what one should do.'

Lord Derby's scheme failed to achieve the required level of recruitment, so conscription was introduced in May 1916. Despite Mr John's insistence that his managers were indispensable, more and more branches came to be managed by women. By the end of the war there were thirty-nine female branch managers, some of them wives or sisters of the peacetime managers. To make the best use of the remaining human resources, the more experienced men were transferred to larger branches, and women were made managers of the smaller stores.

J W Taylor, manager, with his staff at 160 Cricklewood Broadway, pictured in front of the Allies' colours.

Coping with food shortages

Sainsbury's was also faced with problems arising from food shortages. In 1914 it was believed that the free market would be the best mechanism for regulating supplies. The only exception was the establishment of the Sugar Commission to allocate the wholesale distribution of sugar. Concern focused on the need for shipping to be used for the war effort, rather than for food imports, and little thought was given to the needs of the consumer. It was left to retailers to do their best to allocate foods in short supply. Home & Colonial announced early in the war that it would sell sugar only with a purchase of margarine. This was ostensibly to discourage hoarding, but was really a ruse to gain market share from Maypole Dairies. The latter did not sell sugar but relied heavily on sales of margarine.

Even Sainsbury's, whose larger product range meant that margarine formed only a small proportion of sales, found it necessary to undertake a massive advertising campaign emphasising the nutritional and patriotic benefits of eating margarine rather than imported butter. Quoting a speech made by Asquith, the Prime

*Mr Paul saw active service during
the Great War.*

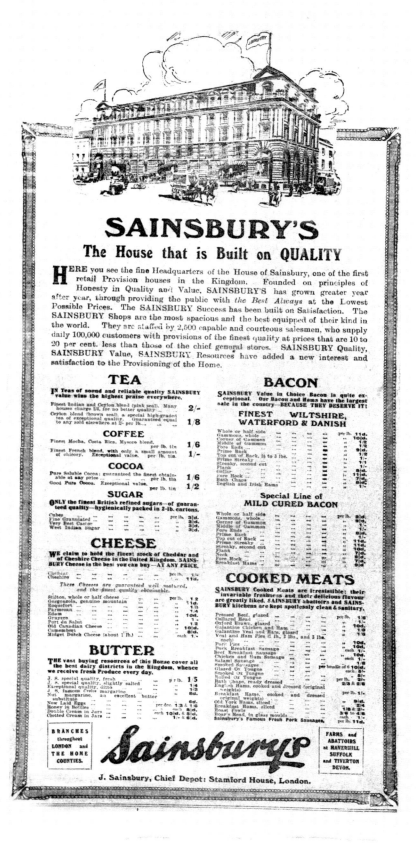

*Despite the exigencies of wartime,
Sainsbury's was still able to offer
its customers a full range of cooked
meats, provisions and groceries.
This newspaper advertisement
dates from 23rd April 1915.*

*Wartime advertisements frequently
referred to contemporary events
such as the sinking of the
SS 'City of Winchester'.*

*A female delivery driver and her
assistant (c 1915) with one of the
firm's first motor delivery vans.*

Minister, on 29th June 1915, the firm declared, 'We must economise!' and went on, 'Economy, desirable always, is a National obligation now, but economy in the food department calls for wisdom. We must reduce food bills, but we must also be on our guard against cutting down food nutriment. We must give a stricter eye now to buying only food that is pure, nourishing, and sustaining; it must be appetising too. And we must not pay a penny more than is necessary. "Crelos" is quite the most delicious, digestible and economic form of fat food you can buy.'

It was not until the U-boat crisis of 1917 that the Government finally accepted that rationing was inevitable. In April 1917 a quarter of the merchant ships sailing to Britain were sunk by the enemy. Proclamations were read out in every church, chapel, synagogue and Salvation Army barracks in the country urging people to buy less, particularly of imported foodstuffs. Even home-produced meats were affected because farmers relied on imported feed for their stock. In July 1917 Sainsbury's warned its customers that 'we do not expect to be able to put more than half the usual quantity of . . . English, Irish and Danish bacon before our customers . . . this month'.

People queued outside the shops when they saw a delivery arrive. To avoid being mobbed by the customers before the goods had been unpacked, shop assistants used coded 'back slang' such as 'nocab' and 'ragus' to disguise the stocks that had arrived. Even so, disturbances did occur. Ethel Jessop, manager of the Woodford branch, phoned the police when rioting broke out among workmen who could not buy cheese. The manager of one of the other shops in Ethel's parade was killed in the disturbance. Eventually a mounted policeman arrived and, on finding that Ethel had only six members of staff, suggested that they close the top half of the shutter across the door. He then stood his horse across the doorway and allowed six customers in at a time under the horse!

Apart from events such as this, few civilians were at risk during the First World War. The only recorded incident of air raid damage to Sainsbury's property was on the night of 23rd–24th September 1916, when the Streatham branch was bombed by a Zeppelin. After attacking Croydon, the airship flew on up the line of the A23, dropping bombs on the way, until it reached Streatham High Road, where Sainsbury's branch was one of several buildings to be hit.

In November 1916 the new Prime

Minister, Lloyd George, created the post of Food Controller, as a first step towards greater government intervention in the distribution of food. The first Food Controller was Hudson Kearley, Lord Devonport, founder of the International Tea Company. Plans were drawn up for the introduction of rationing, but these had still not been implemented when Lord Devonport retired in May 1917 on grounds of ill health.

It was his successor, Lord Rhondda, who finally oversaw the introduction of rationing. In October 1917 a long-awaited Government scheme for the distribution of sugar was introduced. It was not true rationing, because it did not carry with it the promise that customers would definitely receive a fixed quantity, but it marked an important step forward in recognising the need to ensure that supplies were distributed fairly. Local shopkeepers were allocated sugar according to the number of customers registered with them. Sainsbury's eagerly invited customers to 'see that *your* card, filled in with the name "J. Sainsbury" (and address of the branch usually dealt with) is brought to us *at once*'.

The new scheme helped to ease the pressure on sugar supplies but the situation with regard to other goods remained chaotic. Advertisements for bacon and cheese placed in the *Evening News* and *Daily Chronicle* caused Sainsbury's serious embarrassment. The firm was obliged to apologise the following week: 'We did not foresee that as a result of advertising our prices . . . all the World and his Wife would attempt to obtain supplies from Sainsbury's. The outcome of the rush was that our stocks lasted but a few hours, yet it proves that the public realise who is protecting them against inflated prices.'

The same problem recurred when rationing for butter and margarine was announced in January 1918. 'Our invitation to regular customers to register for butter and margarine supplies brought so many thousands to our doors that many of our Branches were temporarily overwhelmed. We regret that . . . many of our friends suffered inconvenience that was beyond our power to prevent.' In particular, customers were urged to remember 'the strain imposed upon our women employees . . . on whom the present difficulties fall with peculiar severity. The firm of Sainsbury does everything possible to help their employees through each trying day, but it is in the power of each individual customer to make things just a little easier for those who are doing their work in most trying circumstances.'

Gradually other products were rationed. The amounts varied slightly as the supply situation changed, but were generally 8 ounces sugar, 5 ounces of butter or margarine, 4 ounces of jam and 2 ounces of tea a week. Fresh meat and bacon were rationed by value, rather than weight, with an allowance which bought about 1 pound of meat and 4–8 ounces of bacon. Sainsbury's welcomed rationing as a

Many young men were promoted during the early part of the war. Arthur Leggett advanced from counterhand to manager before enlisting in the British Expeditionary Forces. He rejoined Sainsbury's on his demobilisation.

fairer way to share out foodstuffs in short supply but was frustrated at the imposition of fixed prices. Several times the firm was threatened with prosecution for selling goods at prices below those set by the Board of Trade.

Under the rationing system, only retailers who sold a full choice of fresh meats were allowed to accept customers' registrations. This was a problem for Sainsbury's as only four of its shops stocked the full choice of meats, although almost all branches offered pork and frozen lamb. To overcome this, wherever possible 'home killed' fresh beef and mutton were hurriedly added to the range.

The impact of rationing on Sainsbury's business is difficult to assess. Although the company's sales increased from just under £2.7m in 1914 to nearly £3.7m in 1918, this disguises an element of distortion caused by wartime inflation. In real terms, turnover fell by over 20 per cent.

Profit margins were squeezed. Gross margins fell from 11.2 per cent in the 1917–18 financial year to 9.95 per cent the following year. This was the result of intense competition between retailers for customers' rationing registrations, and the erosion by inflation of the profit margins allowed by the government's maximum prices for basic foodstuffs. Costs also increased. Providing customers with information about rationing led to a huge rise in advertising expenditure. From £1,220 in the 1917–18 financial year, this increased sevenfold to £8,450 in 1918–19. Although there are no complete figures for the latter part of the war, there were also sharp rises in wages, fuel prices and taxation. As a result, profits after tax fell from £119,306 in 1918 to £71,888 in 1919.

The war also halted Sainsbury's programme of new branch openings. Although eight stores had opened during the early part of the war, between November 1916 and July 1919 no further branches were added to the chain.

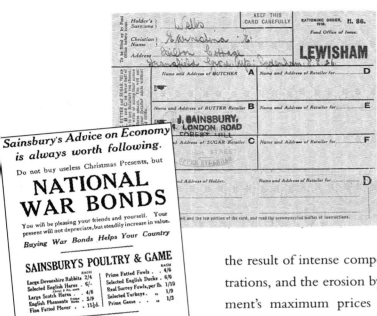

TOP *Ration card for meat, sugar and butter from 1918.*
ABOVE *Sainsbury's wartime advertising frequently appealed to customers' patriotism.*

Returning to normal

After the Armistice it took many months for life to return to normal. Foreign trade had been permanently altered and it was not possible to return to the pre-war reliance on cheap food imports. Nevertheless, prices had returned to their pre-war levels by the end of 1918. Encouraged by this, the government discontinued rationing in May 1919. However, when prices began to rise sharply later that summer, rationing had to be re-introduced for meat, butter and sugar. The situation with regard to meat and butter eased fairly quickly and these were decontrolled in

A display at Wealdstone branch, c1919, showing high prices after rationing was withdrawn. Many goods shown in this photograph were soon to be replaced by own brands.

J.SAINSBURY

THE Premier House in the Provision Trade would like to hear from all employees now serving with the colours, both at home and abroad, with a view to re-engagement directly they are released from the Country's service.

Demobilisation will necessarily be slow, but those men anxious to resume their civil occupations should communicate without delay with the Staff Office, Blackfriars, S.E. 1.

GOD SAVE THE KING!

J.SAINSBURY

This 1919 advertisement shows Sainsbury's eagerness to re-recruit its trained staff.

October 1919; but only in November 1920, when sugar finally ceased to be rationed, was the retail trade freed from restrictions. It was not until the financial year 1920–21 that Sainsbury's sales and profits returned to their former levels.

It took just as long for staffing arrangements to return to normal. In early 1920 thirty branches were still managed by women. Demobilised men were sent to the Blackfriars training school for refresher courses before returning to their pre-war jobs. Most of the women who had taken their places were either paid off or given jobs in the new grocery departments which were added to larger branches from 1920 onwards.

A few women, however, kept their wartime seniority. Alice Hayes, who had been manager of the store at 43 High Street, Islington, was demoted to saleswoman when a new male manager was appointed in December 1919; but her talents had been recognised, and when the post of manager at 159 Queen's Crescent, Kentish Town, became vacant three months later, she was offered the job and remained there until July 1931. Another female manager was Rebecca Juniper who had been in charge of the Coulsdon branch. Like Alice Hayes, she was demoted on the return of the manager, but became manager of 35 London Road, Croydon, in February 1922 and remained there until May 1928.

There were many men who did not return. Nearly one in three of the young men who had been aged twenty to twenty-four in 1914 did not come home. Evidence about the number of Sainsbury's staff who served in the Great War is patchy. At the outbreak of war, Sainsbury's employed about 2,800 staff, most of whom were young men aged between fifteen and thirty. As each new age group became eligible for military service they were replaced by more young men and by women. Even before the introduction of conscription in 1916 over 1,000 men had enlisted from Sainsbury's. It is likely that around 500 male employees died during the war and that twice as many sustained serious injuries. This means that, on average, every one of Sainsbury's 128 branches lost four of its staff.

Another link in the chain

Victory in the Great War brought optimism. In 1920, Sainsbury's had 129 shops and a turnover of just over £5 million. By 1939 this had risen to 255 shops and a turnover of £12.6 million. During the same period the volume of Sainsbury's trade quadrupled. This was in marked contrast to many of the company's competitors and the British economy as a whole. After a short post-war boom, national income fell sharply and the interwar period saw the worst slump in living memory. One reason for Sainsbury's success during this period was that it was a well-managed business. The *Financial Times* in 1928, for example, praised its 'efficient distributing organisation . . . as wonderful in its present-day aspects as it was humble in its origin'. Mr John, like his father, had proved himself to be a businessman of considerable ability. He had an intimate knowledge of the firm, gained through many years' experience working alongside his father. This provided continuity. In 1922, when Sainsbury's became a private limited company, John James became chairman and governing director, and Mr John, Mr Arthur and Mr Alfred were made directors. The share capital of the new company was valued at £1.3 million. The Sainsbury family was not answerable to shareholders and so could take a long-term view of the future and invest a high proportion of the company's profits back into the business.

Sainsbury's was better placed than the larger multiples to respond to changes in Government policy. The pre-war belief in free trade was abandoned in favour of protectionism in an attempt to reduce Britain's huge trade deficit, which by 1928 was running at £123 million. Among the measures introduced by Ramsay Mac-Donald in the 1930s were subsidies for home-produced foods and import quotas which gave preference to goods produced in the British Empire.

These measures were damaging to the large national multiples because they relied heavily on a small product range and the competitive advantage to be gained from cheap foreign imports. By 1934 bacon quotas were estimated to have cost the Allied group – which now embraced Maypole Dairies, Lipton's and Home & Colonial – £150,000 in lost profits.

These restrictions had little effect on Sainsbury's, where imported produce did not form a crucial part of the firm's business. Indeed the measures only encouraged Sainsbury's reliance on the home market. A list of wholesale purchases dating from 1928 reveals £137,000 being spent on British sugar and over £400,000 each on English eggs and pork. The firm exploited the publicity to be gained from its patriotic buying policies. From 1931 onwards its advertisements were

J. SAINSBURY'S

Special Offer
To Personal Shoppers

BRITISH GROWN
GRANULATED SUGAR
(FROM CAMBRIDGESHIRE AND SUFFOLK)

BUY BRITISH!

To enable our Customers to test the quality of this real Home Product we will include

2-lbs. FREE
with each general purchase in the Grocery Department to the value of . . **2/6**

BUY BRITISH!

Monday to Saturday inclusive
July 3rd to 8th

J. SAINSBURY
for QUALITY and VALUE

This offer applies only to those shops with complete Grocery Departments.

As part of its 'Buy British' campaign Sainsbury's promoted home-produced beet sugar.

full of references to 'Empire' butter and 'Colonial' mutton and cheese. Own brand teas were billed as 'Indian and Ceylon' to reassure customers that they were produced in the British Empire.

Steady growth

The national multiples' problems were partly the result of their earlier rapid expansion. In the pre-war years they had opened large numbers of small shops. By the 1930s these had become outdated but their poor performance made it difficult to find the necessary investment funds to carry out a programme of modernisation. In 1939 Home & Colonial's 798 shops only managed a turnover of £9.9 million while the ailing Lipton chain's 449 branches had sales of less than £7 million. Maypole Dairies fared even worse with its 977 shops achieving sales of only £9.1 million. In contrast Sainsbury's 255 stores had sales of nearly £12.6 million. Sainsbury's average sales per branch were three to five times those of its main rivals.

Before the Great War Sainsbury's trading area had grown steadily, so that it extended as far south as Folkestone, Eastbourne and Bournemouth, and to Norwich and Ipswich in the east. The northern and western limits were Watford and Oxford. By far the greatest number of stores were in the London area. During the interwar years most of the new branches added to the chain were within this 'heartland'. Between 1921 and 1937 the population of London and the Home Counties grew twice as fast as that of the rest of the country (18 per cent compared with 7.5 per cent). The new housing estates of West London and Essex, and especially the rapidly growing suburban 'metroland' of Wembley and Harrow, offered ideal locations for Sainsbury's stores, while the building of the North Circular Road not only stimulated industrial and housing development in locations such as Colindale, Barnet and Edmonton, but also made them more accessible to Sainsbury's fleet.

The South Harrow branch, decorated for George V's Silver Jubilee in May 1935.

There was an important exception to Sainsbury's policy of concentrating its expansion in London and the Home Counties. The company established itself in the Midlands by taking advantage of the failure of Thoroughgoods, a chain founded by Alfred Banton, who had started out as an employee of John James. He later established a small chain of shops in the Midlands and along the South Coast and joined the turn-of-the-century trading pact. On his retirement in 1928 he sold his shops on the South Coast to another pact member, Henry Frost. The other shops passed to his five sons. In 1936 the Banton brothers went bankrupt and Sainsbury's acquired most of their shops. Those furthest from the Blackfriars depot were subsequently sold. However, nine were retained in Coventry, Derby, Kettering, Leicester, Northampton, Nottingham and Walsall.

Horses versus motor vehicles

The expansion in the number of Sainsbury's branches necessitated the development of a more efficient distribution system. The proximity of the Blackfriars depot to the wholesale markets and the Thames wharves had enabled the firm to maintain the strictest quality controls and ensure the freshness of its provisions, meat and poultry. It was company policy that each branch should receive at least one delivery a day.

In 1919 it was decided to purchase six Leyland lorries from the RAF to service some of the more distant branches. These vehicles took over most of the long-distance deliveries to the South Coast branches like Bournemouth, Brighton, Eastbourne and Folkestone.

Despite the success of these lorries on longer journeys, Mr John still favoured horse vans for work in central London. He took a personal interest in the animals'

High standards were expected of Sainsbury's horses. Mr John required them to be 'capable of trotting both with and without a load'.

Driver Harry Bearman with one of the firm's first Leyland lorries, c1919. The founder personally presented each driver of the new lorries with a pair of gauntlets and a Thermos flask.

welfare and insisted that each driver carried a bucket for use at water pumps so that the horses were protected from drinking contaminated water at public troughs. He inspected the cleanliness of the horses' tack and commended those who won medals in the annual May Day horse parade at Regents Park.

The horses still had to prove their efficiency. Mr John described the type of horse he required to a farming contact of Mr Frank's: 'We prefer bays or browns, and we are not particular as to sex, height sixteen hands or sixteen and a half. They must be quite clean and with plenty of bone, well bred and active, because the Horse Department has to compete with the Mechanical Department and the time taken on the journey is the essence of the contract.'

The competition between horse transport and motor vehicles was part of a wider debate. Sir Walter Gilbey, president of the National Horse Association and head of the eponymous firm of wine and spirit merchants, stated in the *Daily Express* in 1928 that 'any disinterested observer will find in the various main thoroughfares of London – Piccadilly, Strand, Regent Street, Oxford Street and in the City of London – a long line of motors of over 100 yards in length without a single horse-drawn vehicle . . . It is the half-empty omnibuses, the steam lorries, and the traction engines that are the chief cause of the congestion.' Mr John wrote privately to Sir Walter, 'I can fully confirm your contention that the horse represents the most economical form of transport for short distance work such as is involved in the area of the Docks and wharves. My personal experience is that the saving on this class of cartage compared with mechanical transport is 1/- to 1/6 per ton.'

Nevertheless, motor vehicles were able to work longer hours than horses. The heavy Leyland lorries were on the road for an average of sixty-six hours per week compared with only fifty-three hours for

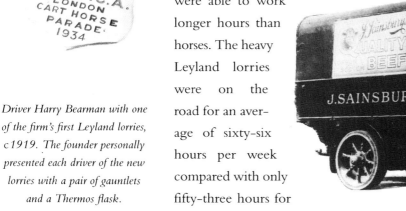

the horse vans. As the petrol engine became more efficient, even the horse van's relative advantage for shorter distances was lost. Reluctantly, Sainsbury's sold its remaining horses in 1937.

The Road and Rail Traffic Act of 1934 limited vehicles over 50cwts unladen to a speed limit of 20 miles per hour and fixed drivers' hours at a maximum of eleven hours in any twenty-four. As a result the heavy Leylands could only serve the furthest branches, like Norwich and Bournemouth, by sharing the driving between two carmen. This restriction was overcome by building special lightweight bodies onto Bedford chassis to create vehicles which were permitted to travel at 30 miles per hour. The new vehicles were loaded at night. This meant they could make the round trip to the most distant branches and still arrive back in time for a relief driver to make a second trip to a suburban branch the same day.

Selecting new sites

The process of selecting a site for a new Sainsbury's store varied from one location to another. The firm often took several years to find the ideal location in a cathedral city and market town like Cambridge or St Albans. Mr John conducted his own market research and counted the shoppers passing a prospective site to satisfy himself that the street was busy enough. His ability to predict how new markets would develop was remarkable. He would take his family out at weekends to look for sites in green field areas. On other occasions he would arrive an hour or so late at the office having agreed the purchase of a site that morning. Plans would be ready before the sale was completed and the new branch would be trading within a year. A new opening was proudly announced as 'Another Link in the Chain'.

Mr John built shopping parades under the auspices of Sainsbury's own development company, Cheyne Investments Ltd. Parades were built at Kenton, Wembley, Ruislip and Haywards Heath. These Sainsbury-planned developments generally took the form of a complete 'market' of complementary businesses.

Developers courted the firm in the knowledge that a Sainsbury's shop would attract other traders to their parade. George Cross remembered the lengths to which he had to go to entice Sainsbury's to come to his Edgware site. Mr John said he would consider it if he were offered a twenty-four foot plot at a nominal price of 'a couple of hundred pounds, or say ten pounds a foot'. Cross objected that this would be 'giving it away'. 'Wise people have done that before now,' Mr John replied. It did not take Cross long to make up his mind: 'You can have it at your figure if you will

A prototype lightweight van, specially built for Sainsbury's onto a Bedford chassis.

J. SAINSBURY.

Chiltern Parade, Amersham, in 1937. Sainsbury's built the parade and took the central shop. The others were occupied by a newsagent's, a shoe shop, a greengrocer's, a gentlemen's outfitters, a branch of Boots, an electrical shop and a milliner's.

let me put up a board stating it has been sold to you.' Cross recalled, 'With this card to play, I laid siege to other desirable firms.'

This status could be double-edged. An expression of interest in a site by Sainsbury's could push up its value. Mr Alan recalled how his father would send out a 'scout' to make enquiries about a site: 'The estate agents were not supposed to know that he worked for Sainsbury's, but of course they all did.' Even less successful was the occasion on which Mr John sent his personal assistant, timid Mr Vallance, to buy a site at Luton. The space was badly needed to extend the cramped loading area at the back of the shop. Hoping to get the site cheaply, he primed Mr Vallance to hold out as long as possible before making his bid. Vallance returned from the auction looking rather pale. 'Well,' said Mr John, 'how much did you pay?' Poor Mr Vallance had to confess that, as the hammer fell, he had fainted!

Perfecting the design

Once a site was purchased, one of the firms of architects regularly used by Sainsbury's would be employed to design a store to meet the company's specifications.

Like the interiors Sainsbury's shopfronts were largely standardised, but occasionally local touches were added. Percival Blow, the architect who designed Sainsbury's 1924 St Albans shop, echoed the classical columns and pediment of the nearby Town Hall in the elaborate office screen at the back of the shop. The speed of development during the interwar years meant that sometimes two shops in different locations were 'twins', like those designed by Belfrage, Saville & Hooper for the new parades at Morden and Gerrards Cross, which opened in 1933.

To the untutored eye the appearance of a new shop of the 1920s and '30s differed little from those of the 1890s. However, refinements were constantly being introduced to perfect the design which the founder had initiated in 1882 at

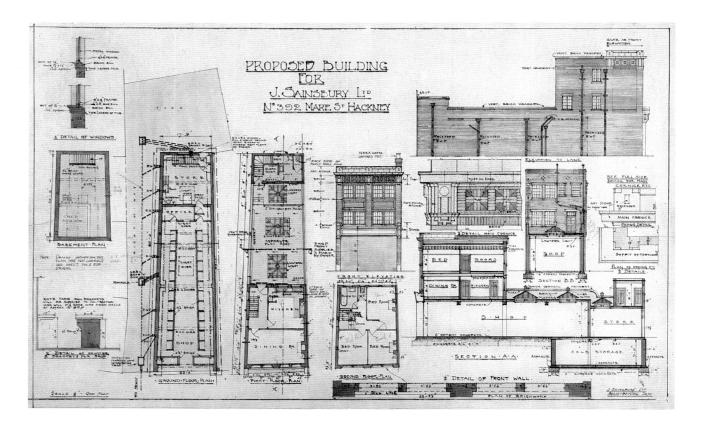

Architectural drawings for 392 Mare Street, Hackney, 1929. Staff accommodation was provided at the front of the building, while the rear was single-storied, allowing the use of roof lights to illuminate the back of the shop.

Croydon. These included moulded plaster 'stick and rag' decoration for the ceilings, curved copings on the counter fronts, and slightly different designs for the floor mosaic and the fronts of the counters. The *Cambridge Chronicle* waxed lyrical about the Sidney Street shop, which opened in December 1925: 'There is probably no finer provision store in the whole country . . . the shop itself is a hall of fine proportions, with a length of one hundred feet and a width of twenty-four feet. The walls are panelled with tiles from floor to ceiling, the floor is of stone mosaic and the ceiling has a beauty of line that would give dignity to the most austere of apartments.' At Bedford, the local paper applauded the 'six-inch fence

of plate glass' used to protect the edge of the counters and claimed that this had been suggested by Mr Sainsbury himself, who 'one day . . . observed a customer's child, whose head was on a level with the counter, breathing on the bacon'.

'Open days' gave customers the opportunity to inspect their new store before it began trading. So enthusiastic were the customers who viewed the Cambridge branch that Sainsbury's had to publish newspaper advertisements apologising for the crush. In its first two days the takings at Cambridge equalled those achieved in a week by some of the busiest London branches. Thereafter, staff in the 'private office' at Blackfriars began to telephone the Cambridge branch to find out the latest record. This practice finally led Mr John to write to Mr Snow, the manager, instructing him not to give such information over the telephone.

Sainsbury's standards of hygiene were envied throughout the retail industry. The counterhands worked diligently to keep every surface spotless. Each day, after closing, the marble counters, tiled walls and counter fronts were scrubbed, and ball whitening was used to polish the tiles afterwards. The floor was sprinkled with sawdust, or later with a compound called 'speedi dri' (which absorbed moisture) and was then carefully swept and scrubbed. Brass weights and scales were polished weekly, and spare sets of cutting boards for cheese, cooked meats and bacon were provided, so that the porter could scrub the set not in use. Once a week the bacon rails were taken down and burnished with sandpaper; sometimes patterns were made on them by carefully rubbing in different directions. Even the grocery displays of cans and jars were dismantled each week and carefully rebuilt using small strips of white paper to 'tie' the stacks together. The older stock was brought to the top of the stack, ensuring that even unperishable goods did not remain long on the shelf. The same care and attention was paid to the cleaning of the preparation rooms behind the shop.

J. SAINSBURY'S
New Store
FORSET COURT
EDGWARE ROAD, W.2

Opening on Wednesday, May 20th

This leaflet advertised the opening of the Edgware Road branch on 20th May 1936.

The six departments

Most new stores of the interwar years had six departments: dairy, bacon and hams, poultry and game, cooked meats, fresh meat, and groceries. This meant that most Sainsbury's stores were larger than its competitors'. There were no hard-and-fast rules about the relative positions of the departments in a Sainsbury's shop of this period. However, the 'top spot' was considered to be nearest the window at the front of the shop, and was used for seasonal specialities, such as cooked meats in the summer months, or poultry and game in the run-up to Christmas. The showmanship of the butterman 'knocking up' butter and Crelos margarine was a strong candidate for this location at other times of year.

On a busy Friday it could take quite a while to queue at each department and wait to be served. To avoid this problem, assistants would, whenever possible, 'serve through' several departments. Some customers deputed a son or daughter to join the next queue while they were being served elsewhere.

The first stop might be the dairy department, where there was a minimum of four kinds of butter and three of margarine. Although some packs would have been made up when trade was quiet, the buttermen would be constantly at work preparing more, weighing it on the elaborate pink and white butter scales, and wrapping it to suit the customer's requirements. If both Sainsbury's best butter and Crelos margarine were purchased, a slip of paper wrapped into the package ensured that they were easily identifiable.

An egg box dating from the early 1930s.

82

A pottery jug which was used for own brand cream.

Ken Boston, manager at 159 Queen's Crescent, Kentish Town, slicing bacon, 1939.

Eggs were displayed in baskets with hay or straw bedding. The range included preserved foreign eggs, as well as fresh English new laid from Mr Frank's Haverhill egg-collection business. Extra large English new laid eggs were renowned as double-yolkers. Small quantities were sold loose in paper bags, while special cardboard boxes were available for multiples of a dozen.

At the cheese counter it was difficult to decide between the forty or fifty varieties available. The biggest trade by far was in Cheddar, with a choice between home-produced and the slightly cheaper red and white Empire Cheddars. Contemporary price lists described the 'delicate Cheshires snug in their special linen shirts, rich red cheese from the low countries, luscious Gorgons from the mountain pastures' of Italy. There were Stiltons decorated with ribbon rosettes, genuine Swiss Gruyère, and specialities such as Gervais, Roquefort and Port Salut. Cream cheeses were protected under a glass dome. A polished cheese iron was kept ready so that customers could be offered a sample of new or unfamiliar cheeses.

The customer might then move on to the bacon counter. Whole sides of bacon were hung from rails above the shelf behind the counter. The Berkel slicer could offer a range of thicknesses, from thickly sliced gammon rashers at number 20 to thin rashers for crisp streaky at number 5. The commonest request was for 'frying thickness' at number 7. Preferences varied from one locality to another. Shoppers in poorer areas, such as Kentish Town or Kilburn, bought streaky bacon and wanted it sliced thinly to make it go further. In more prosperous neighbourhoods such as Brondesbury or Muswell Hill, the greatest demand was for back bacon, and streaky was hard to sell. Sainsbury's imported huge consignments of back bacon from Canada – where streaky was more popular than back – and built up a long-standing relationship with the McLean family of Toronto, who had developed a highly successful bacon-curing business. Uncooked hams, again displayed on the rails high up on the wall behind the counter, were graded for size and hung at an angle so that their plumpness could be seen. 'Under no circumstances,' stipulated the rule book, 'should they be allowed to touch each other.'

Poultry was available both ready-trussed and untrussed, although in hot weather only the minimum number of birds were displayed on the counter. It was important not to have too many birds ready-prepared as they could deteriorate quickly once gutted. Any that remained at the end of a warm day would be sold at bargain prices. When a customer selected an untrussed bird, it was sent to the poultry room behind the shop to be prepared while she waited.

In season, the range of game was tremendous: wild duck, widgeon, capercailzie, hazel hen, pheasant, grouse, black cock, partridge, hares and rabbits. British game was available only when there was an 'r' in the month, but frozen game such as Manchurian partridges, Hungarian pheasants and cheap Australian rabbits were available all the year. A special price list was published for game with recipe suggestions devised by Mrs Eumorfopoulos of the shop services department at head office.

On to the cooked meats department. This stocked Oxford brawn, roast beef, chicken and ham roll, nonpareil (a chicken and ham loaf, 'cooked in a delightfully new and unusual manner'), boar's head, galantines, ox tongue (sliced or in shallow glass jars), pressed pork and meat and fish pastes. The premium product was cooked York ham, which was displayed on pink and white china stands. An order of half a pound or more would be placed in a white box with green edging and tied with a green ribbon. 'Hand-raised' pork pies came in boxes with designs of poppies and corn on the lid. The manufacture and sale of Sainsbury's own brand cooked meats was the most profitable part of the company's business.

The cooked meats department also sold sausages: pork, Paris (pork chipolatas) and beef. In the summer months, when the demand for picnic foods was at its height, the cooked meats counter could take over space from the bacon counter. Judging the demand, however, was a skilled task, since the company's rules stipulated that in summer most cooked meats should remain in stock for no more than two or three days. In the winter these goods had a maximum shelf life of four days.

The display of fresh meats was impressive. Sainsbury's sold two types of beef: Scottish and Argentinian. 'Scotch' beef from the Aberdeen area was regarded as the best available and was introduced to Sainsbury's range from *c*1927. It was originally supplied by a butcher from Stonehaven, near Aberdeen, named Blacklaw. From 1930 onwards, beef was bought for Sainsbury's from local farmers by William Donald. George V's Balmoral herd was kept on one of the farms in this area, and each year eighteen fat cattle were offered for sale on the open market. London retailers would vie with each other for

A painted glass panel from one of Sainsbury's game departments.

Sainsbury's 'famous' meat pies were displayed unwrapped on the cooked meats counter and placed in cardboard boxes for presentation to the customer.

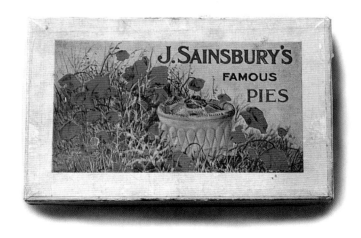

GOOD FOOD

SAINSBURY

November 22nd, 1938

This list is issued fortnightly but prices are subject to market fluctuations

Price lists were published fortnightly for the benefit of customers who had their orders delivered.

'Blue Kaddy' was Sainsbury's premium tea. This illustration, from a 1931 price list, is said to depict the intrepid female aviator Amy Johnson.

the publicity of selling the King's beef, with the result that more 'royal' beef appeared in the shops than could possibly have come from the beasts which were sold.

In 1933 Mr John and William Donald decided to buy the whole of the King's herd. As the sale progressed, the prices rose from £62 for the first heifer to £150 for the final ox. Mr Donald, fearing he had overstepped the mark in paying these prices, wrote nervously to Mr John that 'there were buyers from Barkers, Harrods, and Selfridges, and they were pretty desperate'. In fact, Mr John was delighted by the publicity coup and arranged prominent displays in several of the firm's shops.

The best cheap beef arrived chilled from Argentina. This was the furthest it could be shipped without freezing being necessary. At 2d to 3d per pound less than Scottish beef, Argentinian beef was a popular choice for Sunday lunch. Also available in season were Scottish and Devon lamb, and Dorset veal. The most important supplier of pork was Mr Frank. New Zealand lamb was purchased from another long-standing supplier, the Canterbury Frozen Meat Company. It was shipped frozen and was stored in Sainsbury's cold stores at Blackfriars. However, neither Sainsbury's lorry fleet nor its branches had facilities to keep it frozen so it was sold defrosted. Very often it was still frozen when it came into the shop. Assistants were warned not to sell it partially defrosted unless the customer was able to confirm that it would not be used for some hours. Sainsbury's trade in fresh meats grew rapidly during the interwar years. By the 1930s the company sold more meat than multiple butchers such as Dewhurst's.

At the far end of the shop was the grocery department, with its tall, polished wooden shelves laden with cans, packaged goods and jars of bottled fruit and jams. Although earlier shops had sold Sainsbury's teas, coffees, sugar and some canned goods, it was not until 1920 that Mr John introduced a full range of groceries. Because the work was lighter and less skilled than that of the provisions departments, it was considered suitable for women. They were required to learn the firm's code markings, to be proficient in display techniques, and to 'introduce' new lines and special offers to customers.

Many of the grocery lines were Sainsbury brand goods. 'Gay Friar' pickles and sauces (named after the company's Blackfriars headquarters) were introduced in 1920. 'Broadacres' oats, 'Basket Brand' canned fruits and 'Blue Kaddy' tea all appeared during the 1930s. By 1938 the 'Selsa' brand was used for over eighty product lines, including spices, fruit squashes, calves' feet jelly, custard and blancmange

powders and tinned soups. Introduced in c1930, its name was said to have been devised when Mr Whitworth, the grocery buyer, was shown a new Sainsbury brand line by Mr John. He remarked, 'That'll sell, sir!'

One reason for the popularity of Sainsbury's groceries in the 1920s and '30s was the growth of resale price maintenance. Manufacturers made agreements with independent retailers to fix minimum prices for many of the new packaged proprietary goods, thereby keeping their prices artificially high. They refused to supply any of their products to shopkeepers who offered any price maintained item below the published price. Sainsbury's strongly resisted such attempts by manufacturers to dictate the prices charged in its stores. By offering own label products it avoided the need to sell most price maintained articles and offered its customers better value for money. The company's reputation for own brand provisions, particularly cooked meats, helped to ensure that its groceries became as well regarded as their proprietary equivalents. By 1938 almost all the groceries Sainsbury's sold were own brands. In the financial year 1937–38 Sainsbury's dealt with only six suppliers which supported price maintenance.

Most types of groceries were sold ready packed, rather than being weighed up at the counter, but assistants were told to treat them with the same care as perishable goods. The rule book warned that 'many items, such as cereals and dried fruits, will be found to lose weight if kept in stock; it is imperative that the weight of a few packages are checked daily.' The importance of strict stock rotation as a safeguard of quality was also emphasised.

Despite its growing importance, the grocery department remained 'junior' to the main provisions business. As late as 1938, G Lovegrove, manager of one of the Brighton shops, was

This postcard advertising Sainsbury's 'pure concentrated' cocoa dates from c1920.

A selection of Sainsbury brand lines dating from the interwar period.

SAINSBURY'S
AND THE COAL STRIKE.

The shortage of Coal and necessary economy of gas fuel for cooking will cause you no inconvenience if you are a Sainsbury customer.

SAINSBURY'S

READY COOKED MEAT DEPARTMENT
with large assortment of
DAINTY TABLE DELICACIES
will solve the catering problem for you, whether for Breakfast, Luncheon or Supper.

Local Branch
SIDNEY STREET, CAMBRIDGE.
'Phone 1807.

The industrial strife of 1926 provided an unusual opportunity to promote Sainsbury's products. This advertisement appeared on 2nd July 1926.

roundly chastised by Mr Goldup of the shop services department at head office for wishing to increase his biscuit sales: 'Many years ago when you were at 158 Rushey Green you developed "biscuitomania". We thought, however, that the bracing air of Portslade would have effected a cure, but now that you are in charge of our palatial premises at 3, London Road you seem to have caught it again!! We want to sell Butter, Bacon, Cheese, Lamb, Pork and Cooked Meats; Grocery, of course, is a useful addition, but it is an "also ran" where the main departments are concerned.'

Free delivery service

Almost all Sainsbury's branches offered a free delivery service. For customers who lived within a mile or two of the branch, deliveries were made by lads on bicycles or tricycles. There were four rounds a day. The first left soon after opening time and guaranteed delivery in time for lunch. This was followed by further rounds at 11.30, 2.30 and 5.00. Delivery lads and roundsmen were regarded as the firm's ambassadors and were expected to live up to the same standards as the salesmen.

Loading up customers' orders required considerable skill. Care had to be taken to ensure that strong-smelling cheeses were kept separate from other goods and that paper bags full of eggs were properly protected. Pieces of wood were used so that bicycle baskets could be stacked high with parcels. A delivery lad, if he proved conscientious and hard-working, could expect to be promoted to roundsman driving a motor van, or to become a porter, warehouseman, or poulterer.

Where trade was heavy, or the distances too great for delivery lads, deliveries were made by horse and trap or by motor van. Sainsbury's first Model T Ford van was purchased in 1915. By 1928 the retail delivery fleet consisted of thirty-seven Fords and eighty Morris vans. These were painted a handsome dark red, with gold lettering and a cream roof.

Roundsmen delivered the orders placed by account customers at the branches and were not permitted to carry goods for chance sale. One of their duties was to encourage the purchase of as wide a variety of products as possible. The 1937 branch instruction book emphasised that 'this rule must be particularly enforced in country districts, where roundsmen have some miles to go from a branch, as they have not sufficient time to waste on customers who are simply making a convenience of us.'

*A retail delivery van, c1925.
The rules stated that
'Roundsmen and Delivery Lads
must deliver all parcels to the
customer's house and on no
account to surrender goods in the
street or at the gate of a house'.*

The cost of providing a free delivery service became a cause for concern, as the firm was reluctant to offset it by raising prices. With great reluctance Sainsbury's was forced to introduce a charge of 6d on small orders in 1934. Free delivery continued, however, on orders over 15s or £1, depending on the area. Mr RJ – Mr John's younger son – pointed out that 'we simply cannot continue to supply the finest goods at such low prices and to give in addition a "family" service without some change in our system. It would have been quite easy for us to have made a slight alteration in our Price List, but we have always tried to maintain the same prices in every district.' Retail deliveries were finally discontinued in 1955.

Customer accounts required extra administration, but they could be used to provide a target for advertising. A letter dated 6th March 1932 was sent to seventy customers with accounts at the new Westbourne Grove branch who were not buying butter: 'We are instructing our local manager to send you a free sample of our Delicious Empire Butter at 1/– per 1lb.' Some shops had prodigious numbers of account customers; Marylebone, for example, had over 4,600 on its books. By 1939 the database held by the 'circularising department' at head office comprised over 250,000 names and addresses. In 1935 this became the first department to use the mechanised Powers-Samas punched card system.

Maintaining traditions

On Tuesday, 3rd January 1928, John James died at his house in Highgate, aged eighty-three. His wife Mary Ann had died six months earlier, on 9th June 1927. The *Evening News* described him as 'a man who disliked the limelight so much that he remained almost unknown to the general public throughout his career'. On the day of his funeral all the shops closed as a mark of respect and to allow staff to join the funeral procession from Stamford House to Putney Vale cemetery.

The standards which John James and Mary Ann had set themselves in 1869 were timeless. Chief among these was the commitment to quality which had led John James to purchase foodstuffs direct from the producer and to manufacture himself the cooked meats for which he could not find a satisfactory supplier. By controlling the distribution chain from the producer to the customer he was able to enforce strict quality standards. It also helped him to cut costs and to pass the benefit on to the consumer. Having themselves grown up in humble circumstances, Sainsbury's founders believed that the poor had as much right to high quality food as the rich. They never forgot the competitive lessons of the market street and remained determined to offer the same service to their most impoverished customers as to their richest. A high turnover at low prices, combined with a product range equal to that of the most exclusive high class provision merchant, meant that the poor of Stepney were as well served as the wealthy of Kensington.

The business had grown from a small rented shop in one of London's poorest districts to one which, as the *Financial Times* put it in their obituary, 'had been regarded with a covetous eye by certain finance houses'. The City's interest in the business was not surprising. With 182 branches, a share capital of nearly £2 million and a turnover of almost £9 million Sainsbury's success was in marked contrast to the performance of other multiples. Thomas Lipton, for example, had sold out to Van den Berghs in 1927, declaring net losses of £88,000.

There was no prospect that Sainsbury's would cease to be controlled by its founding family. The articles of association, dating from the company's incorporation in 1922, provided that only direct descendants of the founders and their families could hold shares. Mr John's elder son, Mr Alan, had joined the firm in 1921 at the age of seventeen and was already demonstrating his aptitude for the family business. John James played an active part in the running of the company almost to the end. His last day in the office was said to have been 2nd November 1927. On that very day, John D Sainsbury (Mr JD), Mr Alan's eldest son and the first of the fourth generation, was born.

The death of the founder led to many glowing tributes. This obituary appeared in the Evening News *on 4th January 1928.*

These matching gold watches belonged to John James and Mary Ann.

A career for your boys

' The Retail Provision and Grocery trade has distinct advantages as a career, it is both congenial and remunerative, and what is even more important, is rarely affected by labour differences and trade depressions.' So read one of Sainsbury's recruitment advertisements in the early 1930s. The company's expansion during the interwar years necessitated a vigorous programme of recruitment of 'tall, well-educated young men'. As counter service shopping was labour-intensive, any increase in sales required a corresponding increase in staff. By 1932 the average number of employees per branch was about thirty and some of the larger new stores had as many as seventy. In order to maintain its expansion during the interwar period Sainsbury's had to recruit seven or eight hundred new staff each year. New recruits came from as far away as Yorkshire, Devon and the Welsh Borders.

Some parents were anxious about allowing their sons to take a first job so far away from home. Most recognised, however, that in the depressed 1920s and '30s a job with a respected London firm offered better prospects than the dole queue at home. This point was reinforced by the firm's recruitment brochure, entitled *A Career for Your Boys*. Managers of Sainsbury's 'country' shops were particularly asked to cultivate links with local schools, and the firm's personnel department sent out officials to interview applicants who had responded to advertisements for 'keen young men' in local newspapers.

Applications were also encouraged from school-leavers (aged fourteen to fifteen) in London, the South-east and East Anglia. One lad got a job after sending in a school essay in which he gave his reasons for wishing to work for Sainsbury's. Likely boys were invited to London with a parent or other adult for an interview and arithmetic test.

Training new recruits

The new boys were known as 'learners'. They were boarded at one of the larger London branches or in private lodgings while they attended a fortnight's course at Blackfriars. Practical instruction in the preparation and handling of foodstuffs was complemented with lectures on the origins of the products they were to sell; Dutch butter, New Zealand lamb, Australian rabbits and Russian eggs were a geography lesson in themselves. They drew in chalk on papier mâché models of sides of bacon to learn the proper way to cut the real item. The course included tours of the bacon stoves and the cooked meats factory, where sausages, veal and

---

A CAREER FOR KEEN YOUNG MEN

A Family Business which is rapidly expanding in London, the Midlands and the South has some positions vacant offering security and prospects for suitable young men in the Provision Trade. Applicants must be between 15 and 30 years of age and they will be paid the Highest Wages in the Trade, with an increase after each year of satisfactory service.

at 15 - 20s. per week	at 18 - 40s. per week
„ 16 - 25s. „ „	„ 19 - 45s. „ „
„ 17 - 30s. „ „	„ 20 - 50s. „ „

Assistants	Qualified Salesmen
at 21 - - 53s. per week	60s. per week
„ 22 - - 56s. „ „	63s. „ „
„ 23 - - 59s. „ „	66s. „ „
„ 24 - - 60s. „ „	69s. „ „
„ 25	72s. „ „
„ 26	75s. „ „
„ 27	78s. „ „
„ 28	83s. „ „

- FULL WAGES DURING TRAINING.
- NO EXPERIENCE NEEDED IF THE APPLICANT IS UNDER 21 YEARS OF AGE.
- DINNER AND TEAS 7/6 PER WEEK.
- WELL-MANAGED HOSTELS FOR THOSE WHO LIVE TOO FAR FROM THE NEAREST BRANCH.
- HOLIDAYS WITH PAY.
- ALL MANAGERS CHOSEN FROM COUNTER STAFF.
- PENSIONS AT SIXTY
- FREE MEDICAL ADVICE.
- FREE LIFE INSURANCE.

Call or write, J. SAINSBURY, Staff Engager, Blackfriars, London, S.E.1

Sainsbury's pay and benefits were well ahead of its competitors, as shown by this 1937 recruitment advertisement.

ham pies and bloater paste were made. Not surprisingly, to boys for whom such delicacies were something of a treat, it was thereafter *always* possible to recommend them to customers. One boy later recalled his frustration when customers doubted the freshness of Sainsbury's sausages. After all, he had seen them made.

The boys learnt the arts of egg candling, 'scaling' (balancing the scales to within one-eighth of an ounce), and dividing a barrel of butter into neat

The Blackfriars training school as it was in c1930. This photograph appeared in the company's recruitment brochure.

half-pound packs using 'The Sainsbury Method of Wiring'. They were also taught to respect the equipment they used: to keep the slate inside the butter blocks damp and scrupulously clean; and to take care not to disturb the fine balance of the butter scales. If a pat of butter was less than the required weight, it had to be removed from the scale pan before more butter was added.

The boys' first taste of salesmanship came on the final Saturday, when they were despatched to a London branch for the day. The next evening they moved out of their temporary lodgings and into the branch to which they had been allocated. Boys were sent, if possible, to a branch near home, but for a lad like Stan Rayner, who came from Selby in Yorkshire, the first few days at Victoria Road,

Butter beater and slice. The slice was used to cut the butter to the required size, after which it was knocked into shape using the grooved beater.

Surbiton, were the loneliest of his life. However, it did not take long to become one of the 'Sainsbury family'.

Despite the strict rules the boys got up to all manner of pranks. Little did the housekeeper of the Eastbourne branch know that on hot summer evenings Arthur Grogan and his mates regularly went for a midnight swim. With the help of a room-mate, a drainpipe and an open window, you didn't need to take the 10.30 curfew too seriously. At George Ridgway's branch, he and his colleagues bought a wind-up gramophone and organised dances with the female staff.

The food was good and plentiful – better than many boys had at home. On at least one occasion, however, it was not to their taste. George Hoare recalled that when Mr John discovered that herrings were cheap and nutritious it nearly caused a strike. For a short time herrings were served up with monotonous regularity. As George wryly remarked, 'There were no half measures about the menu.'

Housekeepers were often strict but they stood up to the manager if one of 'their boys' was ill, no matter how much he wanted the boy to go to work. 'A couple of aspirin and back to bed' was a universal remedy for minor ailments. The housekeeper also had to account for every detail of her expenditure. For a household of perhaps twenty young men this was a demanding task. Controls on expenditure were so strict in the early 1920s that in hostels which had no electric light, boys who required a new candle had to give back the stub of the old one!

The Shops Act of 1934 limited lads under the age of eighteen to working no more than forty-eight hours per week except for seasonal overtime. This led Sainsbury's to consider carefully how the boys should use their extra spare time. Libraries were provided, including textbooks on the trade, but also adventure stories and thrillers. Realising that energetic young boys needed to let off steam in more active ways, in 1922 Mr John purchased a sports ground at Dulwich for the company. Boys formed football teams to compete for the Sainsbury Cup. The Dulwich ground was also used for tennis and cricket and served as the venue for the annual summer sports day.

This football team from the Lewisham area won the Sainsbury Cup in 1921.

Staff from the St Albans branch on a summer charabanc outing to Dunstable Downs in 1923. The party enjoyed a half-crown high tea at Wingrave.

Developing new skills

Work started at 7.30am, preceded by an inspection by the manager. Woe betide the lad with dirty fingernails or unpolished shoes. Every boy was issued with six white coats and twelve white aprons. The coats were double-breasted tunics and buttoned to the neck so the front could be changed over and the coats worn on two days. The buttons were black and the second one from the top left-hand side carried a number, so that customers and officials could identify each counterhand. A clean, starched apron was put on after the early morning cleaning jobs were finished.

The first task for new boys was selling eggs. Huge wooden crates of eggs arrived from Poland, Russia and even China. These were in addition to the English new laid ones from Mr Frank in Suffolk and from Lloyd Maunder at Tiverton. Foreign eggs were sometimes very small, very cheap or even bad, which made the egg boy's candling duties all the more important. After checking the eggs, the boy's next duty would be to display them on the wooden stall outside. Small wicker baskets were provided so that customers could select their own eggs if they wished. Eggs could be bought singly, as well as by the dozen, and mental arithmetic such as 'seven eggs at three-farthings each' was a useful test of a boy's head for figures. In the trade, eggs had their own special arithmetic which was used when ordering or checking the contents of a crate: six eggs equalled one Hand (three eggs in each human hand); twenty Hands equalled one Long Hundred; three Long Hundreds equalled one Box; and four Boxes equalled one Case. Selling eggs also tested a boy's honesty: one egg boy was sacked for cracking three hundred eggs and selling them off cheaply to his friends.

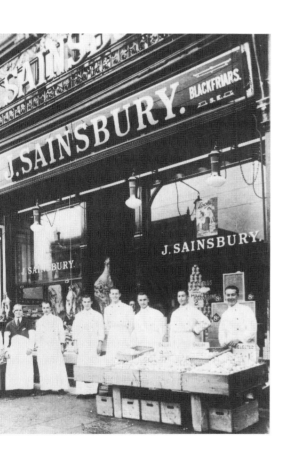

The manager and staff at 87 Broadway, West Ealing, photographed in 1938.

Working outside on the egg stall could be pleasurable on a warm morning, especially in a busy market street where the traders' rivalry in 'barking' the price and quality of their wares added spice to the work. On a cold day, however, it could be miserable. Despite the concession of mid-morning cocoa, being allowed to wear a coat under your tunic and taking turns with the other lads, chilblains were common. S D Dyer even remembered the eggs freezing in their shells.

After the egg stall, a boy would progress to one of the other departments. To begin with, the 'junior' worked alongside an experienced salesman, wrapping bacon, cheese or cooked meats and taking money. Thus he became assiduous in serving the customers, practised his 'scaling', learnt how to take care of butter pats, knives and other equipment and in quiet moments observed the care with which his mentor boned a side of bacon.

Every department had its particular skill which took months of practice to learn. For example, it required great precision to carve ham. Plucking and dressing poultry was also a skilled task. The rule book sternly pointed out that 'efforts to obtain the finest quality goods are nullified if they are badly prepared for the table'. Stiltons had to be kept out of draughts and Gorgonzolas displayed separately from other cheeses lest their strong flavour taint the Bel Paese and Port Salut. Long veal and ham pies were cut so that the golden egg yolks were neatly halved. Handling a side of bacon correctly involved learning how to hang it upright on the rail above your head using a hooked pole known as a 'long arm' – a feat which required both strength and balance.

BELOW A motto displayed behind the scenes in Sainsbury's shops.
BELOW RIGHT Experience card and uniform buttons. Sainsbury's training programmes were greatly respected in the trade and other retailers advertised for 'Sainsbury-trained men'.

The Wedge.

❋

A
man
w h o
does a
little more
work than
h e's a s k e d
to—who takes
a little more care
than he's expected to—
who puts the small details
on an equal footing with the
more important ones—he's the
man who is going to make a
success of his job. Each little thing
done better, is the thin end of
the wedge into something bigger.

Promoting from within

The company's policy was to promote existing hands rather than recruit from outside. This ensured that managers had risen through the ranks and had experience of most of the jobs they would require their staff to perform. It was also intended to encourage managers to place the highest importance on training staff to fill new positions. A steady programme of branch openings, together with a high rate of turnover among junior staff, ensured that there was always a need for young men who showed potential to become managers. Promoting from within was also good for morale.

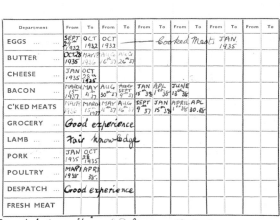

Department	From	To	From	To	From	To	From	To	From	To	From	To
EGGS	SEPT 29 1932	OCT 1932	OCT 1932		Cooked Meats			JAN 1935				
BUTTER	OCT 28 1935	MAY 1936	AUG 16 37	AUG 26 37								
CHEESE	JAN 1935	OCT 26 1935										
BACON	MARCH 15 1937	MAY 1 37	AUG 30 37	AUG SEPT 9 37	JAN 15 38	APL 1 38	JUNE 18 38					
C'KED MEATS	MARCH 1936	MARCH 15 1937	MAY 4 37	AUG 16 37	SEPT 9 37	JAN 15 38	APRIL 1 38	APL 30.38				
GROCERY	Good experience											
LAMB	Fair knowledge											
PORK	JAN 1935	OCT 28 1935										
POULTRY	MAR 1938	APRI 38.										
DESPATCH	Good experience											
FRESH MEAT												

Promoted to position of Salesman 12.2.38.

ow **Wages are Earned.**

the full use of the
wer of Observation.
e creation of General
stomers.
the Instruction of
niors.
a sense of
sponsibility.

?

ting,
ghing,

Maximum

60/-

at do **YOU** earn
ABOVE the line ?

*Employees were constantly
reminded of their duties. This
leaflet, issued in the mid-1930s,
was inserted into the experience
card pictured opposite.*

Promotion often meant moving to another branch. It was expected that fully qualified salesmen would be sufficiently adaptable to work in any Sainsbury's store. Indeed, ambitious young men were actively encouraged to seek out opportunities to move. Some did their best to exploit this; Arthur Grogan, for example, decided he would enjoy spending the summer at a seaside branch and asked for a transfer. His district supervisor suggested Norwich. It was not until he got there that he discovered Norwich was not, after all, on the coast. Happily Arthur got his wish within a few weeks, when he was transferred to Eastbourne.

From a starting salary of £1 a week, of which 12s was deducted for board and lodging, a boy might progress to £2 by the time he was eighteen. Pay rises were given each year on the employee's birthday but they were not automatically awarded. They depended on a young man's willingness to learn, his manner with customers, and whether his manager recommended an increase.

In the early 1930s the introduction of 'red buttons' helped to improve the prospects of salesmen. New recruits and assistants who had not yet reached the status of salesmen wore black buttons on their double-breasted tunics. Red buttons denoted a fully qualified salesman who had gained experience in every department of the shop (this normally excluded the fresh meat department, as butchery was regarded as a separate skill). Whereas an assistant aged twenty-one could expect a salary of 53s, the qualified salesman would receive a handsome £5 per week. Red buttons also brought with them the prospect of further promotion to first hand and ultimately branch manager. It took several years to earn the prestigious first hand's identification button, which bore a number 1 (none of the other buttons denoted a specific ranking).

Under scrutiny

High standards of training and service were assured by unannounced visits from a team of 'samplers'. Posing as ordinary shoppers, this group of ladies was trained to notice how well branch staff did their jobs. They bought goods from several departments in the shop and noted the number of the assistant who served each item. The samplers recorded whether salesmen were pleasant to customers and whether they recommended a product on special offer (a 'feature'). The samples purchased were taken back to head office for examination. The manager would then receive a report about the conduct and skill of each assistant from whom a purchase had been made. Inevitably, experienced salesmen came to recognise the sampling team and, although it was forbidden, would signal to the rest of the staff that they were in the shop. One trick was to make the bacon slicer 'clang' by opening and closing it noisily.

Visits from senior officials were frequent and although these had other purposes, such as to discuss local trading patterns or staffing needs, they were also intended to keep staff on their toes. 'I'm not sure that we ever had anything to hide,' said George Ridgway, 'but we felt better if we knew when a visit was due.' A district supervisor could order the re-dressing of a display, check for dust in any nook and cranny he could reach – or use a stepladder to check those he couldn't – and examine the cheese or bacon already cut to ensure it was in good condition. Each district supervisor, often known as an 'inspector', oversaw fifteen to twenty branches and reported to the company's superintendent.

For many years the superintendent was Mr S E Smith. He was so portly that when he wanted to examine behind a counter all the staff had to file out at one end, walk around the front, and then file in again at the other end. Mr Smith had the power to dismiss staff on the spot. One might have thought that this was the ultimate sanction. Not a bit of it, as Ivor Barrett discovered. One Saturday morning, he found that his last clean overall of the week was missing a hook and eye so that it did not fasten right up to the neck as it should. Lacking time to replace it, Ivor put on the tunic, and although his manager failed to notice, the omission caught the eagle eye of Mr Smith. 'My chauffeur will take you to Blackfriars and back – I want Mr Sainsbury to see what a bad shop assistant looks like,' he roared. Ivor was sent, in Mr Smith's chauffeur-driven car, to Stamford House. In trepidation, he awaited the inevitable sentence. To his amazement, the great man smiled and stood up, emerging from behind his desk to demonstrate that he, too, was improperly dressed. Mr Sainsbury (although it's not clear *which* Mr Sainsbury) was wearing plus-fours!

Despite his fearsome reputation, S E Smith was capable of offering a word of encouragement and praise when it was due. He followed the progress of 'his' managers with particular interest. Edward Tupman received a letter in October 1928 congratulating him for the Watford branch's success in the local Shopping Week's window-dressing competition. The letter also included praise for the success of the other Watford branch, at St Albans Road, whose manager had been trained by Mr Tupman: 'It is indeed good to hear the old shop once again in the limelight, and what joy for you to see the "offspring" following in father's footsteps.'

Window Dressing

. This is to be completed by 10 o'clock each morning, including Mondays.

Boxes of Butter and Margarine are not to be shown in the window for more than half a day, as they deteriorate very quickly when exposed to the light and air. This particularly applies to the produce of Australia or New Zealand, which has been frozen. It is better not to cut packages in half, but to show them complete, this ensures minimum surface exposure.

Butter displayed in the morning should be sold in the afternoon and that on show in the afternoon sold first thing the following morning. Where prints and rolls are made they should be changed at least twice daily and the Butter and Margarine from which they are made sold the same day. When making a display of Butter or Margarine it is better to obliterate the impressed mark or brand.

Elaborate window displays like this at Victoria in 1934 were photographed to provide examples of excellence for the guidance of other branches.

The guiding influence

If attention to detail and the maintenance of standards were Mr Smith's *raison d'être*, the guiding influence was that of Mr John. He had played an important role in the day-to-day running of the business even before he was taken into partnership by his father in 1915. Although the founder remained chairman until his death in 1928, well before that date Mr John took charge of the trading side of the business. Indeed, he decided that the name of the department at head office which looked after such matters as branch takings, customer accounts and shop equipment should be changed from 'Branch Management Department' to 'Shop Services Department'. 'I,' he said, 'am the Branch Management Department.'

It was true: Mr John had the most fantastic grasp of the business. He combined an eye for minutiae with great energy and a desire for perfection. After a visit to the Watford branch in July 1923, he wrote to brief the manager on his views about the way the shop should be laid out. 'I suggested to Mr Smith that we should put the grocery at the bottom of the left hand counter, and to bring the cooked meats forward during the summer months, but he did not approve, as he thought there would be congestion near the doorway, but I thought that might be overcome by putting the bacon scale a little lower down.' The letter, however, also contained a brickbat: 'I noticed when at your branch on Friday that there was a glass shield or two missing; I have made enquiries in the stores dept here, but they can trace no orders for the same.'

A particular concern of Mr John's was that a manager's priority should be 'to give his whole attention to the practical part of the business at the counter'. He ordered the appointment of clerks – usually young women – to ensure that no unnecessary time was spent on administrative duties. This allowed managers to set an example to their staff by being constantly available to the customers.

Mr John consulted managers about local matters, seeking their advice on whether it was worth cultivating an additional delivery round in advance of the opening of a new store, or on advertising in local newspapers. He also reminded them of their duty to 'build up the staff to replace those who, as time goes on, are obliged to take a lighter job. I am sure that when my time and your time comes to make way for younger men, nothing will give us more pleasure than to see the "old firm" maintaining its position in the trade.' He also recognised the stresses that the business placed upon his managers. Mr Tyler, manager of the branch at 44/46 Lewisham High Street, was granted an extra three days' holiday, but Mr John made it clear that 'if he does not take the 10 days right off the object of the holiday is defeated as it is not for his amusement: I am granting the extension for the benefit of his health.'

His concern for the health of A E Snow, manager of the Cambridge branch, was out of the ordinary. In 1926, Cambridge was the company's busiest branch, and the stress told on Mr Snow. After a bad bout of influenza, Snow was sent to a doctor in Cambridge recommended by Mr John's own physician. The doctor's report was very carefully studied by Mr John:

> The Doctor does not consider it necessary for you to leave Cambridge, in other words the district is quite suitable for you, but you have got to conserve your energy, and take things quieter for a time to build up your strength. He strongly recommends you to take an hour's rest each day with your mid-day meal. This will necessitate Mr Underwood [the deputy manager], going to dinner in the first party and you in the second, but you cannot go from breakfast time to 1.45 without a mid-morning lunch *upstairs*, and we recommend you to have either milk, cocoa or Ovaltine and something to eat.

Mr John also recognised the efforts of more junior members of staff. Bonuses were paid to those who took part in local carnivals or carried responsibility above that normally expected. Underwood, for example, was paid handsomely for taking charge of the Cambridge shop when Mr Snow was ill. Mottoes such as 'A man without a smile should never keep a shop' and 'A place for everything and everything in its place' were strategically positioned around the preparation rooms behind the shop floor for the day-to-day encouragement of the staff. Telegrams, like the one received by Howard Bell's branch at Colchester on Christmas Eve 1935 to 'keep a stout heart through the last lap', demonstrated Mr John's understanding of the pressures of branch life.

A leaflet advertising Christmas fruits, sent to account customers in 1929.

Christmas trading

A stout heart was certainly necessary for Christmas trading as it was by far the busiest time of the year. The festive season was heralded in November by the arrival of the new season's dried fruits: choicest Vostizza currants, finest Empire raisins and figs from Smyrna. Elaborate window displays of these, together with suet, ready-made puddings and jars of mincemeat, reminded customers of their culinary responsibilities.

As few households had refrigerators, customers left the purchase of perishable goods, especially poultry, which formed the centrepiece of the Christmas feasting, as late as possible. This meant that there was a terrific surge in trade during the last few days before the festivities. The arrival of the first turkeys during the week before Christmas signalled the start of the rush. A busy branch could sell over two thousand turkeys. They arrived 'rough plucked' – with soft feathers still attached and uneviscerated – as this ensured that they stayed fresh for as long as possible. The junior staff sat on wooden crates in the warehouse, surrounded by a mounting sea of feathers, as they 'clean-plucked' the birds. The first priority was to create the displays. Inside the shop, birds were hung in order of size along the rails usually employed for bacon, while outside, row upon row of birds were suspended over the whole shop fascia. During the week before Christmas, as orders increased, finishing time for almost everyone grew later and later. Sunday working was inevitable when Christmas Day fell early in the week.

Preparing the birds for sale was left as late as possible in order that they reached the customer in peak condition. The preparation of the poultry began two days

Sainsbury's paper bags often carried attractive advertisements for own brand products.

The 'open show' at the Boscombe branch. On early closing day an elaborate display of Christmas goods was arranged across the shop and illuminated so that it was visible from the street.

before Christmas. Work on drawing, dressing and trussing the turkeys, chickens, ducks and geese would go on all night with a sausage-and-mash supper served between 9pm and 10pm. The poulterers' task was the most demanding of all, for the presentation of the birds was their responsibility. No one expected a customer to accept a poorly trussed fowl for Christmas lunch.

Life was hectic in the despatch department too. Every order had to be matched with a bird, which was then wrapped in brown paper, with a greaseproof paper lining, and laid out ready for delivery or for collection by the customer. Before

A 1930s Christmas poultry display. This is typical of those which adorned all Sainsbury's shops during the week before Christmas.

dawn on Christmas Eve the orders were ready, and the van drivers and tricycle lads loaded their vehicles for the first of several journeys. Shop staff who lived out would then go home for an hour or two, while those who lived in simply staggered upstairs for a wash, a shave and breakfast, before the shop opened again. B G Jones, who worked at Surbiton, was one of those who lived out. Sent home exhausted at 4.30am one Christmas Eve, he was later discovered by a policeman fast asleep in a doorway, having fallen off his bicycle. 'Fortunately, I was known to him – he was a customer!'

All day the shop would be crowded with customers collecting orders, remembering extra items or hoping to find a bargain late in the day. An understanding manager would try to let his staff go as early as possible. He knew that many of those who lived in had long train journeys home. Sometimes, however, leaving early was not possible. Bill Bridgeman remembered telephoning customers at

10pm to ask after a roundsman who had not returned. The poor man had retraced his steps to deliver to customers who had not been in to receive their orders.

After all the effort which they had put into ensuring the success of customers' Christmas lunches, many lads were too tired to enjoy their own. After 'knocking up' three and a quarter tons of butter and margarine over one Christmas week, B G Jones couldn't even hold his knife and fork. His mother fed his meal to him like a baby. Young Arthur Grogan found a touch of irony in the prize he won in a local Christmas raffle – a turkey!

Despite its hardships, the excitement of Christmas trading brought job satisfaction to many. Howard Bell's manager offered a 5s prize out of his own pocket for the best essay from the boys at his branch on 'my first Christmas at Sainsbury's'. Later Howard was to recall his 'jovial hard-working colleagues, a new manager for whom I had immense respect and a transfer closer to home. I was possibly happier that first Christmas at Sainsbury's than I have ever been in life since.' It was customary for everyone involved in the frenetic last-minute preparations of a Sainsbury's Christmas to receive double wages for the week. Mr John wrote wistfully to Mr Snow at Cambridge on 23rd December 1926, 'I suppose you are right in the thick of it now, and I am sorry not to be with you to make new records. I would like you to convey to all your staff my high appreciation of what you have achieved.'

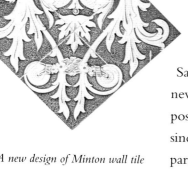

A new design of Minton wall tile used from 1936.

Stamford House

The centralised nature of the business meant that, as it grew, so did the importance of efficient support from the Blackfriars headquarters. In 1932 there were 945 staff employed at head office, in the warehouse and in the factory. Almost every aspect of the work was labour-intensive, from the manual calculation of branch stock results and supplier invoices in the offices, to the hand linking of sausages in the factory.

Stamford House was built in 1912–13 to provide new offices and warehouse space. The top floor of the building housed the offices: those for senior officials (mainly members of the Sainsbury family) at one end, and clerical staff and their supervisors at the other. Here row upon row of clerks 'extended' endless columns of figures with pencil and paper. Branch sales of every commodity were calculated and aggregated to give the weekly turnover. Despatch notes which listed the deliveries that went from the depot were matched against the receiving branch's debit note. Suppliers' invoices were checked against the goods received by the depot. For the young men who worked in the offices the regime was as tough as that of the branch staff. Speed and accuracy were essential and anyone making errors was quickly weeded out. Two mistakes in a week meant a visit to the company secretary; the second visit meant dismissal.

The buyers also occupied the top floor. While some products, such as biscuits, were simply ordered by clerks who used the sales figures as a guide, the purchase of perishable products was a skilful task which involved close links with suppliers. It was regarded as such an important job that at first only members of the Sainsbury family were permitted to do it. Mr Alan, for example, began his career working alongside his uncles, Mr Arthur and Mr Alfred, buying eggs and dairy products. Even after the business became too large for this to be possible, every buying decision was closely supervised by a Sainsbury.

The lower floors of Stamford House were originally designed as warehouse space. However, in 1920 machinery was installed on the first and second floors for packing Sainsbury brand dry groceries such as rice, pulses and oats. On the ground floor were the loading banks where the horse vans and motor lorries were loaded up with goods for despatch to the branches. The lower basement was used as a cheese store.

Stamford House, shortly after its completion in 1913. It is believed that the wrought ironwork on top of the building was taken down and used for scrap during the Great War.

On the opposite side of Stamford Street were the old 'kitchens'. The smell of baking pies attracted local boys, who hung around in the hope of earning a bite to eat in exchange for running an errand. The fish used to make bloater paste to Sainsbury's closely guarded recipe was particularly smelly. By the 1930s the kitchens were badly in need of modernisation as the firm's growth had outstripped their capacity. The butchers had to work outside in the yard and the old premises were impossible to keep up to Sainsbury's hygiene standards.

The new factory

Sir Owen Williams was commissioned to design a model factory to replace the old kitchens. The new building was a marvel of modernity and was the first pre-stressed concrete building to be approved by the London County Council. The factory's cantilevered design allowed for wide areas of floor space uninterrupted by supports, thus allowing the efficient arrangement of the production lines.

The project was supervised by Mr James, whose father, Mr Arthur, had managed the old factory. Athough still in his twenties Mr James relished his new responsibilities. He insisted the factory be equipped with quality control laboratories to ensure the goods produced could be regularly tasted and analysed. He also decreed that there should be no cupboards to attract clutter and that every worker on the production lines be provided each day with a freshly laundered hand cloth.

The new factory opened in 1936. Branch staff could visit for an organised tour on their early closing afternoon. They marvelled at how it was possible to follow the progress of pork carcasses, newly arrived from Mr Frank's Haverhill abattoir, as they travelled through the factory from the receiving bay on the ground floor. The pigs' heads were chopped off for use in the brawn and Bath chaps which were made in the basement. An overhead rail system carried the rest of the carcasses up to the second floor where they were jointed. Some meat was sold as fresh pork while the rest was boned and minced for use in the sausages and 'table delicacies' for which Sainsbury's was renowned. Next to the butchers were the sausage-makers: rows of girls who deftly filled great lengths of sausage-skins with the meat extruded from their machines. The end product could be despatched within an hour of the carcasses entering the building.

On the third floor was the bakery. Here Sainsbury's veal and ham pies, pork piekins, and steak and kidney pies were made. Bread was baked and allowed to go stale for seventy-two hours so that there was always a supply of breadcrumbs in perfect condition for sausage-making. Here too was the spice and seasonings room, described by the workforce as the 'holy of holies'. Mr John's own gardener grew thyme and marjoram for the factory. From the oven the pies went

J. Sainsbury's

HIGH GRADE GROCERIES

December 3rd, 1928

This List is issued fortnightly, but prices are subject to market fluctuations.
PREVIOUS LISTS CANCELLED.

This colourful price list was one of a series showing the production and transport of Sainsbury's groceries.

The sausage-filling and linking lines at the Blackfriars factory. The girls wore neat blue overalls with white detachable collars and white hats.

1 lb. Pies.
lbs.
Flour   14
Lard   4 1/2
Butter   3
Salt   6 ozs
Pie Meat   22.
Seasoning   5 ozs
Eggs. 3
Water   3 1/2 pints
Makes. 44 x 1 lb. Pies
Cooking 50 minutes 380 temp.
Pie Meat.   lbs.
Fresh Pork.   20
Salt   8
Veal   8
Salt   14
Seasoning. 6 ozs: 1 dram Pepper.
6 ozs to Salt
Sage Thyme Marjoram 3 ozs each

down to the first floor. Here they were packed in wicker baskets for despatch to the branches, where they sometimes arrived still warm from the ovens.

The two premium lines were long pie and breakfast sausage. Joe Barnes recalled how, when he joined the company in the 1950s, Mr James still made twice-daily inspections which included the tasting of pies from every single batch. He was an absolute perfectionist. 'It was not unusual for him to reject an entire batch of long pie because somewhere on the one he tasted the crust was a little too wide, or a little too narrow, or was a little under-baked on the crust. The seasoning might be a little weak or a little strong, or the chopping a little large or a little small.' Though up-to-date in the 1930s, production techniques still depended on judgement. Breakfast sausage had to be perfect. 'There was just one man in the whole factory who knew how to smoke it properly. He would vary the heat of the ovens according to the humidity of the weather, and would reject the lot if he didn't like it.'

Mr John's life work

In 1938 Mr John retired from the business at the age of sixty-seven following a minor heart attack. His whole life had been devoted to the business. One of his earliest memories was of helping his parents in their shop at 159 Queen's Crescent. Thereafter he had been schooled in every aspect of the business by his father, who had acknowledged his eldest son's contribution to the firm's success when, in 1915, he took Mr John into partnership. The *Grocers' Gazette* described him as 'the architect who drew up the plans for the expansion of the empire of high class provisions shops . . . the builder who personally directed the growth of the firm [and] . . . an unapologetic dictator' who controlled the entire organisation 'from buying right through to the retail level in the branches'. The article added: 'The orderliness of his nature, plus the amazing organising ability he possessed, were the instruments he used to build up an unrivalled system of retail distribution which has been copied by the vast majority of multiple companies that have since come into existence.'

Mr John's achievements had indeed been phenomenal. Between 1915 and 1938 the number of Sainsbury's shops had more than doubled, from 122 to 248. Turnover in real terms had risen fourfold. Sainsbury's had become a household name throughout its trading areas in the Midlands, East Anglia and the South. Mr John had continued to pursue his father's policy of offering a wider product range than competitors and selling goods of exceptional quality at highly competitive prices. The number of products sold by Sainsbury's had increased from about 200 in 1915 to over 550 in 1938. The addition of fresh meats and numerous own brand groceries had encouraged customers to rely on Sainsbury's for most of their families' food needs.

Although Mr John could have continued to influence the management of the business, he made a conscious decision to pass full control to his sons, Alan and Robert, in whom he had complete confidence. They became joint general managers, an arrangement which took advantage of their complementary skills and characters. Mr Alan had joined the firm in 1921 and become experienced in every aspect of trading. He had worked at the counter of the Boscombe branch under the alias 'Mr Allan'. Robert Sainsbury (Mr RJ) had trained as an accountant before joining the firm in 1930. He spent seven years as company secretary and became responsible for personnel and administration. This arrangement was to last for over thirty years and was the key to Sainsbury's survival in the difficult years ahead.

ABOVE *Piemaking in Sainsbury's factory as depicted in a stained-glass window at Christchurch, Blackfriars.*

OPPOSITE *Recipes for Sainsbury's cooked meats were closely guarded secrets. This example for 1lb veal and ham pies was written on the back of a handbill dating from 1932.*

SECTION 3

War
and
Postwar

FOOD IS A MUNITION OF WAR

WELCOME TO SELF-SERVICE SHOPPING

HONEST TO GOODNESS

Sainsbury's East Grinstead branch was badly damaged during the Second World War and the business was transferred to this disused Wesleyan church where it remained until 1951. After the war the 'shop in a church' even appeared in tourist brochures aimed at American visitors.

F o o d   i s   a   m u n i t i o n   o f   w a r

At 11am on Sunday, 3rd September 1939, the people of Britain gathered around their wireless sets to hear the Prime Minister's announcement that they were at war with Germany. There was little surprise that Hitler had refused to withdraw his troops from Poland, but few people would ever forget the sense of foreboding at the enormity of the task ahead and at the changes they knew war would bring to their daily lives.

The most immediate fear was of gas attacks during air raids. Recalling the dreadful injuries suffered by the soldiers fighting at the front during the First World War, the authorities had already issued the entire civilian population with gas masks. Sainsbury's had also made contingency plans for such an emergency. Before the outbreak of war, detailed instructions had been sent out to all Sainsbury's managers outlining the drill to be followed in the event of an air raid. These plans were put into effect almost immediately after the Prime Minister's announcement, when the sirens sounded unexpectedly in London. Ken Boston, one of the three managers at the Sainsbury's shops at 98, 151 and 159 Queen's Crescent, Kentish Town, recalled how 'when the sirens went the two other managers and I were unloading a Sainsbury's lorry out in the Crescent [the shops at 98 and 159 Queen's Crescent did not have loading bays so all deliveries had to be carried through the stores]. We all dived for cover at 98, which had been set up as an anti-gas chamber, leaving the lorry and the shops unlocked. I made myself busy throwing buckets of water at the blankets we'd hung over the windows to keep the gas out. We really thought it was going to happen, but that didn't stop me taking great satisfaction in leaving Mr Walder, the manager of 98, to clear up the mess when the "raid" proved to be a false alarm!' In the event it was to be several months before the air raids began in earnest.

A price list cover, 1939. Due to rationing, it was to be fifteen years before customers could again enjoy 'Christmas as usual'.

Preparing for staff shortages

The company was better prepared than it had been during the First World War to avoid the staffing problems caused by conscription. Thousands of letters had already been sent out to former female employees guaranteeing them re-engagement if they presented their letter to the manager of the nearest Sainsbury branch. It was felt that the women would already have a knowledge of the high standards expected by Sainsbury's.

Even this initiative proved insufficient, as the evacuation of many former employees from London and the South-east made them unavailable for work.

Others felt unable to make a long-term commitment to Sainsbury's while the situation remained so uncertain. For this reason a bulletin was issued to managers the day after war was declared pointing out that a further recruitment drive was necessary: 'unless we enroll an enormous number of women within the next few weeks, there is a strong possibility that in a few months as our male staff begin to go, we should find it very difficult to carry on.'

As in the Great War, women took on jobs traditionally regarded as male preserves. However, the general managers ruled that terms such as 'butcheress' were not to be used.

A well-structured training programme was introduced for these new female recruits in which they received on-the-spot instruction from the men they were to replace. This meant that they were already known to customers and familiar with their new work when their instructors were eventually conscripted. From the middle of 1940 a variety of short courses were introduced at Blackfriars to ensure as far as possible that standards of customer service were maintained.

This policy did mean that staffing levels rose rapidly during the first few months of the war at a time when the trade of many branches fell, due to the evacuation of women and children to safer areas. The result was that the company's wage bill increased by £100,000 per week. This problem was exacerbated by conscription proceeding more slowly than anticipated. Nevertheless, the general managers considered the additional expense was justified as long as it ensured the highest possible level of staff training: 'as in peacetime the "JS" standard of employees is immeasurably higher than our competitors, so shall it be in wartime.'

Even so, difficulties were encountered in employing women, as they were subject to different regulations under existing employment legislation. The 1912

"*Please go easy with the BACON!*" After all, there are plenty of other good things to choose from. Here are a few — the famous Sainsbury quality at Sainsbury's fair prices.

Sainsbury's SUGGEST:

Hot breakfasts with a difference—all but one of them actually cheaper than a couple of rashers of bacon:

Enough SALMON-CAKES for six persons are made with a ½lb. tin of Sainsbury's Salmon, one egg, and a little mashed potato and golden crumbs. A novel, substantial easy-to-make meal at only 2½d a portion all in!

If you haven't had PORRIDGE lately, try it at its very best—" Broadacres " flaked Scotch oats. A 7½d packet (2lbs) gives no less than 30 handsome helpings. Reckon milk at ½d each extra and you still have a wonderfully cheap meal. Real porridge fans eat it with salt and pepper (don't despise this without trying it !) but if you have a sweet tooth try a spoonful of honey for sweetening.

ENGLISH NEW-LAID EGGS cost 2½d at Sainsbury's—a saving of 3d a dozen on the maximum " controlled " price. These eggs are so good that they don't call for anything fancier than just plain boiling.

SAINSBURY'S PORK SAUSAGES are specially delicious. Although the cost of a couple is nearly ½d more than a bacon breakfast, you get for it an outsize helping of a great delicacy.

When the weather gets colder BAKED BEANS will be sure of a welcome. In a 5d tin at Sainsbury's you have enough for four people or three boy-scouts . . .

Everyone will want to have fuel-saving days. That will give you a chance of discovering how pleasant a cold breakfast can be if you trust to Sainsbury's :

For its first meal Hollywood contents itself with GRAPEFRUIT. In one of Sainsbury's 5½d tins you get three good helpings. Much cheaper than bacon, and healthier too.

For only 3d you can have no less than 6 slices of SAINSBURY'S SMOKED SAUSAGE cut thin as it deserves to be — one of the most delicious of dishes.

SARDINES are tasty and nourishing and surprisingly cheap. A tin costing 5½d at Sainsbury's gives four sufficient helpings. BRISLING costs only 7d for four breakfasts, or even less if you find six fish too many for a single portion. What is left over can be served hot on toast with only a trifle of trouble.

In the interests of national economy buyers of bacon are asked to **' grin and share it !'**

J. Sainsbury

Head Office : Stamford House, Blackfriars, S.E.1

This wartime advertisement, designed by Leonard Beaumont under the supervision of Francis Meynell, pre-dates the introduction of rationing in January 1940.

Shops Act, for example, required that women should be provided with seats behind the counters. As many of Sainsbury's branches had been operated exclusively by men, such seating was often unavailable. Managers were therefore advised to make do with wooden corned beef boxes and padding covered with material.

The pre-war staff also had doubts about the quality of some of the new recruits. Howard Bell, who at the age of seventeen was given the task of devising a training programme for the new girls at the Colchester branch, recalled how many of those taken on from competitors fell 'very much below the standard of our training'. Some allowances were therefore made. For example, whereas male employees were expected to be able to add up prices in their heads, pads were provided for women whose mental arithmetic was rusty.

The rigid discipline of the pre-war period was relaxed. Managers were told not to expect the same standards of discipline from their female staff as from the young boys they replaced. They were warned not to make an issue over minor irregularities of dress and to be tactful over the use of make-up and the wearing of jewellery. The company recognised that it could not afford to lose staff due to petty disagreements. In July 1943, when staffing levels became dangerously low, Mr RJ sent a letter to the district supervisors stating that 'only if it can be said that the particular branch will definitely be better off without the employee . . . should one make no effort to retain that employee'.

Of national importance

A second recruitment campaign was undertaken in the spring of 1940 when many of the remaining male employees were conscripted. To begin with, reserved status was given to managers, butchers and warehousemen over the age of thirty, as the authorities recognised that experienced managers and butchers had an important part to play in ensuring the efficient operation of the rationing regulations. Warehousemen were reserved because it was felt that their heavy work could not be done by women. As the war progressed, however, the needs of the armed services took priority. In May 1941 the age at which reserved status for managers took effect was raised to thirty-five, and finally, in January 1942, reserved status was abolished altogether. Thereafter, the company could apply for the deferment of individuals' call-up only by justifying each case. For Sainsbury's this was a serious blow, because the retention of experienced male staff was regarded as essential to the maintenance of standards and the smooth running of the business.

Young, single women were also subject to conscription. To begin with, it was expected that women working in the food industry – whose work was officially classified as of 'national importance' – would be exempt both from conscription into the services and from direction into war-work. This confidence was misplaced, however, and the company faced an ongoing battle with the authorities to convince them just how much training was required to do the work of its branch employees. Its efforts in this area were not helped by the fact that rival companies such as Home & Colonial, Maypole Dairies and the Co-operative spent less on training and employed fewer staff per branch. Although women working in food shops were officially reserved until early 1942, local labour exchanges often tried to pressurise individual women into war-work.

In February 1942 the already severe staff shortages were made more acute when it was announced that the call-up would immediately be extended to all single women in the twenty to twenty-one age group. The general managers responded to this development by stating in a memorandum sent to all district supervisors that 'it is up to us to find a prior substitute . . . if we wish to avoid the possibility of the Ministry of Labour getting tired of our refusing the often unsatisfactory substitutes they send and taking away the employee without prior substitute'. A third recruitment drive was therefore undertaken which paralleled that of the first weeks of the war, with the new recruits working alongside those they were to replace. This completed the transition from a work-force composed mainly of young unmarried men to one of part-time married women, older men, and young people under the age of eighteen.

Special care was taken by Sainsbury's to retain its female employees. It was recognised that working women were frequently juggling the demands of their work with looking after a family. New staff were given 'mentors' to help them settle into the job, while managers were instructed to take a personal interest in their training. Every member of the staff was paid personally by the manager so that problems could be discussed in private. The general managers asked to be informed when any member of an employee's family was reported missing, wounded, killed or captured by the enemy: 'we think the least we can do is to express the sympathy of the firm in their anxiety or sorrow.'

It was realised that women who had families and worked full-time might have difficulty in finding time to do their shopping. A discretionary 'shopping time' allowance of one hour a fortnight was therefore granted in 1943 and became a right for all female staff over the age of eighteen in April 1944. Soon afterwards,

Fresh eggs were 'allocated' rather than rationed. In practice this meant that most consumers – other than expectant mothers, infants and invalids – received about thirty eggs a year.

during the flying bomb raids, when many schools were closed, married women were even permitted to bring their children to work.

Women were given permission in October 1941 to dispense with wearing stockings, which were by then very scarce and precious, during business hours. During a cold snap in November 1943 they were allowed to wear slacks and 'woollies' under their overalls and to wear warm bootees instead of shoes.

Wartime communication network

Rationing also caused problems. Before the outbreak of war, local food offices had been set up to manage the day-to-day administration of rationing. This included the issue of ration books and dealing with changes of address (no small task as 2¼ million people left their homes during the first month of the war and over the whole war there were 60 million changes of address). Each local food office reported through a divisional office to headquarters at the Ministry of Food.

Sainsbury's set up its own rationing department at head office with the task of establishing a communications network to ensure that the Ministry of Food's regulations were correctly interpreted. Important changes in the system were communicated through a system of 'contact clerks' who telephoned selected branches as soon as they had been notified by the Ministry of a change in the regulations. These branches were then responsible for passing the messages on to a further group of shops in their area.

So efficient was this 'contact clerk' system that some local food officers believed that Sainsbury's had prior knowledge of the regulations issued by the Ministry. Margery Farrell, Mr RJ's secretary, recalled that 'this caused some resentment with local officials, until they realised that we sat up all night, phoning instructions through to the branches'. Thereafter, many local food offices discovered that it was quicker to telephone Sainsbury's rationing office to obtain advice on the regulations, than to go through their own complicated official channels.

At the centre of the whole system was the head office at Stamford Street. This was manned day and night with staff taking turns to co-ordinate the requirements of individual branches and pass on reports of bomb damage to the engineers and building staff. An air raid shelter and canteen were set up in the lower basement and a dormitory for fire watchers and duty staff on the third floor.

Frederick Juby with his staff at 41 Magdalen Street, Norwich, in July 1940. Already more than half Frederick's staff were women.

Although a few key personnel remained at Blackfriars, most of the staff was evacuated. Office workers who lived north of the Thames were sent to premises above the Cockfosters branch, while those from south of the river went to Ewell. This resulted in many people doing unfamiliar jobs. Further problems were caused by the rapid conscription of experienced staff into the armed forces, as few clerical jobs had reserved status.

Depot staff were evacuated from Blackfriars to temporary premises at Bramshott in Hampshire, Saffron Walden in Essex, Fleckney near Leicester, and Woolmer Green in Hertfordshire. This was partly because it was recognised that a

'C' Company, 17th London battalion, Home Guard. This unit was comprised of members of Sainsbury's staff at Blackfriars. They were drilled at the Union Street bacon yard by an officer from Chelsea barracks.

The Saffron Walden depot in July 1941. This was one of four decentralised wartime depots.

distribution system based entirely in central London was vulnerable to enemy air attack. There were also practical reasons for decentralisation. Firstly, it saved on fuel, which was strictly controlled by the government. Secondly, it enabled the company to supply branches which it would have been prohibited from serving from the capital because the government had banned the movement of most foodstuffs between the various designated zones within the country.

Registration strategies

At the beginning of November 1939 families were told by the Ministry of Food to register with a retailer as a preliminary to the introduction of rationing. As registration committed a customer to using a particular shop, Sainsbury's was anxious to obtain as many registrations as possible. However, staff were instructed not to 'tout' for registrations as this was considered likely to be counterproductive. Instead they were told to rely on Sainsbury's reputation for quality and hygiene: 'Efficient, polite service, "JS" standards of cleanliness and orderliness – an air of cheerfulness and willingness, the maintenance of the public's confidence – will do far more for the registration than the slips of paper on the window panes of our competitors saying "Register Here" will achieve for them.'

The general managers sent out detailed instructions to be followed for registration. Each branch was told to clear two sections of counter on opposite sides of the shop. One side was to offer customers help in filling in their ration books, the other to accept completed books. The paperwork involved in each registration was complex and time-consuming. Separate counterfoils had to be detached from the customer's ration book for every member of the family. These had to be checked to make certain they contained the correct name and address of the applicant and the Sainsbury's branch with which they wished to register. They were then sorted into alphabetical order, collated, and despatched to the local food office. Finally, a card-file register had to be kept with detailed records of every registration.

Although in theory these registration procedures were foolproof, in practice their implementation caused some problems. William Guest, manager of the branch at 66 Watney Street, was inundated with semi-literate customers who were unable to fill in their ration books. This caused the staff at the small branch so much additional work that he had to apply to Mr Butcher, the district supervisor, for help. Mr Butcher in turn referred the matter to head office. William recalled, 'The very next day a taxi drew up outside, and out stepped Miss Potter and a group of her clerical staff. They loaded the ration books into the taxi and took them to Blackfriars, returning 24 hours later with a perfectly ordered filing system and several thousand ration books immaculately filled in.'

Introduction of rationing

The system was extremely complex as products were rationed at different times and in different ways. Butter, bacon and sugar were the first goods to be rationed in January 1940. They were followed by meat and preserves in March 1940, tea, margarine and cooking fats in July 1940, and cheese in 1941. Sugar, bacon, butter, cheese and cooking fats were rationed by weight, and the relevant coupons had to be cancelled in the book. Meat was rationed by value, with each coupon entitling the customer to spend up to a given sum. Jam and other preserves were rationed as a group, so that the customer could choose whether to buy jam, marmalade or syrup or, at some point in the war, to 'swap' the jam ration for extra sugar. Tea coupons had to be clipped out of the book. To complicate matters further, an individual's entitlement varied according to the food supply and their occupation.

Customers were required to re-register for rationed goods twice a year. This caused problems for Sainsbury's because as the war progressed the trading advantages that had made the company so successful in the interwar years actually made it more difficult to retain registrations. One reason for this was that the core of Sainsbury's business was the sale of meat and provisions such as bacon and dairy produce. As these were rationed, the company was particularly vulnerable if customers transferred their registrations to other retailers. Another reason was that Sainsbury's trading heartland in London and the South-east was the area most affected by evacuation. Many regular customers left their homes for long periods in the war. A third factor was that the high street sites, which had been so profitable in the interwar years, became less attractive to customers faced with air raids, a disrupted public transport system and the blackout. For many people it was more convenient to register at their local corner shop.

Ration books were distributed during the early months of the war. Sainsbury's own ration card (BOTTOM LEFT) *gave regular customers priority for non-rationed goods in short supply.*

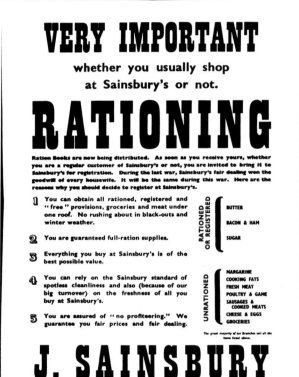

Sainsbury's responded to these difficulties by emphasising its traditional strengths. Advertisements were placed in the national newspapers giving general advice about rationing and stressing the far greater choice of goods to be found in a Sainsbury's store compared with its main competitors. These were devised by the company's advertising agents, Mather & Crowther, under the supervision of Francis Meynell – who also produced the Government's 'Food Facts' advertisements and was later knighted for this service. Customers were reminded that a trip to Sainsbury's was more convenient than visiting half a dozen specialist shops during the blackout.

Sainsbury's also introduced a 'Fair Shares' scheme using 'points'. The objective of this was to ensure that goods in short supply – such as sausages, cake, meat pies, blancmanges and custard powder – were distributed equably. Customers were allocated a number of points, up to a maximum of fourteen, according to the number of rationed goods for which they were registered. The scheme encouraged customers to register for all rationed goods at Sainsbury's.

Sainsbury's scheme was noted by the Ministry of Food. On 1st December 1941 the government introduced its own points scheme covering a wide range of grocery lines. Every adult was allocated sixteen points per four week period which they could spend on goods covered by the scheme. This had a number of advantages over conventional rationing. In the first place it enabled individuals to choose the items they purchased rather than restricting them to a specified quantity of each product.

It also allowed the authorities to manipulate the market by requiring more points for scarce commodities than for those which were plentiful.

Rationing placed an additional burden on staff. Despite Sainsbury's 'Fair Shares' scheme, many customers became frustrated at the long queues that formed for unrationed items. As the daily bulletin put it: 'The knack of keeping happy those customers who are waiting is one of the greatest gifts which a saleswoman can possess.' To ease the situation Sainsbury's developed a system known as 'call-backs'. This enabled a customer to leave her shopping list at the store and call back later to collect her purchases. The scheme was designed to give priority to working people who had less time to do their shopping. In areas where there were large numbers of factory workers Sainsbury's made arrangements for stores to remain open late one evening a week to enable workers to collect their orders.

"NO, MA'AM, I'M NOT QUEUEING, I'M JUST WAITING FOR MY GIRL FRIEND."

Keeping the company afloat

Even these measures could not prevent a serious falling off in the company's business. By March 1942 sales were only 65 per cent of their value in 1939. In real terms turnover had fallen to half its pre-war level. At no point in its history had Sainsbury's come closer to collapse. As Mr RJ later put it, sales had reached 'the lowest possible level – any lower and we couldn't have survived'. Keeping the company afloat became an act of faith. 'You couldn't deal with the situation if you had doubts. You had to assume that you would survive.'

In a further attempt to cut costs the number of deliveries to customers' houses was reduced. At the beginning of the war it had been argued by some that delivery services should be abandoned completely in order to save fuel. However, the government took the view that some people would face hardship if retailers were to cease all their deliveries. Sainsbury's therefore maintained a limited delivery service throughout the war to cater for those people who found shopping difficult because of their health, age or working hours. The firm was torn between the desire to offer pre-war standards of service and the knowledge that under wartime conditions compromises had to be made. Sainsbury's managers were encouraged to persuade customers to collect their groceries in person if at all possible, as it was considered that 'customers who do . . . their shopping personally but omit to bring a shopping basket are definite saboteurs'.

On one matter, however, there was no room for compromise. Staff were told that no matter how persuasive a

Customers were urged to re-use cotton flour bags such as the faded example pictured on the right.

customer might be, the rationing regulations were to be obeyed to the letter. Every branch employee was required to sign a declaration that they understood that if they broke the rationing regulations they would face instant dismissal. The declaration was headed 'Food is a Munition of War'. This rule was carried out however much it inconvenienced the company. Reporting a particularly bad case in the daily bulletin – when six members of a butchers' department had been sacked for overcharging – the general managers explained that 'by committing these offences, those concerned indicate their unwillingness to "run in the same harness" with us'. The situation was potentially serious for the company, as the government had the power to cancel a retailer's right to distribute rationed food. The general managers made it clear that, for those whose work was classified as of national importance, the very security of the nation was at stake. When a manager was dismissed in July 1943 for stealing rationed foods they wrote, 'we think it hard indeed to think of a more despicable act for a man of military age deferred because he is manager of a food store'.

Surviving the Battle of Britain

Rationing was by no means the only problem to be faced by staff. By the early summer of 1940, air raids were a nightly occurrence and daytime raids intensified as the Battle of Britain commenced. The general managers advised staff 'to take

Over six hundred incidents occurred involving bomb damage to Sainsbury's shops, frequently necessitating emergency measures. Improvised counters such as these exemplified Londoners' determination to beat the Blitz.

every possible opportunity of conserving . . . energy and making up for lost sleep by going to bed early and getting as many hours sleep as possible before midnight'.

At the start of the war, managers were instructed to close their shops as soon as the sirens sounded. Each store was required to post a notice on the doorpost stating the location of the nearest ARP shelter. However, many customers preferred to stay on the premises than go to the crowded shelters. Whenever possible, benches, made of egg stall boards and trestles, were set up in the branch basements to accommodate them. Where no basement was available, it was suggested that 'quite good cover is to be had beneath the counter or back shelf'.

At the height of the Blitz, daytime raids were so common that the decision to close a shop was left to the discretion of the manager. If the branch remained open members of staff with whistles were posted at the door to act as 'spotters' and, when explosions or aircraft were heard, warn customers to take cover. Although managers were told not to pressurise staff to work during an alert, some customers could be extremely demanding. On one occasion the general managers were appalled to discover that the staff at a London branch had remained serving at their positions behind the counters while an air raid was actually taking place.

Many members of staff displayed great stoicism during the Blitz. Mrs Eleanor Batey, a customer at one of the Walthamstow branches, remembered with affection the efforts of the elderly manager to reopen his store following a raid: 'After a bad night of bombing we queued up outside the wrecked shop – it was boarded up – no door on – no lights. The police had brought the old chap from home at 2am that morning and he'd spent the time "dusting the bacon" and scraping soot etc. off the margarine.'

The East End suffered particularly badly during the air raids. William Guest's branch at 66 Watney Street had to be closed when an unexploded bomb crashed through the wall of the adjacent Maypole Dairy and settled in the foundations of his shop. 'For several days we traded from another shop and stall up the street. A van from head office kept us supplied with a good selection of perishables and we kept our customers reasonably happy. The van took away the surplus food at night and brought us fresh supplies each day.' During this period William was visited by Mr Goldup, a head office official, and the district supervisor, Mr Butcher. Mr Goldup enquired if there was any cash in the safe of the closed shop. 'I told him how much approximately and he said we ought to get it out. I was a little startled at the suggestion and without thinking gave him the keys. There was a slight pause,

AIR RAID WARNINGS

his shop will remain open for business until such time as the Manager t his absolute discretion considers it necessary for those on the remises to take cover. Customers then in the shop will be welcome, t their own risk, to take cover with the staff.

MID-DAY CLOSING.

n the event of a warning between 12 noon and 1 p.m., this shop will ot close as usual during the dinner hour.

EVENING CLOSING.

n the event of a warning during the last half hour of business this hop will remain open till 6.30 p.m. (Friday and Saturday 7.30 p.m.). f the shop has to close for business it will re-open for half an hour ubject to closing not later than approx. 7 p.m. (Friday and Saturday pprox. 8 p.m.).

TELEPHONE ORDERS.

Ve shall be grateful if, in accordance with the Government's request, ur customers will refrain from telephoning our branches during eriods when an air raid warning is on.

J. SAINSBURY

Managers took responsibility for deciding whether or not to trade during an air raid, as this notice indicates.

Mr Butcher looked at me with a twinkle in his eyes and then Mr Goldup handed the keys back saying perhaps it wasn't a good idea.'

Head office was bombed. There were direct hits on the garage workshops, the 'kitchens' and the Union Street bacon stoves. The latter were being used by the Ministry of Food to store frozen meat, and Sainsbury's staff struggled throughout the night to save as much as possible. Mr RJ was summoned immediately and set off from his home to walk to Blackfriars. He flagged down a passing fire engine and asked the driver, 'Are you going to Sainsbury's? Can I have a lift?' As he and Fred Salisbury stood watching the blaze, Fred remarked sadly, 'This war will set us back fifteen years.'

The board room at Stamford House after it was badly damaged by blast during an air raid.

There were also casualties during the Blitz. The biggest tragedy was at the Marylebone branch, where four staff were killed when a direct hit was scored on the shop during the night of 19th September 1940. It took five hours for two others to be rescued from the debris of one of Sainsbury's finest shops.

The situation was so bleak for a time that Sainsbury's actually made preparations for an invasion. Detailed instructions were sent out to all branches within thirty miles of the coast. In the event of an invasion, staff at Folkestone, Hythe and Ashford were to go to Tonbridge, those from the Brighton branches to Haywards Heath and those from Norwich and Ipswich to Cambridge. Staff at the Bournemouth and Winchester branches were to report to the temporary depot Sainsbury's had set up at Bramshott in Hampshire. Each of the managers was instructed to requisition one of the branch vans for their family and take with them all ledgers, cash books, registration particulars and cash. Anticipating that this might not be as simple a task as it appeared, it was added, 'If transport is commandeered, you must do your best to persuade the powers that be of the necessity of keeping your own transport to move goods from the shop which would be of value to the enemy. If the roads are blocked you must use your own initiative.'

Air raids outside London

By the beginning of October 1940 the Battle of Britain had been won and the danger of imminent invasion receded. Daytime raids on London became less frequent as the Germans changed their tactics and launched devastating air attacks on

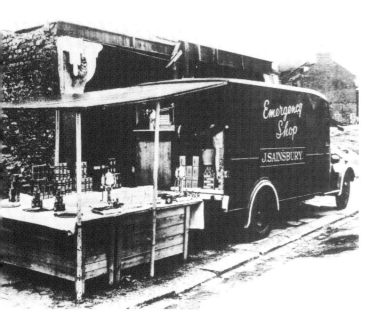

other important cities. One of the worst affected was Coventry. In a single night the centre of the city was almost totally destroyed. Glynn Harrison, a relief manager, recalled the scene as he and his staff struggled to work the next morning: 'Owen Owen's was a complete wreck . . . the roads were littered with debris from the buildings and we had to pick our way.' To Glynn's astonishment, the Sainsbury's shop had survived intact. 'The only thing that was out of place was one of the main beams of the shutters. I opened up, we got inside, and there wasn't a thing broken, not even an egg!'

Many other areas suffered bombing. Norwich experienced heavy raids during the first week of May 1942, in which six members of staff were made homeless. Even so, everyone reported for work the next day. At East Grinstead the branch was bombed twice. On the first occasion, on 9th July 1943, the damage was relatively slight and manager Laurie Holmes and his staff were able to set up a temporary shop in a disused Wesleyan chapel for six weeks while it was being repaired. A year later, on 12th July 1944, the shop was totally destroyed. This time Laurie and his staff transferred permanently to the Wesleyan chapel. The interior served as the shop and Sainsbury's engineers built a prefabricated store and cutting rooms at the rear.

Improved working conditions

Despite these problems the war years saw a steady improvement in the working conditions of the company's staff. In July 1941 a new wage structure was introduced comprised of three elements. The first was a 'wage for age' payment, guaranteeing that all those under the age of twenty-one would receive an annual increase of salary on each birthday. The second was the introduction of new 'proficiency payments' for staff who mastered specified skills within their department. Finally a bonus, up to a maximum of £12, was introduced for each year of service.

The East Grinstead branch was one of several totally destroyed during the Blitz.

Hours of working were also improved. A forty-eight hour week for women, announced before the outbreak of war, came into force from the beginning of October 1939. In August 1941 this was extended to all staff over the age of eighteen, with younger employees working a maximum of forty-four hours. Overtime payments were introduced for members of staff who worked more than fifty-one hours a week. In April 1944 the hours for staff under sixteen were limited to forty hours per week. 'It is clear,' wrote the general managers, 'that the Government's post-war plans will require young people to work considerably shorter hours in order to complete their education and to obtain further technical experience.'

These measures were progressive by contemporary standards and underlined Sainsbury's commitment to a better standard of living for the post-war period. Mr Alan and Mr RJ expressed whole-hearted support for the newly published Beveridge Report, which outlined plans for a national insurance scheme. Beveridge's objective was to provide a welfare state which offered protection 'from cradle to grave'. In a letter published in *The Times* on 3rd December 1942, Mr Alan and Mr RJ wrote, 'We would like to record our spontaneous welcome to the report of Sir William Beveridge and our agreement in principle with the extension of the system of social insurance outlined therein.'

Sainsbury's was keen to reassure its customers that its sausages contained a high meat content.

It was not surprising that Mr Alan and Mr RJ should have been such enthusiastic supporters of Beveridge's proposals, which were very much in the spirit of Sainsbury's own welfare arrangements for staff. As long ago as 1922, Mr John and his father had set up a fund known as the 'Good Fellowship Trust' which provided discretionary payments to staff in times of sickness or adversity. In 1934 a staff welfare scheme had been introduced which gave employees the right to sickness and disability payments and provided them with pensions. These benefits were available to Sainsbury's staff some fourteen years before the new welfare state provided them for everyone.

Originally, married women were not covered by this scheme because in the 1930s female shop staff were required to leave when they married. Women who left to get married were paid a lump sum 'dowry'. In 1942 the Staff Welfare Scheme was extended to married women in recognition of their work for the company. The pre-war 'marriage bar' was never reinstated.

Preparing for peace

Dried eggs were supplied under the Lend-Lease agreement.

By 1944 Sainsbury's had begun to prepare for peace. One of the company's chief concerns was to clarify the position of its many temporary members of staff. In

October the general managers stated in the branch bulletin, 'It is our earnest hope that our war-time staff will be willing to continue with their present duties at least until the Japanese war is over. We shall expect to retain all those engaged as juniors (those under 18), and we hope to be able to offer permanent positions to . . . a proportion of *wartime* engagements over 18 who may desire to continue with us. It is the declared policy of the Firm not to draw any distinction between single women, married women and widows.'

The company also made plans for the return of its employees from the forces. Throughout the war Sainsbury's had kept in touch by sending each an annual newsletter and a token Christmas gift. It was decided that all male employees on national service would be offered the same basic salary if they chose to return to Sainsbury's. A pamphlet detailing the post-war conditions of service was sent to all members of staff on national service. No one was to be allocated to a specific post until the process of demobilisation was complete. It was felt that this would allow a fair appraisal to be made of everyone who decided to remain with the company. Once permanent jobs were allocated, the company promised that any individual's promotion would be backdated to the date on which they rejoined Sainsbury's. In making these promises, Mr Alan and Mr RJ admitted that they were 'going the limit' – stretching the firm's depleted resources to their utmost. Nevertheless, they believed that the long-term future of the business depended upon mutual trust between staff and management.

Plans were also made for VE day. Three weeks before the official announcement, branch managers were instructed to make ready at short notice for a two day bank holiday in celebration. The main concern of the general managers was to ensure that there was a fair balance between customers' needs and the right of employees to join in the celebrations. It was also realised that, after nearly six years of war, the release of tension might lead to rowdiness. Managers were authorised to close early if the celebrations got out of hand.

At last, on 8th May 1945, it was announced that the war in Europe was over. To mark the event, Mr John wrote to all the Sainsbury's staff on national service expressing the pride the company felt for their contribution to victory:

At this moment of Europe's deliverance it is the spontaneous wish of your colleagues in the business and the Sainsbury Family to send you greeting. I realise that for many the fight is far from over and that even when all hostilities cease much will remain to be done. To all of you who, wherever you have been called upon to serve, have by your individual exertions and sacrifices made possible the successful conclusion of the first part of the great task, and brought nearer the day of final victory, we send this expression of our deep and lasting gratitude.

Half-labels saved paper on own brand goods.

Welcome to self-service shopping

*A*lthough VJ day was celebrated with great enthusiasm on 14th August 1945, the end of the war did not bring immediate prosperity. The nation had to face the task of paying for a war which had brought it to the verge of bankruptcy. There were soon shortages of food, fuel and raw materials. On 21st August 1945 the United States ended the Lend–Lease arrangement which had allowed Britain to buy essential supplies, including food, on credit. The much less favourable terms imposed on subsequent dollar loans, coupled with the devaluation of sterling, made the repayment of these debts a significant burden in the post-war years. Moreover, the diversion of food supplies to the newly liberated peoples of continental Europe made the shortages even more acute. In Britain the rations of bacon, cooking fat and fresh meat were reduced within three weeks of VE day (27th May), while bread and potatoes – neither of which had been rationed during the war – were both soon subject to post-war controls.

After the Second World War shop work was no longer a male preserve. This photograph was taken at the Catford branch in 1955.

These shortages were not confined to the late 1940s. In November 1951 the *JS Journal* (the company's in-house magazine founded in December 1946) reported that the Chancellor of the Exchequer had announced another campaign to reduce a projected trade gap of £350 million in 1952. Once again, great emphasis was placed on reducing food imports. This was because the rise in disposable income after the war had enabled consumers to substitute expensive imported canned meats and convenience foods for rationed goods like fresh meat, fats and sugar. So acute was this problem that the value of imported canned meats actually exceeded the money spent by the Ministry of Food on imported fresh and frozen meat.

It was not until 1954 that Sainsbury's sales in real terms exceeded their pre-war levels, so there was little scope for expansion. Even so, shops like those at Hythe, Hastings and 159 Queen's Crescent, Kentish Town, which had been 'mothballed' for most of the war were reopened, as were most of those which had sustained bomb damage. Even if funds had been available, it was virtually impossible to obtain the necessary licences to modernise existing shops or build new ones. Sainsbury's was at a particular disadvantage in this respect because many of its interwar shops were of far better design and construction than those of the smaller independent retailers. This made it very difficult to convince the Board of Trade that they needed urgent modernisation.

It was largely as a result of building restrictions that the company had to wait until 23rd February 1950 to open its first modernised store at Selsdon, near Croydon. This store was a radical departure in design from the pre-war shops. For the first time the old open windows were replaced with single sheets of armoured plate glass and the central shutters with permanent doors. The external fascia was also changed from the pre-war black on gold to one where Sainsbury's name appeared in gold on a background of 'blue pearl' granite with a red granite surround. Internally, a less elaborate floor mosaic was used and the old green, cream and 'teapot' brown wall and counter tiles replaced with lighter shades.

Sainsbury's Self-service shopping is EASY and QUICK

you go in you are given a special wire
t for your purchases.

'—The prices and weight of all goods are clearly marked. You just take what you want.

you a fast shopper or a slow? You can
er when you shop at Sainsbury's!

4—Dairy produce, cooked meats, pies, sausages, bacon, poultry, rabbits and cheese—all hygienically packed.

at is served from Sainsbury's special
erated counters   Or you can serve
elf from the cabinets.

6—Pay as you go out.   The assistant puts what you have bought into your own basket and gives you a receipt.

This 1955 advertisement was one of a series that helped familiarise customers with the new self-service methods.

The potentiality of self-service

The Selsdon branch served as a testing-ground for many of the new ideas incorporated into Sainsbury's first self-service store, which opened four months later at 9/11 London Road, Croydon. This experimental conversion was the culmination of twelve months' research and development. After the war, the Ministry of Food had decided to promote improvements in food retailing methods. As part of this campaign Mr Alan, together with fellow director Fred Salisbury, were presented with diplomatic passports in March 1949 to study recent developments in food retailing in the United States. Mr Alan recalled: 'We went to study the display and sale of frozen foods in American stores but we both came back so thrilled and stimulated at the potentiality of self-service trading that we became convinced that the future lay with what we thought were large stores of 10,000 square feet of selling space.'

This was an astute assessment by Mr Alan, for at the time of his visit there were no supermarkets in Britain. Self-service had become widespread in America during the Depression, when vacant warehouses had been converted into supermarkets selling packaged groceries with the minimum of customer service. Since then they had grown in sophistication to become a highly efficient method of retailing. Supermarkets were cheap to develop in America because land prices were much lower than in Britain. The higher wages in America also meant that the less labour-intensive nature of self-service trading was attractive to food retailers in the United States.

'Train for a Career in the Food Trade.' This recruitment advertisement appeared in the services magazine Blighty *in January 1957.*

America's affluence contrasted sharply with the poverty of post-war Britain. In 1950, 59 per cent of American households had one or more cars compared with only 12 per cent in Britain. Many American customers travelled by car to do their shopping, so supermarkets tended to be situated near busy road junctions in suburban areas rather than in town centres. Mr Alan and Fred Salisbury were struck by the infrequency with which many Americans shopped: 'In contrast to our customers, who in these days of shortage like to be in the branches as frequently as possible, the American car shopper can well purchase 7–10 days' supplies of goods at a time.' So great were the differences between the American situation and the British, that J Edward Hammond, a leading retail commentator, stated in 1951 that it was 'improbable that this class of emporium will ever be introduced into Great Britain'.

Although Mr Alan realised it would be impossible to build an American-style store under prevailing British conditions, the conversion of the Croydon branch to self-service was a significant achievement. Before this date a few retailers, most notably the London Co-operative Society, had converted stores to self-service by simply rearranging existing fittings to house a limited range of groceries. The small size of these shops and the administrative complexity of operating them while rationing was still in force made full-scale self-service impossible to introduce.

Pioneering new standards

These minor conversions were quite different from Mr Alan's plans for the Croydon store. With a floor area of 3,300 square feet, this was one of the few existing Sainsbury's stores large enough to be suitable for conversion to self-service. Mr Alan's intention was to pioneer new standards of food preparation and handling and to offer customers a greater choice of non-rationed foodstuffs. The Croydon store was completely refurbished under one of a hundred special building licences offered by the Ministry of Food. These licences were given to retailers who were

Sainsbury's first self-service branch at 9/11 London Road, Croydon, which opened in June 1950. Rationed goods, including meat, were sold from the counter on the left-hand side of the shop.

The Harlow branch, which opened in December 1957, had a 'lumenated' ceiling and was also equipped with 'nesting' trolley frames.

prepared to experiment with self-service conversion and share their experiences with other interested parties. The Croydon store required extensive redevelopment as part of it had traded for over seventy years. Even the 'newer' part of the shop dated back to 1896.

The branch at 9/11 London Road, Croydon, remained open throughout these alterations. Branch staff (dubbed 'the workers') and customers found themselves continually adapting to the demands of the building staff (known as 'the wreckers'). As Fred Salisbury recalled, 'customers arriving on a Monday morning seemed to take it for granted that there had been yet another re-arrangement during the weekend.' The *JS Journal* wryly remarked that 'the symbol "9/11" had become practically a password to panic'.

The Croydon store incorporated many technical improvements which were to become standard in all new stores. One of the most important of these was fluorescent lighting, which had been developed for use in wartime factories, as it produced a brighter and more evenly distributed light than conventional lamps. At Croydon, fluorescent lamps were initially used in conjunction with spotlights as it was discovered that when used alone they produced a bluish glow which made food look unappetising. Over time, however, colour rendering was improved and by 1957 fluorescent lighting was used to create sophisticated 'lumenated' ceilings.

Another innovation was the use of perspex. During the war this had been used to make the cockpit covers of aircraft like the Spitfire and Lancaster. In peacetime it was found to be an ideal and hygienic substitute for glass, as it was clear, light and easily shaped. Perspex was used to make canopies for counters, lighting covers and display equipment such as bins for tea and the ingenious 'waterfall' stand that was developed by Sainsbury's to display its eggs.

The most important technical advance was the introduction of refrigerated cabinets. So far only a few Sainsbury branches had been equipped with refrigerated bins, known as 'coffins', in which a small range of frozen foods such as peas and ice creams were kept. These were clearly inadequate for the demands of a self-service store. In 1949 Sainsbury's had therefore converted part of the Selsdon store into a laboratory in which Ralph Hall, the company's chief engineer was set the task of developing more efficient units. Ralph designed the open-topped refrigerated cabinets piloted at the Chelsea branch in 1950. At Croydon these cabinets became a standard fitment and were later installed in all the new self-service branches and counter service shops. The Selsdon laboratory also developed special air-cooled counters patented by Sainsbury's. These allowed perishable foods, which had previously been exposed on open counters, to be kept chilled under a simple curved perspex canopy.

John Jones, of Frederick Sage & Co, worked with Fred Salisbury on the design and layout of the early self-service stores. He recalled the lengths to which Sainsbury's went in combining good design, the best materials, and an almost obsessive regard for hygiene. John Jones designed special display shelving – known as gondolas – which had legs encased in stainless steel sleeves. These could be lifted up when the floor was cleaned so that no smears were left around the legs. One mistake, however, was made. The original specification for the width of the top shelf of the gondolas was seven inches. This was based on the assumption that the turnover of stock would be similar to that of the grocery departments in the counter service shops. However, it was soon found that seven inches was far too narrow to cope with the massive increase in demand for self-service groceries, and the shelf width had to be increased.

Another interesting experiment at the store was the introduction of primitive shopping trolleys known as 'prams'. The first prams consisted of a simple metal frame on wheels on which two wire baskets could be placed. While their small capacity was adequate for the relatively modest demands of customers who made frequent small purchases in the early self-service stores of the 1950s, they were gradually superseded by the more familiar shopping trolleys.

Public reaction to self-service

The formal reopening of 9/11 London Road, Croydon – at 8.30am on 26th June 1950 – was something of an anticlimax. It appears that many regular customers had become so used to the disruption caused by the store's conversion that its

F T Fowler, manager of 9/11 London Road, Croydon, stayed on beyond normal retirement age to help his customers adjust to self-service shopping.

completion generated little excitement. Indeed, it was reported that when the doors were opened the staff found a queue of just one . . . the manager's wife! It was only later in the day that crowds began to fill the shop.

Accolades soon appeared in the press. *Good Taste* described it as a 'splendid combination of efficiency and hygiene', while *Store* praised the pram park. In November 1950 Ernest Wilkinson, a Co-operative Society market research expert, warned the readers of *The Producer* that 'this particular shop is certainly doing a weekly volume of trade greater than that of any grocery shop in this country . . . Whilst one swallow does not make a summer, this self-service store may well be the first of a flight. If it is, a number of self-service co-operative shops will be out of date in the very near future.' When Mr John, who had been sceptical about the merits of self-service, paid an early visit to the store, he was so impressed that he demanded to know why all Sainsbury's stores were not undergoing a similar conversion.

Most customers were impressed by self-service. After years of shortages and queuing, the experience of choosing one's own groceries at leisure was irresistible. Jim Woods later remarked

One of the checkouts at Croydon in 1950. Goods were placed in a hand-operated rake which the cashier would pull forward by means of a wooden handle.

that 'unlimited supplies of sausages . . . cream biscuits and canned fruit [which] were still rarities . . . did a great deal to "sell" self-service to our customers'. *Home News* found the temptations of the new Croydon store almost too seductive: 'We collected a basket and wandered around, leisurely choosing a tin of fruit here, a packet of biscuits there, a meat pie from one of the refrigerated containers until our basket was full. There was no queuing, no need to ask "what do you have in stock?", for it was all there to see. Our only criticism – it's the easiest way in the world of spending too much money. It's such fun to pop things in the basket yourself that you forget you have to pay on the way out!'

There were a few customers who were less impressed. These were usually elderly people who found it difficult to adapt to the new system or the more prosperous who felt the idea of self-service was an affront to their dignity. At the opening of each self-service store Sainsbury's ensured that there were plenty of assistants on hand to offer advice about the new procedures. Retired branch managers were employed to give help to the elderly. Even so, there were some amusing incidents. One customer when offered a wire basket at the entrance of the shop by Mr Alan simply threw it back at him in contempt. At the newly opened Purley branch a judge's wife screamed abuse at Mr Alan when she discovered that she was required to do the work of a shop assistant and carry home her own purchases! Even others in the trade were not altogether convinced: a competitor told Mr Alan that the British public would never take to self-service. 'How wrong they were,' Mr Alan said. 'How lucky we were that they were wrong!'

Slow progress

Sainsbury's first self-service display of fresh meat was opened at 32/4 Above Bar Street, Southampton, in 1954.

A basket of own brand groceries from 1947.

Despite the success of the Croydon branch, the introduction of self-service in Sainsbury's stores proceeded only slowly during the 1950s. While the tight building restrictions remained, it was often only possible to obtain permission to rebuild bombed-out branches. Many of these were old stores on small sites and unsuitable for conversion to self-service. In rebuilding these, Sainsbury's placed great emphasis on hygiene and technological improvements. When the East Grinstead branch was rebuilt, for example, it incorporated many of the features used at the Selsdon branch along with the first use of Ralph Hall's prefabricated chilled counters and air-conditioned preparation rooms. Prior to its opening, local residents were offered guided tours of the preparation areas to prove they satisfied the highest standards of cleanliness. When the shop opened for business on 18th September 1951, one reporter described it as 'the most modern hygienic food shop in the South of England, and possibly in the whole country'.

It was not until 25th February 1952 that Sainsbury's first purpose-built self-service shop was opened, on the site of the bombed-out Eastbourne branch. Another showpiece store was opened at Southampton in September 1954. This was Sainsbury's first store in the town and was also built on a former bombsite.

Other early self-service branches were opened on the new London County Council (LCC) estates built to rehouse East-Enders who had been made homeless in the Blitz. The first of these estates were at Debden and Grange Hill in Essex. The visionary aspirations of the LCC were not always apparent when these stores were built. At Debden Sainsbury's branch was the first shop in the main parade and fronted an unmade road. The estate was built on marshland and was so far out in the Essex wilds that head office staff dubbed it 'Fort Debden'.

The move towards self-service was aided by the gradual deregulation of foodstuffs. In December 1948 jams and preserves were the first products to be taken off the ration. This offered Dick Welham, manager of the Colchester branch, an opportunity to demonstrate the salesmanship of his team. He set his staff the incredible sales target of 10,000 pounds of jam for the first week of deregulation. After the first weekend his allocated stocks had already been exhausted and he had to persuade Blackfriars to send him more preserves: 'raspberry, apricot, gooseberry, lime marmalade and LEMON CURD'. Amid growing excitement, the staff volunteered to stay behind to take stock after the branch closed on Saturday evening. Much to their disappointment, they had only sold 8,575 pounds but this was still 2,000 pounds more than their nearest rivals!

'All glass' frontages such as this one at 250/4 Kentish Town Road, pictured in 1955, gave customers an uninterrupted view of the shop's interior.

Other products took longer to be deregulated. Milk was not decontrolled until January 1950, and the points system remained until May 1950. Thereafter things only gradually improved. Tea was derationed in October 1952, sweets in February 1953, sugar and eggs during the autumn of 1953, and butter, margarine and cheese seven months later. It was not until bacon and meat came off the ration on 3rd July 1954 that wartime restrictions finally ended.

The availability of these previously rationed goods made it much easier to extend the size of new stores. In 1955 Sainsbury's opened the largest self-service food store in Europe in Lewisham High Street. With a sales area of 7,500 square feet, this shop had over twice the trading area of the Croydon branch. It was enthusiastically welcomed by the *Lewisham Mercury* which carried a long editorial deploring the planning battles which had delayed the rebuilding of the town's bomb-damaged shopping centre. Sainsbury's advertisement in the paper expressed the company's pride at participating in the regeneration of the town. It went on to promise that the 'friendly touch' which had characterised its business would 'not be lost even in self-service [as] . . . the Sainsbury Family know that the firm's success and expansion are the result of a good understanding between the men at the top and the customer in the shop'.

By December 1955 Sainsbury's had eleven self-service branches, of which four were conversions of existing stores and three were on LCC estates. The first five years of self-service had seen a full recovery in the company's turnover, so that in real terms it was now well above the pre-war level. By the end of 1959 a further fifteen self-service branches had opened. Four of these were in the new towns of Hemel Hempstead, Crawley, Harlow and Stevenage.

These new developments were encouraged by politicians. The Prime Minister, Harold Macmillan, visited the self-service store in Harlow in August 1959 and declared it to be 'a very clean and most ingenious way of serving the public and doing business'. He later had tea with Harold Weight, the store's head butcher, whose house had been selected as typical of those in the new town. The opposition's Lord Morrison was entertained at the Crawley store. His verdict was more down to earth. He declared it 'Damn good!'

There was a steady programme of improvement of existing stores. This included the installation of refrigerators, the refurbishment of shopfronts and the replacement of damaged mosaic floors with modern tiling. Twenty-nine of the least profitable branches were closed. The result of this investment, and of the removal of wartime controls, was that by 1960 sales had risen to nearly £68 million – four times their 1950 level. In real terms this represented a trebling of turnover in ten years. Profits had also increased dramatically, from £560,000 in 1950 to £2.6 million in 1960.

The effects of self-service

The demands of self-service influenced the company's trading practices, although not always in the manner envisaged by the Ministry of Food. The latter had encouraged self-service in order to economise on labour and help to alleviate the manpower shortage caused by full employment. In practice the most labour-intensive element of retailing – the packaging and preparing of foods – was merely transferred from the counter to preparation rooms behind the scenes.

It was not until the late 1950s, when most of the responsibility for preparing and packaging goods was shifted from the retailer to the manufacturer, that savings were made in this area. Even so, many manufacturers were slow to respond to the needs of a progressive retailer like Sainsbury's. Wartime restrictions had led to a seller's market in which manufacturers had become used to allocating rather than marketing their products. These allocations were often made on the basis of pre-war sales and took no account of the requirements of an expanding retailer. John D Sainsbury (Mr Alan's eldest son, known in the business as 'Mr JD' because Mr John, his grandfather, was still alive) joined the company in 1950 after national service and university. His first job was in the grocery department, where in 1951 he became biscuit buyer. He recalled that shortages of some products were still

Many of the labour economies predicted for self-service retailing were slow to materialise. Here staff at Sainsbury's Lewisham branch are shown carefully wrapping biscuits in cellophane.

acute and that 'a buyer's enterprise and powers of persuasion were very much needed' to persuade manufacturers to supply products that Sainsbury's had not stocked before the war.

Sainsbury's gained first-hand knowledge of the problems facing producers when it purchased the Kinermony herd of pedigree Aberdeen Angus cattle and five hundred acres of farmland at Inverquhomery in 1944. The company's aim was to produce top quality Scottish beef and to improve its understanding of farming techniques. It also allowed the company to demonstrate its strong commitment to improving the quality of British meat. This was important at a time when rationing placed emphasis on the quantity, rather than the quality, of the meat produced.

The project was supervised by Fred Salisbury, who in 1941 had become the first non-Sainsbury family director of the company. Fred combined responsibility for the farms and fresh meat buying with the supervision of Sainsbury's estates and building development. His work also achieved wider recognition. During the war he had been an advisor to the Ministry of Food on meat supplies and distribution and from 1955 to 1961 served on the government's technical and advisory committee on meat research.

Sainsbury's also moved into production with the development of Tendersweet bacon. This was a project masterminded by Mr JD. As he recalled:

> I soon realised that Britain was years behind the rest of the world in bacon production and marketing. As wartime controls were lifted, the producers would soon experience something they had almost forgotten – competition. The growth of self-service was another factor – we just could not get pre-cut bacon for our self-service stores. So I suggested to my father that I should visit North America, where Canada Packers were our good friends and suppliers, to see what had been going on in their bacon market over the past twenty years. He was not entirely convinced as to my motives, but I offered to pay half the cost and he eventually agreed.

As a result of Mr JD's visit to Canada, a pilot plant was set up for the production of sweetcure bacon at Blunt's Hall abattoir at Haverhill. This proved a great success and it was decided to build a permanent plant to be run by a partly owned associate company named Haverhill Meat Products (Sainsbury's and Canada Meat Packers each owning a 50 per cent stake in the company). One of the pioneers of this enterprise was Dan Pillar, who answered a mysterious advertisement for somebody 'willing to spend time in a commonwealth country'. After a two week induction course with Sainsbury's, he spent the next six months in Canada learning about modern bacon production methods. Haverhill Meat Products began production in 1958 and was soon supplying all Sainsbury's self-service stores with bacon.

Mr JD examining bacon in Sainsbury's sampling rooms in 1957.

Sainsbury's popularised chicken as an inexpensive family meal. This leaflet was one of a series offering novel recipe ideas to suit different lifestyles.

Another example of product innovation stimulated by self-service shopping methods was the introduction of the 'ready-to-cook' frozen chicken. Inspired by American production methods, Mr Alan and Max Justice worked closely with chicken breeders, most notably Geoffrey Sykes, and producers such as Lloyd Maunder, G W Padley, Buxted Chicken and the Western Chicken Growers Association to develop the mass-production of frozen chickens. By transferring responsibility for drawing and dressing the birds from the retailer to the producer – who also froze and packed them – it was possible to increase production enormously. It was largely owing to Max Justice's foresight that Sainsbury's became pioneers in the 'broiler' trade. Chicken soon became an inexpensive product which everyone could afford.

In 1958 Sainsbury's ventured for the first time into television advertising to promote its frozen chicken. Jim Woods, who as merchandising manager was responsible for the production of the advertisements, recalled that early methods were refreshingly simple. 'We did the filming at the Putney branch, and every time we started recording, one of us had to dash outside to stop the traffic because of the noise. The actress who played the customer had to take her shoes off, because they made a noise on our mosaic floor, and I carved the chicken myself!' Later television advertisements made use of a set built from 'shop fittings' borrowed from the firm's training school at Blackfriars.

It was an exciting period. 'All the time we were saying "what can we do next? What shall we try now?"' recalled Jim Woods. Tomatoes and cucumbers had already been added to the product range because they were a natural complement to the company's sale of cooked meats. When the Lewisham branch opened in 1955 it was decided to add apples, citrus fruits, grapes, bananas and potatoes to form the first 'produce' department. 'Then we discovered someone who was prepared to shell peas, and pack them in cellulose bags.' Another experiment was with washed and prepared Brussels sprouts.

Sometimes Sainsbury's tailored its new products to a particular locality. At Swiss Cottage, where there was a large Jewish community who had fled from Nazi Europe during the war as well as refugees from the newly created Communist states, the self-service branch offered a range of continental foods rarely seen outside a specialist delicatessen. These included salami from Italy, Hungary and Germany; Polska ham and Krakowska sausages from Poland; Yugoslav kabanos and ring sausage; Belgian liver sausage and continental cuts of meat such as *boeuf à la mode* and noisettes of lamb. There was also ravioli, spaghetti, vermicellini, sauerkraut, continental crispbreads and rolls, Danish and Polish bread, grissini sticks and Norwegian flat bread. At the time it was regarded as revolutionary for a self-service store to offer these products.

A revolution in packaging design

The demands of self-service trading led to a revolution in the design of Sainsbury's food packaging. Packaging needed to be both hygienic and robust to protect food from repeated handling by customers. It also had to be a 'silent salesman' by being pleasing to the eye and informative. To meet this challenge Mr Alan appointed Leonard Beaumont as design consultant to Sainsbury's in 1950. It was to be a happy choice as the two men immediately reached a mutual understanding, Beaumont writing enthusiastically after their first meeting of Mr Alan's receptiveness to 'my spontaneous and bold allusions to your design problem'.

Beaumont's approach was certainly bold. Its essence was simplicity. At a time when most manufacturers were using complex and often garish packaging, Beaumont developed for Sainsbury's a design standard which involved the use of just two typefaces – Albertus and Trajan, with the latter used on shop fascias. Associated with these was the use of stylised graphics and muted colours to create a clean, fresh image which enhanced the uncluttered lines of the new self-service shops.

'Above all,' Mr Alan later told *Design* magazine, 'I wanted to get discipline into the look of things, and an avoidance of fussiness . . . it may be my reaction to Victorianism . . . Simplify, Simplify!' Even manufacturers' point of sale advertising was redesigned to conform to Sainsbury's house style. 'So persuasive was Beaumont's influence,' recalled Jim Woods, 'that we even considered converting the head office typewriters to Albertus. It did, however, have one drawback as a standard typeface for Sainsbury's – the J was weak and looked rather like a T, so Beaumont re-designed the Albertus J with a more emphatic serif.'

New own brand lines

As part of this process of modernisation it was decided to discontinue the old subbrands like 'Selsa' and 'Crelos'. It was felt that in a self-service environment new customers might not realise that they were Sainsbury brand goods. The intention was also to promote own brand groceries as produced *for* Sainsbury's rather than *by* them and to cultivate the image of own brands as equal in quality to branded goods but sold at a more competitive price. This was made possible by passing on to customers the savings made in advertising and distribution costs.

Own brand instant coffee was introduced in 1958 because the high price of the brand leader made it logical to offer a more competitive alternative. In the case of canned fruits, as the buyer, Jack Russell, recalled, 'it was impossible to buy enough of any given packer's brand, and consequently the customer never knew what she

An early Beaumont design for Sainsbury's baking powder.

Egg packs used by Sainsbury's in the 1950s.

was getting. Soon I was on the plane to Australia, South Africa and Italy to persuade packers to pack our own label to our specifications. I used to have to go out and pass every batch code before it was shipped.'

This detailed supervision was characteristic of all Sainsbury's activities. A typical example was the price meeting held by Mr Alan at 10am every Wednesday morning. Buyers were required to justify any price changes. Ron Topp, who was Mr Alan's personal assistant, recalled that 'if a buyer came in with half a dozen price changes and they were all going up, he'd have a hell of a job; if he came in with prices to come down, he would sail through.'

Closure of 173 Drury Lane

Mr Alan and G W Pawsey, manager, on the closing day of 173 Drury Lane. Mr Pawsey handed the branch key to Mr Alan, saying, 'Your Grandfather opened this shop, and I think it's only right that you should close it.'

Self-service transformed British retailing. Nowhere was this more apparent than in Drury Lane, where John James had founded the business. On 11th November 1958 the original shop at 173 Drury Lane was replaced by a new self-service branch. The decision to close the old store had not been easy. As Mr RJ put it: 'Most people seemed to assume that we should never, under any circumstances, part with it.' In the end, the realisation that the shop was no longer safe forced the issue. On their annual Christmas visit to Drury Lane, Mr Alan and Mr RJ found the shop so crowded that they feared the floor would give way. 'We decided that it was not for us to indulge in the primitive custom of ancestor worship and that we could best show our respect for our forebears by trying to take care of the future.'

J Edward Hammond had no doubt that they had made the right decision when he reported for the *Grocers' Gazette* on the opening of the new shop:

I visited both. In the little old shop the manager and his staff were jostling and sidling past each other and lining up at the counter, and assistants were darting and fetching and carrying in the good old-fashioned way . . . At the big, bright food store over the road they were filling the shelves, bins and gondolas in readiness to let customers do all the carrying, but without having to dart or fetch. This store, like the little old shop it has displaced, has become very busy indeed. But in such a different way. Although the customers are multiplied many times over there is no jostling or scrambling. The selling goes on with smooth and apparently effortless precision. The work that makes it so easy for women to buy from such a vast variety of food is carried on out of sight – like the work of the stage productions nearby.

The following day 173 Drury Lane closed. It was the end of an era.

H o n e s t   t o   g o o d n e s s

The self-service experiments of the 1950s were the beginning of a programme of modernisation and development which was to transform Sainsbury's. In 1960 only 10 per cent of the company's shops had been converted to self-service. By the end of the decade this figure had risen to almost 50 per cent. During the same period sales increased two and a half times and profits before tax almost doubled. The conversion to self-service, although ultimately highly profitable, involved a massive capital investment. In this respect Sainsbury's was better placed than some of its major competitors in still being a family business. As *Management Today* remarked in 1967, 'the Sainsburys say that one of the advantages of a family-controlled firm is that you can take the long view and not necessarily turn in bigger profits today or tomorrow.'

The famous slogan 'Good food costs less at Sainsbury's' was first used in 1959.

Preparing the next generation

Mr Alan and Mr RJ – both in their fifties at the beginning of the decade – realised that it was essential to prepare the next generation of the family to take over the running of the company. In a memo to senior executives dated 3rd April 1959, Mr Alan envisaged a 'transitional period before the fourth generation become responsible for the day-to-day functioning of the business'. He added, 'We firmly believe that it is in the interests of the business that whilst we are both still able to be fully active and thus to guide the destinies of the business those who will, in due course, succeed us should take a greater responsibility in its daily functioning.'

All three of Mr Alan's sons assumed active roles in the company's management. Mr JD, Mr Alan's eldest son, had joined the firm in 1950 and was already playing a major part in the business. He was appointed a director in 1958. Mr Alan's second son, Mr Simon, became a director a year later. He gradually took over the administrative, financial and personnel management responsibilities of Mr RJ, working alongside NC Turner, who had joined the board in 1945. Fred Salisbury, who in 1941 had become the first non-Sainsbury family director, was also nearing retirement age. His responsibilities for poultry and fresh meat buying and for the farms were gradually taken over by Max Justice, who was appointed a director on the same day as Mr Simon. Fred Salisbury's other specialism was estates and building development. Mr Timothy Sainsbury became his deputy in 1959 and was appointed director of estates, architects and engineers in 1962. The company's chief statistician, Bernard Ramm, became a director at the same time as Mr

Timothy. A year later Mr RJ's only son, Mr David, joined the company. He was made a director in 1966. By grooming the next generation to take over the running of the company, Mr Alan and Mr RJ hoped to avoid their own experience back in 1938, when on their father's sudden retirement they had been – as Mr RJ put it – 'thrown in at the deep end'.

As a result of these changes, Mr Alan and Mr RJ were able to delegate much of

Sainsbury's 'empties' depot at Running Horses Yard, Blackfriars, soon after it opened in 1951. Each day two hundred vehicles passed through the yard returning and collecting boxes, feathers and rabbit skins to be recycled.

their day-to-day 'hands on' control of the business. They acknowledged this in 1962 when they relinquished the title of joint general managers. In future they were to be known respectively as chairman and deputy chairman. These were posts which they had combined with the joint general managership since their father's death in 1956.

In 1962 Mr Alan was made a life peer in the New Year's Honours on the recommendation of Hugh Gaitskell, the leader of the Opposition. This was a fitting tribute as he had always taken an active interest in politics and even stood as a Liberal candidate in the general elections of 1929, 1931 and 1935. In the *JS Journal* Mr RJ predicted an active role for his brother in the upper chamber: 'the long experience of Mr Alan in the world of business and particularly in the field of retailing, together with his highly specialised knowledge of the food trade, must be of great value in the House of Lords, and I am sure that he will be able to render much service to the community through his participation in the debates and committee work of that House.' This proved to be an accurate prediction, as Mr Alan (who took the title Lord Sainsbury of Drury Lane) became an active champion of consumer rights.

Modernising the distribution system

One of the most pressing problems facing the new management team was the inadequacy of the Blackfriars depot, whose facilities had not improved in line with the growth in Sainsbury's trade. Its methods had changed little – except in scale – since it was established in the 1890s. Goods still had to be manhandled from each specialist department to the ground floor loading bays, and then stacked carefully – again by hand – onto vans for delivery to the branches. The loading of cooked meats, pies and sausages took place on the other side of Stamford Street at the factory, while meat, butter and bacon were stored and loaded around the corner at Union Street, off Blackfriars Road.

A further problem was the congestion caused by Sainsbury's lorries and those of its suppliers. It was not unusual for vehicles to have to queue for over an hour at the loading banks. The tight schedule of the night loading of more than three hundred vehicles meant that any delay caused disruption to the whole timetable.

The system was clearly outdated. The constraints placed on it by lorry capacity and the size of the warehouse meant that deliveries were almost always made at the last minute. It was not uncommon for an 'emergency' delivery of a single hamper of perishable goods to be rushed out to a branch by passenger train or by special van. Whereas in a well-ordered depot 'just in time' deliveries are a mark of efficiency, at Sainsbury's in the late 1950s they showed just how close the whole distribution system was to a complete breakdown.

In 1959 it was decided to begin a process of decentralisation by looking for sites for regional distribution centres. As a first step the company began to search for suitable warehouse accommodation outside London. Eventually Fred McManus, who was then assistant to the transport manager, spotted an advertisement in the *Daily Telegraph* for the auction of a former Royal Army Ordnance depot at Buntingford on the A10 north of Ware. Peter Ruff, head of the newly established work study department, visited the site and realised it was ideal, as very little building work was needed to make it usable. He reported back, 'We've got to have this!'

The new Buntingford warehouse opened in late 1960. It took over the delivery of 500 non-perishable grocery lines and 'stores goods', such as paper bags, to branches in North London, East Anglia and the Midlands. The Blackfriars depot continued to supply perishable goods to these shops as well as servicing the remaining branches. Sainsbury's were able to introduce new working practices at the warehouse. Whereas at Blackfriars each man had belonged to a single department, at Buntingford they were required to 'pick' a complete order from the 500 lines laid out in the 40,000 square foot warehouse. Another change was that, instead of daily deliveries to each branch, the non-perishable lines handled by the Buntingford warehouse were supplied only two or three times a week.

Plans were made for a series of regional depots to supply branches with the

whole product range. The first site, at Basingstoke, was acquired in April 1962. The location was attractive because the town's status as a new town meant that Sainsbury's development was likely to be well received by planners and that housing would be available for staff who transferred to the new depot. It was also felt that Basingstoke's proximity to the proposed M3 and M4 motorways would aid the company's expansion in the South and West. The new depot was provided with facilities for handling chilled and frozen foods, which were transported to the branches using the firm's new fleet of 12-ton TK Bedford refrigerated lorries.

The Basingstoke depot also took over much of the work formerly undertaken at the Union Street

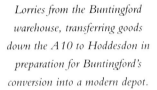

Lorries from the Buntingford warehouse, transferring goods down the A10 to Hoddesdon in preparation for Buntingford's conversion into a modern depot.

One of the firm's first refrigerated lorries, a 12-ton TK Bedford van, pictured in Reading in c1964.

bacon stoves. This enabled important changes to be made in the way Wiltshire bacon was prepared. The Blackfriars depot had received the unsmoked bacon and then transferred it to the Union Street bacon stoves to be smoked. It was despatched to the branches as whole sides or prime cuts and was prepared for sale on the premises. This process was revolutionised at Basingstoke. Not only were the depot's modern bacon kilns more efficient, but Sainsbury's engineers had designed packaging lines which sliced, wrapped and priced the product. This enabled ready-packed bacon to be sent direct to the self-service branches. By centralising the process at the depot, less space was needed for preparation areas at the branches and labour productivity was greatly increased. When the Basingstoke facilities opened they were acknowledged to be the most advanced in the world.

Air freight was used to transport fresh produce from abroad and to enable customers to purchase fruit and vegetables outside their normal seasons.

The company also carried out successful experiments at Basingstoke with the prepacking of frozen New Zealand lamb and fresh beef. This was particularly ambitious because of the perishability of these products. In a speech to senior executives in October 1967 Mr JD predicted that by early 1969 the depot would be able to supply 50 per cent of the frozen lamb and fresh beef requirements of the branches it served. The depot also took over the packaging of Cheddar cheese and of dry groceries, which had formerly been done at Blackfriars.

The Basingstoke depot opened in January 1964. Its 350,000 square foot working space was roughly equal to the combined sales areas of all Sainsbury's branches. Angus Clark, who later became depot manager and subsequently a director of the company, recalled that at the time many people felt it was too large to function efficiently. In the event it was less than three years before the depot had to be extended.

While Basingstoke was still under construction a specialist depot for the distribution of fresh fruit and vegetables was established at Hoddesdon in November 1962. The perishable and seasonal nature of fresh 'produce' – an American term for fresh fruit and vegetables that was adopted by the British trade – meant that it needed different handling methods from other lines. Daily deliveries had to be made by 7.30am to each of the thirty-two self-service branches which carried the full range of fresh produce. W J Sims, an outside contractor who had already been engaged to deliver produce from Cook's Yard at Blackfriars, provided transport at the new Hoddesdon depot. The site had the advantage that it was conveniently situated for deliveries from the growers of the Lea Valley.

The first winter at Hoddesdon was the coldest since 1947. With temperatures as low as two degrees Fahrenheit, the tomatoes froze solid like cricket balls. At one point, twenty-seven vehicles were immobilised when diesel froze in their tanks. Nevertheless, when the thaw came the new depot was able to claim that it had never missed a delivery.

The next stage of depot decentralisation was to bring Buntingford up to the standard of a full depot. In order that the site could be redeveloped its entire operation was moved temporarily to Hoddesdon, which was enlarged to accommodate it. Like Basingstoke, Buntingford was provided with a chilled warehouse for perishables. It was also equipped with the latest facilities for frozen foods as this was a sector of the market that was expected to expand in the future.

Once Buntingford had returned to its own site, the additional accommodation at Hoddesdon was given over to non-foods such as soaps and detergents. Later, beers, wines and spirits were also added. These new product ranges needed separate storage areas away from the foodstuffs kept in the composite depots. This was because strong-smelling soaps and detergents could contaminate foodstuffs while off-licence goods required special security arrangements.

The site chosen for the third of Sainsbury's regional distribution centres – its fourth depot – was Charlton in South London. This was designed to serve the eighty branches in London and the South-east which still received their supplies from Blackfriars. The company was anxious that in transferring the last of its distribution activities away from the head office site it should not break the link between the buyers and the goods they purchased. It was felt that Charlton's proximity to head office would enable it to be visited frequently by the buyers.

The new depot was handed over on 31st December 1969. It had a floor area of 228,400 square feet – half of it devoted to cold storage – and forty-six loading bays.

Sainsbury's first EMIDEC computer arriving at Stamford House in 1961. The computer was so complex that it had been ordered two years earlier.

This brought the total floor area of Sainsbury's depots to over 1½ million square feet. At the time it was considered that Charlton's location on the Thames was ideal for its function, but this proved not to be the case. The infamous Blackwall tunnel was a persistent problem for drivers trying to leave the capital.

The decentralisation of the depots made it more than ever necessary for the standards set at head office to be monitored and enforced. To achieve this, Sainsbury's became the first food retailer to enter the computer age. In May 1961 an EMIDEC 1100 computer was installed at Stamford

52/5 Friar Street, Reading, which opened in October 1963, was typical of the design of Sainsbury's stores in the early 1960s.

House. It took over the stock control of non-perishable lines, which had previously been performed by the mechanised Powers-Samas punched card system. The computer allowed information about the sales of non-perishables to be gathered and analysed with greater speed and accuracy. These products included the rapidly growing range of Sainsbury brand groceries.

Extending the own brand range

Mr JD described the development of own brand groceries at Sainsbury's as the firm's 'greatest postwar trading success'. From its earliest years the company had established an enviable reputation for its perishable goods. During the interwar period this had been extended to non-perishable goods marketed under Sainsbury's 'Selsa' and 'Basket Brand'. For its customers the name 'Sainsbury's' was synonymous with 'quality'. As *Management Today* reported in April 1967, Sainsbury's had 'created an image of freshness that rubs off onto all the other goods that [it] sells.'

In the 1960s the company was able to extend this association when it launched new own brand lines. During the decade, approximately 1,000 Sainsbury brand products were introduced. The greatest expansion was in non-perishable lines ranging from soup to soap, from catfood to cornflakes, and from biscuits to baby food. By the end of the 1960s, own brand lines accounted for over 50 per cent of Sainsbury's turnover, with some products enjoying a much greater share of trade than this. Sainsbury brand biscuits had a 65 per cent share of sales, jams and marmalades 70 per cent and soft drinks 85 per cent.

Central to Sainsbury's buying policy was that all products bearing the Sainsbury brand must be as good as the market leader and offer better value for money. 'It is our hope and ambition,' said Mr JD to Sainsbury's staff in 1965, 'that this development in own brands enhances and increases [our] reputation with our customers.' Every supplier of Sainsbury brand products underwent a rigorous inspection procedure which covered the entire production process. This included checks to ensure that the product specification – the technical 'recipe' for the product – was consistently met, that hygiene standards throughout the factory were maintained and that the producer's own quality control procedures were properly performed. Further checks were made at Sainsbury's Blackfriars laboratory.

To maintain the competitiveness of all its lines, both own brand and proprietary, only a director was allowed to fix the prices at which goods were sold. This contrasted with the practice of other retailers who often allowed buyers, or even store managers, to determine prices. The rule ensured consistency throughout the company.

Own brand products were offered alongside national brands in order to give customers more choice. 'I do not mind whether a product has a Sainsbury's label or a proprietary one,' Mr JD told the Marketing Society in October 1969, 'I am concerned only with the demand for that product in our shops.' Nonetheless, as the *JS Journal* explained in February 1965, 'our reputation has given our customers confidence to *try* our own brands even against the very powerful advertising of the most famous national brands. We have even found . . . our customers more willing to try new lines under our label than they are new proprietary lines.'

This policy avoided the need to sell cheap, inferior brands which would undermine the company's reputation for quality and reliability. The lower prices at which Sainsbury brand goods were offered resulted from suppliers' reduced marketing costs, from the discounts to be obtained by regular orders for large volumes and from the efficiency of distributing goods through Sainsbury's depots. Mr Alan pointed out that the consumer benefited not only from the lower prices of own brands but also from their competitive effect on brand leaders' prices: 'The manufacturer is disinclined to allow too great a margin between the price of his brand and that of the retailer's competing "own label".'

Some examples of the own brand lines introduced during the 1960s.

Another element in the success of the Sainsbury brand was packaging design. It was considered important to convey the 'unobtrusive good value' of the Sainsbury brand. After the retirement of Leonard Beaumont in 1962, his successor, Peter Dixon, carried the company's policy of 'design discipline' a stage further. He set up

Sainsbury's own studio and produced graphics which often made use of stylised, geometric illustrations. *Design* magazine described them as 'austere and even Bauhaus'. Mr JD took as great an interest as his father had done in the subject and personally approved every design.

The company's design standards extended beyond packaging into house style. As Mr Alan told *Design* in November 1967, 'We think our design will have failed if our customers have to read the name over our entrance to know the name of the shop they are entering.' In presenting the Royal Society of Arts Presidential Award for Design Management to Sainsbury's in 1967, the Duke of Edinburgh paid tribute to the company's 'consistent adherence to a family handwriting . . . a planned housestyle that has missed no detail while relating every part to the whole . . . from building to packaging, from shop front lettering to counter ticketing and from store layout to advertising.'

Self-service sales of perishables

Sainsbury's reputation for quality helped to ensure its success in selling perishable goods by self-service methods. This was quite an achievement. A survey by the advertising agency J Walter Thompson in 1963 found that few supermarkets had adopted self-service methods for the

This sculpture by John Wragg was specially commissioned to stand outside the Chelsea store which opened in May 1966.

When the Poole branch opened in 1969 it formed part of a covered mall which was described by Mr JD as 'the only really well-designed enclosed shopping centre in Britain'.

sale of meat, bread and greengrocery. There were two reasons for this. Firstly, most supermarkets were inexperienced at handling fresh foods. This meant that they were often expensive – because of high wastage rates – and inferior. Secondly, housewives frequently associated 'pre-packed' with 'not fresh' or with the concealment of poor quality. 'Can I see the back of that one, please?' was the canny housewife's test of the quality of a joint of meat.

From 1954, Sainsbury's offered the choice of buying meat from self-service cabinets or from traditional service counters. It was only after extensive research had been carried out into the display and marketing of fresh meat that it was decided to open the first all self-service meat department at Basildon in November 1960. A buzzer was provided so that anyone who could not find the joint they required, or who had a query, could summon assistance. Since all Sainsbury's branches employed qualified butchers who continued to prepare joints for sale on the premises, it was a simple matter to provide a customised service for those who required it. By 1967 over 20 per cent of the company's total gross profits were derived from the sale of fresh meats.

Non-food lines

A completely new departure for Sainsbury's was the addition of non-food lines to its range. The Chichester branch, which opened in October 1961, was the first to sell these on a permanent basis. The convenience to customers of buying washing powder, toilet paper, soaps, shampoos and household cleaners with their groceries led to the gradual extension of this department, with many products being introduced under the Sainsbury brand. Housewares, including brushes, buckets and cooking utensils, were introduced at the new Lewisham branch in December 1963. However, these products were only available in larger branches.

Beers, wines and spirits were also introduced to Sainsbury's product range. The first self-service off-licence department was opened at Bristol in June 1962 after a long campaign against what Mr JD described as 'an alliance of brewers and puritans'. The licensed victuallers' association, in particular, vehemently opposed the sale of drinks by self-service food shops. The company's only previous off-licence had been acquired with the purchase of the Weybridge branch in 1922. The Bristol shop offered twenty-four different beers, three ciders, and forty-seven wines and spirits. The first own label products in this department were four Spanish sherries, a selection of British wines and a Spanish Sauternes. Sainsbury brand whisky, at 45s a bottle, was introduced in 1967 and own brand beers two years later. The range of wines grew steadily, with French, German and Portuguese wines taking their place alongside British cherry and ginger wines and Spanish table wines. The

143 High Street, Guildford, had originally been a counter service branch. It was completely refitted and converted to self-service in 1962/3.

1969 price list included descriptions and serving suggestions. Sainsbury's French medium dry rosé, for example, was billed as 'a good all round wine suitable for all occasions. Light. Medium dry. Goes well with all food.' A bargain at 12s a bottle!

Obtaining off-licences for new stores often involved battles with local magistrates. By 1969 only twenty-nine of the seventy-four stores opened since 1960 included this department. The reason for this was that magistrates were reluctant to give licences to shops where customers could help themselves. This was a particular problem for Sainsbury's as it was determined to offer beers, wines and spirits in a self-service environment. Glynn Harrison, manager of the Bristol branch, recalled that both he and Mr JD had to give evidence at the Crown court before a licence was granted. The investigations into his own good character even included interviewing his former neighbours in Derby,

The challenge of success

The huge increase in the product range over the decade – from approximately 2,000 lines to 4,000 – necessitated a steady increase in the size of Sainsbury's stores. The average sales area of Sainsbury's self-service branches increased from

4,750 square feet in 1960 to 10,200 square feet in 1970. These figures would have been bettered if it had been possible to get planning permission for larger new stores. In this respect Sainsbury's was hampered by the legacy of its successful high street stores. The long, narrow shops in high street parades were unsuitable for conversion into supermarkets as they had insufficient frontage width for the checkouts. When Sainsbury's converted its older stores to self-service it was often forced to make compromises. On sites too small for full-scale conversion – for example, New Malden and Wood Green – the shops were only partially converted to self-service while adjacent premises were used for grocery self-service and meat and provisions counter service.

Even where it was possible for a full-scale conversion to be carried out, the increase in trade often caused problems. At Guildford, a two stage conversion to self-service involved a complete rebuilding of the premises during 1962–3. On reopening, the store experienced a 68 per cent increase in trade. The old adage 'No one shops at Sainsbury's because of the queues' became a source of some embarrassment. However, the *Co-operative News* (8th February 1969) pointed out rather wistfully that this was a problem many of Sainsbury's competitors 'would be pleased to have on their agenda'. By 1968 Sainsbury's branches had sales of £4 per square foot, compared with an industry average of around 30s.

Self-service was popular with customers and profitable. In 1962 Tony de Angeli, news editor of the *Grocer*, estimated that the 9,000 self-service shops so far operating in Britain accounted for about a quarter of the food sold by the nation's 140,000 food shops. So far, however, the self-service revolution had been almost entirely confined to London and the South-east. Only the Co-operatives had made substantial progress with the new shopping methods in other areas. Just 51 of Home & Colonial's 649 shops and 62 of Lipton's 434 shops were self-service. The rising stars of supermarket trading were Fine Fare, whose 200 stores were all self-service, and Tesco's, which had 150 shops, only one of which was not run on self-service lines. Sainsbury's rate of conversion was slower, but both the size of its new stores and their turnover, as in the past, were well ahead of its competitors. By 1969 the average sales per week of Sainsbury's 100 supermarkets was £25,000, whilst the average for all its stores was £15,000. This compared with £4,000 for Tesco's branches and £2,700 and £2,100 for Fine Fare and Allied Suppliers

Sainsbury's Family *magazine was published quarterly from 1961 until 1964.*

respectively. This high intensity of trade was one of the company's biggest trading strengths, as it meant that it was achieving higher sales with lower overheads than its competitors.

It was still difficult, however, to find sites which met Sainsbury's requirements. Mr JD and Mr Timothy fought an ongoing battle to persuade the planners, architects and developers of new shopping centres that they should completely revise their notions on the size and layout of town-centre shopping facilities. Few developers used market research, and most local authorities just assumed new shopping centres would better serve existing customers rather than attracting people from elsewhere. As Mr Timothy put it in a speech to the Royal Institute of Chartered Surveyors in 1969, 'in this country . . . we are very backward in providing information which would enable planners and retailers alike to make better decisions, both as to the siting of shops and to their size and number . . . we have a planning system which is designed to prevent bad building, unfortunately it also acts as a deterrent to imagination and design and innovation.'

Under Mr Timothy's direction a strategy for new store development was devised. The first priority was to replace the old counter service shops. Where this proved impossible, the aim was to bring them up to modern standards. By the late 1960s Sainsbury's had also begun to replace some of the older self-service stores such as those at Kentish Town, Stevenage, Debden and the pioneering store at 9/11 London Road, Croydon. The other priorities were to open stores in fast-growing centres in the company's existing trading area – such as Dunstable, Aylesbury and Bracknell – and to extend the trading area itself by building stores in major provincial towns like Bristol, Taunton and Wolverhampton.

Changes in store size and layout

Despite the huge growth in sales area, the overall number of Sainsbury's branches fell from 256 in March 1960 to 225 in March 1970. The reason for this was that often a large new store replaced several smaller older ones. The new branch which opened at 54/55 Chapel Market, Islington, for example, replaced two of the firm's oldest counter service stores as well as a temporary shop. Mr JD recalled that 'at the time these new branches looked enormous to us'. The total sales area of the new self-service shops increased from 95,000 square feet in March 1960 to 806,000 square feet in March 1970.

As the size of stores increased, their layout became even more important. Mr Alan was determined from the start that the self-service layout should be standardised so that customers would always know where to find the goods they wanted. He had no time for periodic rearranging of the goods to catch the customer's eye.

Shelves were laid out with the smallest size of the cheapest brand of a commodity on the left and the largest size of the most expensive brand on the right. This helped to preserve a sense of order and predictability for both customers and staff. The actual amount of a product displayed was determined solely by its sales. Two other long-standing rules were that larger pack sizes should offer better value for money and that advertised price cuts were genuine reductions.

The battle against trading stamps

Competitiveness and fair dealing were at the heart of a 1960s campaign in which Sainsbury's played a crucial role: the battle against trading stamps. Trading stamps had originated in late nineteenth century America as a means of gaining customer loyalty by encouraging shoppers to save them in exchange for gifts. In Britain, after a series of false starts, trading stamps began to be widely adopted by small chains and independent grocers from early 1961.

The members of the National Association of Multiple Grocers agreed between themselves in November 1961 not to introduce the stamps without first notifying other members. However, on 21st August 1963, Fine Fare, which was owned by the Canadian magnate Garfield Weston, announced it would be issuing Sperry & Hutchinson's pink stamps from 21st November 1963. This caused an immediate split among the members of the National Association of Multiple Grocers. Pricerite introduced stamps in the second week of October 1963, followed by Tesco's and Fine Fare a fortnight later (the latter brought forward its launch date because of the competition).

Sainsbury's was convinced that customers would soon realise that the cost of providing stamps would lead to increased prices. Mr Alan, together with Malcolm Cooper of Allied Suppliers, formed the Distributive Trades Alliance and launched a vociferous campaign against the stamps. He sponsored a bill in the House of Lords which urged that the stamps should be exchangeable for cash and that controls should be placed on misleading advertising. It was, however, a more limited

If
women want stamps
why
are Sainsbury's doing better business than ever before?

"I've always been a Sainsbury's customer—15 years when I lived in London, and 10 down here. You get everything fresh and reasonably priced—that's better than getting Trading Stamps"

says Mrs. J. W. Thompson
FROM SUSSEX, A SAINSBURY SHOPPER FOR 25 YEARS

Honest-to-goodness value at Sainsbury's — no stamps, no stunts

'Honest-to-goodness value at Sainsbury's.' These advertisements from 1963/4 formed part of the company's campaign against trading stamps.

bill sponsored by the Conservative back-bencher John Osborn which became the Trading Stamps Act (1964). At the same time Mr JD supervised Sainsbury's own massive anti-stamp campaign, which included full-page advertisements in the national newspapers and leaflets for customers explaining the company's opposition:

The grocer has to pay for the stamps. On average they cost as much as 12/- per 1,000. This money covers the cost of gifts, printing, administration and, of course, provides the profit of the trading stamp company . . . Sainsbury's make no bones about it. It would cost £2 million a year for Sainsbury's to give trading stamps . . . ! It would be impossible for Sainsbury's to maintain their high standards of quality and freshness and give trading stamps without raising prices.

An anti-stamp leaflet issued to customers in 1963.

Sainsbury's 'Star Buys' programme was re-launched on 12th November 1963 as 'SuperSavers' as a practical demonstration of how the company's anti-stamp policy made it more competitive than its rivals. The use of the slogans 'Good Food Costs Less' (which dated from 1959) and 'Honest-to-Goodness' reinforced the company's reputation for good value and fair dealing.

The publicity generated by this joint assault was beneficial to Sainsbury's image. Mr JD recalled that 'we had probably never had such national publicity. Our advertisements played a part, but the editorial coverage we obtained was even more important.' Robert Heller, editor of *Management Today*, wrote, 'The 95-year-old firm . . . already had a marvellous reputation for quality. But until the stamp battle broke across the front pages and advertising columns few customers saw Sainsbury's as it really is: an efficient, expanding multiple chain which is fiercely competitive . . . very profitable and very much in the firing line of the food revolution.'

Sales increased dramatically. Mr Alan was able to report to the *Financial Times* that in the week that Fine Fare introduced trading stamps, Sainsbury's achieved its biggest week's trading in its entire ninety-four year history. Turnover rose from £88.5 million in 1962–3 to £101.5 million in 1963–4.

The pro-stamp lobby also claimed a spectacular response from customers. The *Sunday Express* reported that Tesco's flagship store at Leicester had been besieged by thousands of battling housewives and that twelve had fainted in the crush. Fyffe Robertson, reporting for the BBC television programme *Tonight*, claimed that trading stamps appealed to the housewife's desire to get 'something for nothing, plus the satisfaction of the feminine squirrel instinct. And the fun of licking and sticking.'

The main focus of the anti-stamp battle, however, was on Garfield Weston's food conglomerate, Associated British Foods (ABF), which owned Fine Fare and, through its bakery company, supplied bread and biscuits to other supermarket companies. Faced with the prospect that ABF would lose the goodwill and trade of members of the Distributive Trades Alliance, Fine Fare stopped issuing stamps in the autumn of 1964. The news that Fine Fare had capitulated was greeted with jubilation at Sainsbury's. Steve Cody, the firm's transport manager, recalled that the staff at the Basingstoke depot wanted to raise the flag in celebration. Permission was sought from Mr RJ who was visiting the depot at the time. 'No,' he replied, 'let's just call it a victory for common sense.'

Resisting resale price maintenance

Mr Alan was also active in opposing resale price maintenance, whereby manufacturers fixed minimum prices for their goods. Sainsbury's sold very few of the lines affected by resale price maintenance so Mr Alan's opposition was based on principle rather than business interest. For Mr Alan, the heart of the issue was the efficient retailer's right to pass on to its customers price reductions achieved through lower distribution costs, buying advantage and economies of scale. In a speech in the House of Lords on the second reading of the Resale Prices Bill he said, 'It has always struck me as socially unjustifiable and economically unsound that a customer who gets credit, home delivery, plus personal service should pay the same price as a customer who goes into a shop, pays cash on the nail and takes the particular article away with her. It is right . . . that competition . . . should result in a variety of prices for the same product, dependent on where it is sold and how much service is attached to it.' The Bill passed into law in July 1964.

New working hours and personnel

Meanwhile Mr RJ had been enhancing Sainsbury's reputation as an enlightened employer. He wanted better conditions for Sainsbury's staff in order to make shop work more attractive at a time when severe labour shortages were making recruitment difficult. In 1949 Sainsbury's trading week had been reduced by the simple, but courageous, expedient of closing at 4pm instead of 5.30pm on Saturdays. Together with the existing mid-week half-day closing, this made it possible to reduce the working week to forty-five hours. These hours now compared favourably with those in industry.

However, it was recognised that the necessity for full-time staff to work on Saturdays still made it impossible for them to have two consecutive days off. In 1961 it was therefore decided to experiment with all-day

OW WAS I TO KNOW IT WAS LORD SAINSBURY ! "

These attractive pale blue Bri-Nylon overalls were designed by Hardy Amies in 1963.

In 1969 there were seven members of the Sainsbury family on the board. Left to right: Mr Alan, Mr RJ, Mr JD, Mr James, Mr Simon, Mr Timothy and Mr David.

closing on Monday. This was the day that generated least trade and accounted for only 8 per cent of the week's takings. As consumers became more affluent, trade was transferred from Saturday to Friday and Thursday. Moving the early closing day from the middle of the week to Monday therefore benefited both customers and staff. By January 1962 the new opening hours had been adopted by all the shops where it did not infringe local by-laws. In 1965, the Shops (Early Closing) Act allowed retailers to choose their preferred early closing day. Until the late 1970s, the only Sainsbury's shops to trade on Monday were five stores in central London which relied on office workers' lunchtime custom.

Among the most important personnel changes associated with the introduction of self-service was the growth in part-time employment for married women. Large self-service branches employed twice as many women as men, most of them as 'gondola girls' and checkout operators. This type of employment was particularly suitable for part-time staff and was increasingly undertaken by married women. By 1968 over 11,000 of the company's 28,000 employees were part-time staff, most of whom were women.

In 1965 women personnel officers were appointed at Sainsbury's larger branches. Their main responsibility was the pastoral care of female staff. Area personnel officers were appointed under the supervision of five superintendents. They took over the work of several specialist departments at Blackfriars, including recruitment, training, administration and welfare. In 1969–70 area offices were established at Kingston, Ealing, Bromley, Romford and Coventry. These became the bases for the area general managers (the new name for the area superintendents) and their personnel teams.

Top management changes

The late 1960s saw the culmination of the top management changes which had been initiated by Mr Alan and Mr RJ in 1959. On 2nd January 1967 Mr Alan retired from the chairmanship of the company to be succeeded by his brother, Mr RJ. Mr JD became vice chairman. Mr RJ paid tribute to his brother in a letter written to senior executives:

Mr Alan's retirement brings to an end a long, close and very happy partnership as executive directors. For roughly a quarter of a century, we have shared the responsibility for the daily management of the business, for our errors and triumphs . . . My pride [in becoming chairman] does not spring just from the past achievements of JS, but also from my knowledge of the present vitality of the business and my conviction of an even greater future, which now lies largely in the hands of a generation of Directors and Staff younger than myself.

It had been a brilliant partnership: Mr Alan with his talent for trading matters, his passion for customers' rights, and his fiery personality; Mr RJ with his compassionate understanding of personnel issues and meticulous grasp of an ever-growing administrative challenge. Together they had steered the firm through the challenges of wartime, postwar conversion to self-service and 1960s growth. Under their leadership Sainsbury's had been transformed. Most important of all they had understood the need to broaden the management basis of the company. Henceforth the business relied increasingly upon its team of professional managers, who helped the Sainsbury family to develop the business and respond to the challenges of an ever more complex retailing environment.

Mr RJ stepped down as chairman on 12th June 1969. He was succeeded by Mr Alan's eldest son, Mr JD, who had already taken on his father's responsibilities for trading policy and served as vice-chairman since 1967. On Mr JD's appointment as chairman, Mr Simon became vice-chairman. These changes coincided with the company's centenary, and a four-candle logo was designed to represent the achievements of four generations of the Sainsbury family.

The centenary celebrations

The company celebrated its centenary on Tuesday, 15th April 1969, by giving customers at every branch a free slice of birthday cake. One customer wrote to say that at her child's playgroup the appearance of Sainsbury's cake among the

Over a million slices of cake were given to customers in celebration of Sainsbury's 100th birthday. Mr JD, Mr RJ and Mr Alan are pictured with a young customer at the Drury Lane branch.

The Sainsbury Centenary Banquet was held at the Savoy Hotel. Among the guests were suppliers, leading figures in the trade and foreign and civic dignitaries.

mid-morning snacks led to the request that everyone sing 'Happy Birthday to Sainsbury's'. There were also celebration lunches and dances for staff, a party for the company's pensioners and a magnificent centenary banquet for senior staff and suppliers. A highly illustrated popular history entitled *JS 100* was published as a record of Sainsbury's achievements. The company also announced a grant of £250,000 for the advancement of research in food science.

On a more practical level, the centenary was a good cause for celebration. There were twenty new openings in 1969: the largest number to be achieved in Sainsbury's hundred year history. The company had also begun to call its new self-service stores 'supermarkets'. For a long time this term had been avoided because of its down-market connotations. The Balham branch – the 100th supermarket – was chosen for a royal visit by Princess Margaret.

Sainsbury's commitment to the future was exemplified by the installation of the most advanced ICL 1906E computer. Mr JD welcomed the new technology, not because of its sophistication, but because it offered the potential to give to 'a large business like ours . . . the quick and flexible response to consumer needs that is more often the characteristic of a really good small retailer – such as we were 100 years ago.'

The candles on the centenary logo represented the four generations of the Sainsbury family.

157

SECTION

4

The

Modern

Company

QUICK CHANGE

A PASSION TO INNOVATE

THE NEW BUSINESSES

The Worle branch,
Weston-super-Mare, part of an
edge-of-town district centre
developed by Sainsbury's.
The store opened in October 1978.

Quick change

Sainsbury's entered its second century with optimism. During the 1960s, as a result of the company's massive investment in new stores, profits had doubled and sales tripled. The programme of store modernisation had also been extremely successful. According to market research carried out by an independent trade index, Sainsbury's food sales were exceeded only by those of the Co-operative societies. This was a remarkable achievement as only 20 per cent of the population lived within reach of a Sainsbury's store. Sainsbury's expansion had been financed by retained profits and a modest amount of borrowing. The company had also drawn on funds derived from the sale of some of its freehold town centre shops which were unsuitable for conversion to supermarket trading. These were valuable assets as Sainsbury's policy had been to choose the most desirable high street locations for its stores. In March 1973 Sainsbury's properties were estimated to be worth nearly £96.6 million: a figure which exceeded their book value by £61 million.

Eager 'shoppers' crowd in for Sainsburys

IT WAS as if Sainsburys was giving away free butter and eggs at one of its supermarkets. The last-minute rush to put in applications for the 10 million shares on offer meant a great seething crowd gathered at the Midland Bank's new issue department in Austin Friars in the City today.

Some City men were complaining that these things ought to be better organised "otherwise one day people are going to get injured."

All kinds of tricky techniques were being employed at the counters by the masses trying to get lucky in the inevitable draw for shares which must follow this massive flood of applications.

With all four counters at the bank open, many were trying to increase their chances by putting in a few applications at each counter.

Bales of envelopes, cheques and application forms were rapidly removed to the back of the bank where some 240 girls were busily sorting the applications.

"We'll still be counting at 6 o'clock tonight," predicted a bank spokesman.

Lists for the offer, oversubscribed, closed at one minute past 10.

A report on the flotation in the Evening Standard.

Flotation on the stock exchange

These sources of finance had been sufficient to fund the company's ambitious programme of modernisation and expansion during the 1960s and early 1970s. However, for some time the Sainsbury family had been carefully considering a flotation on the Stock Exchange as they believed that a company of Sainsbury's scale and stature warranted public status. As Mr JD explained in the 1973 *Report and Accounts,* '. . . it is no longer appropriate for the ownership of the company to be almost wholly confined to members of the Founders' family.' Later he said, 'My brothers and I felt that the ownership should be widened. It seemed right that the public – our customers – and staff should have a share in the business.' While the company had no urgent need for additional investment funds it was also recognised that this extra source of capital would enable further expansion.

A memorandum was circulated to staff which assured them that the flotation 'would in no way affect the control of the Company, its established trading policy, or its style and philosophy of management'. The memorandum continued: 'In the belief that many staff will be interested in becoming shareholders, the Company will ensure that at the time of the flotation the maximum number of shares permitted by the Stock Exchange are made available for full-time staff, subject to a minimum service qualification.'

The details of the offer for sale of ten million ordinary shares in J. Sainsbury

The crowded scene on the floor of the Stock Exchange as dealing began in Sainsbury's shares on 19th July 1973.

Ltd were published on 3rd July 1973. It was at the time the biggest flotation in terms of capitalisation ever mounted on the London Stock Exchange, with the company being valued at £117 million. The shares offered for sale amounted to 12.4 per cent of the company's capital although 85 per cent were still controlled by the Sainsbury family. Sainsbury's kept its pledge to give preference to members of staff wishing to buy a stake in the company by setting aside a million shares for employees. The company also mounted a publicity campaign aimed at the general public rather than institutional investors. This included making share application forms available at every Sainsbury branch and the use of television commercials to advertise the issue. The allocation of shares was also weighted in favour of smaller subscribers.

The share offer opened at 10am on Thursday, 12th July 1973. Within one minute the list of applications was closed, with almost £495m offered for the £14.5m worth of shares available. One institutional pension fund actually bid for the entire issue! The *Guardian* noted approvingly that 'Sainsbury's has not forgotten the thousands of small investors and housewives who decided to take a stake in their local grocery supermarket . . . those who wanted 15,000 or more shares will

161

have to be satisfied with about 2% of the amount applied for with a maximum [for any investor] of 50,000 shares.' Of the 147,577 individual applications 4,772 came from members of Sainsbury's staff.

Dealing in the shares began on 19th July 1973. The Stock Market opened its doors fifteen minutes early to allow dealers to get into position for the expected rush. They were not disappointed. Although the market was sluggish at the time, Sainsbury's shares immediately leapt in value from the offer price of 145p to 165p. By the end of the day their price had stabilised at 162p. The *Yorkshire Evening Post* wryly remarked that 'Good shares cost more . . . [at Sainsbury's]!'

The transition from private to public status was accompanied by important changes in the top management of the company. These reflected the different style of leadership of the fourth generation of the Sainsbury family. At the time of the flotation, five of the ten board directors were members of the Sainsbury family. These were Mr Alan's three sons – Mr JD (chairman), Mr Simon (deputy chairman) and Mr Timothy (estates, architects and engineers) – Mr RJ's son, Mr David (financial controller), and Mr James, who had overseen the Blackfriars cooked meats factory from its opening in 1936 until its closure in 1972.

A popular competition prize in the 1970s was the 'grub grab'. This lucky winner grabbed goods worth £38.67 when let loose for his two minutes at the new Stratford branch in 1973.

The non-family directors were Bernard Ramm (data processing – appointed in 1962); Arthur Trask (provisions buying – appointed in 1965); Gurth Hoyer Millar (distribution), who joined the board in 1967; Roy (later Sir Roy) Griffiths (personnel); Joe Barnes (meat production and subsequently trading director) and Peter Snow (branch operations). Roy Griffiths, Joe Barnes and Peter Snow had all been appointed to the board in 1969. Two further directors were appointed in the first half of the 1970s. They were Len Payne, who became distribution director in 1974 when Gurth Hoyer Millar became development director, and Cecil Roberts, who became joint marketing director in 1975. All these directors were to play a significant role in Sainsbury's spectacular growth. Between 1975 and 1985 both turnover and profits doubled in real terms.

Despite the instant blue-chip status of Sainsbury's shares following the flotation, they were still liable to the market fluctuations caused by the weakness of the British economy. In October 1973 the *Financial Times* 30 share index stood at 430; by the end of the year it had fallen to 304. It continued to decline throughout 1974 until it reached a low of 146 in January 1975. As early as May 1974 the price of Sainsbury's shares had fallen below their flotation price and by the beginning of

1975 they were trading at a mere 74p. Conscious of the many small shareholders in the company – especially among the staff – Sainsbury's reassured them that the fall in value was the result of market forces rather than the company's performance. Mr Simon advised staff to take a long-term view of their investment: 'paper losses aren't real losses any more than paper profits are real profits.'

One did not have to be a financial expert to understand the cause of the stock market crash. The first half of the 1970s was a period of economic instability, with frequent strikes, low productivity and ever larger wage claims which all fed inflation. These problems were compounded by world shortages of food and raw materials. Successive governments' attempts to reduce the rate of inflation by introducing prices and incomes policies, although they had some short-term benefits, failed in the long term.

Decimal currency

There was a popular belief that decimalisation had initiated the inflationary spiral. The decision to abandon the old pounds, shillings and pence in favour of an unfamiliar 'foreign' system was unpopular among a large section of the population, and many older people found it impossible to measure value for money using the new currency.

Sainsbury's made the transition as easy as possible for its customers. The first priority was to ensure that staff were familiar with the new coins and would be confident in offering help to customers. To this end the company set up a special training shop at 9/11 London Road, Croydon, which was laid out to provide on one side a modern self-service area and on the other a counter service display. It was appropriate that the Croydon branch should become Britain's first decimal shop as it had already been associated with two historic stages in Sainsbury's development: in 1882 as the firm's first suburban branch and in 1950 as its first self-service store. From 10th February 1970 until 27th November both parts of the Croydon store traded in decimal currency using plastic coins, and over 1,500 key staff were trained to use the new money in preparation for 'D-day', 15th February 1971. Each of these was then given responsibility for the instruction of staff at their branch.

Groups such as the Townswomen's Guilds and Women's Institutes were invited to the Croydon shop to experience 'decimal shopping' at first hand. Visitors were shown a specially commissioned

This advertisement for the 'decimal' shop at Croydon appeared in Family Circle *in 1970.*

QUICK CHANGE
at
SAINSBURY'S

£. s. d. to £. p. without tears

The price of this 1s 5d pack of dried peas has been 'rounded down' to 7p. The pack is also marked with metric as well as imperial weights.

Sainsbury's quick dried

Garden Peas 2oz. 4dr. **1/5** 7p **4 Servings**

film called 'Quick Change' which was presented in characteristically brusque style by cookery expert Zena Skinner. During the shop's ten months of trading it was visited by over 30,000 customers. On the last day a special demonstration was held for local pensioners and girls from Croydon High School. Each pensioner was given a pound to spend in the store and was allocated a schoolgirl to help with their shopping. Although some pessimists had predicted chaos when decimal currency was introduced it turned out to be, as Mr JD put it, 'the biggest non-event of the year'.

Despite the painless introduction of the new currency many consumers were convinced that decimalisation would be used by retailers to disguise price increases, as the old copper coins had no decimal equivalent. Since the smallest unit in the decimal system – the 'half new p' – was equal to 1.2d, it was inevitable that there would be price increases at the lower end of the range. Long before

D-day Sainsbury's promised customers that decimalisation would not lead to an overall increase in its prices and that it would round down more prices than it rounded up.

An atmosphere of instability

Decimalisation did, however, coincide with a sharp rise in food prices. The rate of inflation for food rose from 6.7 per cent in 1970 to 11.5 per cent in 1971. By 1974 it had reached 18.4 per cent and in July 1975 it peaked at 29 per cent. Over the decade as a whole prices rose by 264 per cent. Although wages also rose sharply, by the mid 1970s real incomes were beginning to fall behind the level of price inflation. In 1976–7 there was a 2 per cent drop in real personal disposable income. This meant that for the first time since the Second World War the standard of living was actually declining.

Britain's decision to join the EEC, on 1st January 1973, was also blamed for inflation. However, it was extremely difficult to establish a causal link at the time as Britain had a higher rate of inflation than its continental neighbours when it joined the EEC. The situation was further complicated by the falling value of the pound following its flotation on 23rd June 1972, Britain's heavy dependence on foreign food imports and government subsidies on staple foods like bread, milk and butter. In May 1975 Mrs Shirley Williams, Minister for Prices and Consumer Protection, told the House of Commons that in her opinion 'the overall level of food prices in the UK . . . is not at present significantly affected one way or the other by Britain's membership of the Community'.

Britain's vulnerability to fluctuations on the world market was illustrated by the sugar and paper shortages of 1974 and the rapid rise in coffee prices of 1976–7. Not only did these events fuel inflation, but they also had a profound effect on the trade. Staff could scarcely keep up with the price changes from one day to the next. As Cecil Roberts, who was the director responsible for grocery buying, recalled: 'One of the most difficult tasks I ever had was to ensure that through all this we maintained the confidence of our customers.'

Labour disputes contributed to the general atmosphere of instability. Strikes by the Bakers Union, the dockers and the Road Haulage Association all caused interruptions to the supply and distribution of food. Things became so bad that one wag at the Leamington Spa branch, where a local bakers' dispute coincided with a national shortage of toilet paper, suggested that products in short supply should

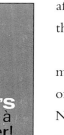

'Cross-channel shopping' was popular with continental housewives in the 1970s. When the Folkestone branch opened in 1970 it accepted French, Belgian and American currency.

be displayed at opposite ends of the store so as to leave 'customers motionless in indecision' as to which end to rush to first!

Sainsbury's also suffered from the imposition of Selective Employment Tax (SET), which service industries – unlike manufacturing industries – had to pay for each employee. In 1971 SET cost Sainsbury's the equivalent of 26 per cent of its net profit before tax. When SET was halved in 1971, Sainsbury's demonstrated the benefit to consumers by reducing prices on selected items so as to make the tax reduction clearly visible. In 1973 SET was replaced by Value Added Tax (VAT). Since VAT was zero-rated for food Sainsbury's were able to make further substantial price reductions which were estimated in the 1973 *Report and Accounts* to be worth approximately £3 million in the first year.

Sainsbury's relief at the abolition of SET was short-lived. The Labour government which took office in March 1974 attacked the high profits of food retailers, claiming that they had contributed to rising food prices. Sainsbury's challenged this view in its 1974 *Report and Accounts*, stating that 'one of the more naive assumptions that is made about profits in food retailing is that those whose profits grow the fastest have the highest retail prices. The contrary is the case, for it is generally the companies with the most competitive prices that have expanded their sales fastest . . . [and] are better placed to invest in the future and so ensure a greater degree of competition and thus lower prices.' Despite the force of these arguments the Price Commission recommended that gross profit margins for retailers during 1974/5 be reduced to only 90 per cent of their 1973/4 level.

This squeeze on profits came at a time when costs were rising sharply as a result of the oil crisis of 1972/3. In the space of four months, the price of crude oil more than doubled and Sainsbury's was faced with a massive increase in its fuel bill. The company's expenditure on gas and electricity increased by nearly 50 per cent between 1974 and 1975. This prompted rigorous efforts to reduce energy consumption.

SUGAR

We regret we must ask customers to limit their purchases to 2LB GRANULATED PLUS 2LB OF ANY OTHER SUGAR

The mid-1970s saw acute shortages of some products. This poster urged self-restraint during the sugar shortage of 1974.

A selection of Sainsbury brand soft drinks from the early 1970s.

Improving efficiency

Ironically, the oil crisis made Sainsbury's much more cost-effective. Sir Roy Griffiths recalled that 'for the first time non-food inflation was higher than food inflation with the result that our costs were increasing faster than our turnover. This made us look very hard at our costs and take much more active steps to control them.' Sir Roy himself was responsible for the implementation of many of the improvements to Sainsbury's organisation and systems. He had already played a key role in modernising the personnel structure and his remit was

now broadened to include the administration of the whole company. At Mr JD's instigation he supervised the setting up of a board-level directors' administrative committee (DAC) aimed at eliminating waste such as the duplication of departmental activities. The DAC approved every new staff position while a board director's authorisation was needed for the replacement of staff in existing posts.

Improvements were made in branch productivity. In real terms sales per branch doubled between 1969 and 1979 while sales per employee increased by 25 per cent. This contributed to a doubling of the company's turnover in real terms during the course of the decade. These remarkable figures were largely due to the introduction of self-service. In 1970 the sales per branch at Sainsbury's 114 supermarkets were almost four times those of the remaining counter service branches. Another result of the introduction of self-service was that the number of branches actually declined during the 1970s as the smaller, less efficient shops were closed. By 1980 Sainsbury's had 231 shops compared with 244 in 1969.

These large, new self-service stores allowed the introduction of modern technology. The most important innovation was the use of more sophisticated computer ordering systems. In the late 1960s Mr JD had been impressed with the systems which were used by the most advanced supermarkets in the United States. As a result of his close contacts with the Super Market Institute of America (SMI) an American consultant, Ned Harwell, was appointed to advise the company on its branch ordering systems and merchandising.

A shop assistant using one of the first Plessey data capture units introduced in 1972. By 1983 the cumbersome trolley housing the equipment had been replaced by a compact handset.

The new system of ordering introduced by Sainsbury's from 1972 brought savings in labour and warehouse space as well as improved stock control. Each branch was supplied with two Plessey data capture units which recorded its orders for a range of non-perishable goods. Attached to each unit was a light pen, which, when passed over a bar code printed on to a shelf edge label, recorded the identity of the product to be ordered. The operator then used a keypad to order the necessary number of cases. The orders were recorded on a magnetic tape inside the data capture unit and sent to Blackfriars down an ordinary telephone line using a transmitter located at the rear of the shop. From there they were relayed to the appropriate depot to be assembled for delivery to the branch. Some orders could be

Display cages, like these pictured at Woolwich in 1975, were popular with competitors as they could be delivered to stores ready filled by suppliers. Sainsbury's soon abandoned their use as they looked untidy and were unsuitable for its centralised distribution system.

In 1973 a spate of 'baby snatching' from prams left outside shops led Sainsbury's to pioneer the use of cradles attached to shopping trolleys.

despatched within twenty-four hours of being received. By relating product ordering to the display methods used instore the new technology gave Sainsbury's a considerable competitive advantage. It also enabled reductions to be made in the level of stock held in the branch warehouses.

Labour economies were made behind the scenes. The first automatic machines for wrapping meat were installed in 1970. Based on an American idea, the equipment was developed jointly by Sainsbury's engineers and the machines' manufacturers and enabled one person to pack, weigh and price the meat. This greatly reduced the number of staff required in branch preparation rooms.

Although these measures were highly successful they could not compensate for the seriousness of the economic situation. The profits announced by Sainsbury's for the first half of 1975/6 were nearly 20 per cent below those of the previous year. It was impossible for the company to pass on its increased costs to the customer due to a combination of the government's prices and incomes policy and increased competition in the retail sector as consumers' expenditure on food fell in real terms. The fall in profits also reflected the effects of continued industrial unrest on the company's store development programme. By September 1975 only four of the seventeen stores planned for the 1975/6 financial year had been opened. The delayed projects added to the company's costs without bringing in any revenue.

Nevertheless, the second half of the year was remarkably successful. During the autumn of 1975 the company's architects, engineers and retail staff worked hard to reverse the delays in the store building programme. These efforts were rewarded when in the course of ten weeks twelve supermarkets and a major extension to the Haywards Heath branch were opened. The new branches contributed to a 20 per cent increase in turnover over the whole financial year and to a creditable 5.4 per cent increase in profits.

Edge-of-town sites

Sainsbury's continued to have problems obtaining planning permission for new town centre stores throughout most of the 1970s. Local planners often appeared to be as hostile to new retail developments as central government was to profitability. In the early 1970s it could take three years to secure planning permission for a new shop. In an attempt to change outdated attitudes Sainsbury's held a two-day seminar at St John's College, Cambridge, in September 1972 for seventy local authority planners on the topic 'Retail Store Location in the 1970s'. The conference was chaired by Professor Peter Hall of Reading University and the speakers included Mr JD, Mr Timothy and John Alpass of the Copenhagen Institute of Centre Planning.

This conference reinforced Sainsbury's point. As part of his presentation Mr Timothy showed a film illustrating the difficulties customers experienced due to poor planning. Among the 'horrors' on view were fire doors that opened in the wrong direction, local authority signs forbidding customers to use trolleys to take their shopping to their cars, and a shopping centre in Bracknell where customers had to manhandle trolleys up an escalator to the car park. The most telling scene was one in which an elderly disabled woman was shown struggling downstairs with her shopping at the Friars Centre at Aylesbury where the local authority had saved money by installing lifts which only stopped at landings between the floors of the car park. Kelsey van Musschenbroek of the *Financial Times* was astonished to hear the planners laughing at these scenes and described their reaction as 'a vivid indication of a lack of identification with the needs of the consumer'.

These planning difficulties led Sainsbury's to open edge-of-town stores. The first of these was at Coldham's Lane, in a non-residential area on the eastern edge of Cambridge, which opened on 3rd December 1974. It was an instant success although the fact that it catered for car-borne shoppers had an unexpected result.

An example of a planning 'horror'. At the multi-storey car park in Kingston-upon-Thames, trolleys were banned from the lifts.

169

A lorry negotiating a difficult corner while delivering to the Sidney Street, Cambridge, branch.

As Mr JD recalled: 'We had taken the unusual step, for Sainsbury's, of inviting a VIP to open the store. Mr Jim – later Lord – Prior was an appropriate choice, as he was a former Minister of Food and had strong East Anglian connections. He later became one of our first non-executive directors. We were therefore rather worried

when, twenty minutes before the store opened, instead of the expected queues there was nobody about. They all arrived at once!' The 376-space car park was filled within minutes and the queues soon stretched for hundreds of yards along both sides of the building.

New product lines

The opening of the Coldham's Lane store was as important a milestone as the conversion to self-service of the Croydon branch twenty-four years earlier. Although a handful of large new branches with adequate car parking had opened before this, they were in the 'new towns' of Bretton,

Customers queuing in the rain at the opening of the Coldham's Lane branch on 3rd December 1974.

Bletchley and Telford where planning requirements were more relaxed. Coldham's Lane, by contrast, was on the edge of a historic city and was complementary to the town centre Sidney Street branch. The store's 24,000 square foot sales area offered space to experiment with new products like electrical goods, kitchen hardware, household linens, cosmetics, stationery, and even gardening and DIY tools.

The most adventurous step was to introduce a range of own brand clothing. Clothes had first been sold in 1973 at the Telford branch where they had included ladies' skinny-rib sweaters at under £2 and fashionable flared jeans at £3.80.

Sainsbury's socks made a star appearance in the 1974 Grand National when they were spotted on the feet of the winning jockey, Brian Fletcher, whose mount was the legendary Red Rum. The clothing range – together with many of the other lines comprising the 'new departments' – was only partly successful. Despite advice from outside consultants Sainsbury's found that it lacked the buying power to make a success of selling a full range of clothing. The lines which most suited Sainsbury's trading style were those which – like foodstuffs – were inexpensive and most frequently purchased. Thus underwear, socks and some children's clothing became a permanent part of the company's 'extended range' for larger branches, while fashion clothing was gradually discontinued as the range of foodstuffs grew during the late 1970s and early 1980s.

The Coldham's Lane store also included counter service for delicatessen and an instore bakery. This new

RIGHT *Early examples of Sainsbury brand clothing, as modelled in 1973.*

BELOW *A 'behind the scenes' view of the instore bakery at the Worle branch, Weston-super-Mare, in 1978.*

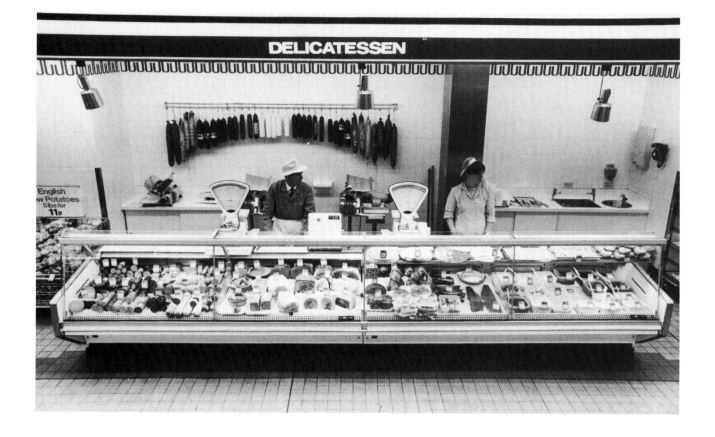

DELICATESSEN

Sainsbury's first delicatessen counter at the Wandsworth branch, which opened on 8th June 1971.

style of counter service was an important departure as Sainsbury's had been committed to self-service trading since 1950. In larger branches, however, there was now room to accommodate this form of personal contact with customers, making the stores more welcoming and offering a greater choice. The first delicatessen counter, at the Wandsworth branch in 1971, stocked 73 items which included pâté, continental sausages, salamis, hams, apfelstrudel, Danish pastries and cream cakes. The first instore bakery was opened at Telford in 1973. To begin with, part-baked frozen bread was bought in from outside and 'baked off', but this method was soon replaced by the use of refrigerated dough, and subsequently by bread made from scratch on the premises. Andy King, who worked at Telford, earned the nickname 'King Alfred' from his weekly ritual of cooking a 'really burnt' loaf for one customer who liked her bread overdone.

The success of the Coldham's Lane branch encouraged Sainsbury's to be even more ambitious in planning its next edge-of-town store, which opened at Kempston, near Bedford, in November 1975. At 37,610 square feet, Kempston's sales area was three and a half times the average size of a contemporary Sainsbury store. However, it was soon apparent that the store was overambitious. The chairman acknowledged this in a speech to senior managers in 1976: 'we were influenced by the huge success of Coldham's Lane and by our desire to have enough room to

ABOVE *The petrol station at Coldham's Lane, Cambridge.* BELOW *An aerial view of the Bretton store, Peterborough, which opened on 25th April 1972. This new town site demonstrated the benefits of good access and adequate surface-level parking.*

experiment with new ranges . . . However, let us be frank and admit that Kempston really has been built too big.' Over the next two years the sales area was reduced by nearly 5,000 square feet, although Kempston remained the largest Sainsbury's branch until the Crystal Palace store opened in April 1983.

A number of important lessons were learnt from the Kempston experiment. As Mr JD explained: 'Planning problems in high street locations had placed constraints on the size of almost all of our new stores. We wanted to discover quite how large the ideal supermarket could become. We were on a learning curve, and we learnt very fast. Larger new stores gave us the opportunity to experiment with new product ranges. They were mutually beneficial to customers and to the company. They delivered what the customer wanted in terms of more choice and better service and also what the company wanted in terms of economies of scale and reduced costs. These stores were therefore both more popular and more profitable than those in cramped high street locations.' The average size of new stores increased steadily – from 10,000 square feet in 1970 to around 18,000 square feet in 1979 – although by the end of the decade only eight stores had sales areas of over 25,000 square feet.

It was also in the 1970s that Sainsbury's diversified into the rapidly growing frozen food market. Between 1972 and 1973 the sales of both frozen foods and

Several former counter service branches were refitted to become freezer centres like this one at East Grinstead, which opened on 9th July 1974.

Early bulk freezer packs such as these gave way to smaller sizes as fridge-freezers grew in popularity.

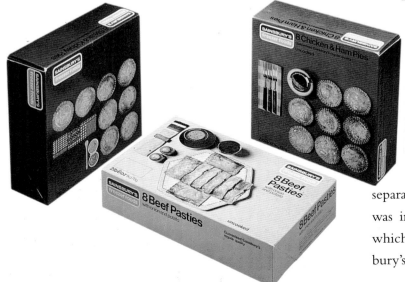

freezers had increased by over 30 per cent. Bejam's success in this area encouraged Sainsbury's to open a chain of freezer centres which operated independently from the main supermarket business. At the time it seemed an ideal use for some of the old counter service branches which were in good locations but were too small for conversion to supermarket trading. The shops also provided extra trading space when planning difficulties for new supermarkets were holding up the company's development programme. The first freezer centre was opened in a former counter service branch at Southbourne near Bournemouth on 25th June 1974. However, few of the town's large population of retired people possessed a freezer, and the shop closed after only ten months of trading.

In the meantime, other more successful freezer centres opened at East Grinstead – adjacent to the newly opened Sainsbury's supermarket – and North Cheam. To begin with, most of the products sold by these shops were large pack sizes which offered considerable price savings over conventional frozen foods. These included a wide range of 5lb packs of vegetables including peas, beans and crinkle-cut chips. There were also bulk packs of meat, fish portions and a huge range of frozen desserts like Danish pastries, jam doughnuts, banana dream pie, and the ever popular Arctic Roll. For the more adventurous, early price lists included 'continental specialities' such as lasagne, pizzas and 'chicken espagnole'. There were even bulk packs of uncooked 'Dinnodog' meat for the family pet.

In 1974 only 11 per cent of households owned a freezer. By 1982 this proportion had risen to 49 per cent. As early as 1975 Sainsbury's decided that the growing popularity of frozen foods meant that it was preferable to 'integrate' them into new supermarkets rather than to sell them in separate shops. The first 'integrated' freezer centre was incorporated into the Chippenham branch, which opened in October 1975. However, Sainsbury's continued to operate 'independent' freezer centres – there were twenty-one of these trading in 1980 – until they were finally sold to Bejam in 1986.

Existing departments also saw a steady increase in their product ranges. One of the most important growth areas was the wine department. By 1970 difficulties in obtaining off-licences had largely been overcome and fifty of Sainsbury's stores sold beers, wines and spirits. The range of wines sold under the Sainsbury label had grown steadily, although early own brand wines were actually bottled in the UK. In 1972, however, Sainsbury's decided to purchase wine bottled at source in order to be able to offer better-quality wines, particularly at the lower end of the price range.

A new range of French wines launched in July 1973 included Gaillac Perlé at 63p, Anjou rosé at 73p and Beaumes de Venise at 83p a bottle. These provincial wines were virtually unknown in Britain at the time. Subsequently Sainsbury's became the first British retailer to bottle Spanish wines and sherries at source. Unfamiliar wines – such as Manzanilla, Vino de Catalonia and Arruda – all proved popular with customers, who had learned to trust the Sainsbury brand. The first Italian wines were introduced at the Kempston branch, where there was a local community of former Italian prisoners of war. By successfully marketing quality wines at competitive prices Sainsbury's transformed wine from an occasional luxury into an everyday purchase. To help customers, a label was added to the back of each bottle, describing the wine and suggesting suitable foods to accompany it. Sweetness indicators were introduced for white wines. Advertisements, informative leaflets and books all helped customers to become more informed about the wine they were drinking.

By 1982 Sainsbury's had the largest wine sales of any British retailer. The ingenuity and originality of Sainsbury's buying team were widely acknowledged. Just as other retailers had advertised for 'Sainsbury-trained men' during the interwar years, they now sought out former members of Sainsbury's off-licence department in order to emulate its success. A more welcome accolade was the award in 1986 to Allan Cheesman, the departmental director for off-licence buying, of the French government's prestigious *Ordre du Merit Agricole* for the role which he and his team had played in encouraging British consumers to appreciate French wines.

The 'produce' department was one of the fastest growing areas. Among the new lines to appear during the early 1970s were globe artichokes, courgettes, aubergines and peppers. Later additions included Galia melons, Chinese leaves, kohl rabi, and Kiwi fruit. There were occasional complaints about the more exotic new lines. One old gentleman was reported to have returned some mangetout peas on the grounds that 'once you've podded them there's nothing left'!

From the early 1970s the produce department was placed near the entrance to

ABOVE *A label designed in 1976 for Sainsbury's* Costières du Gard. BELOW *Some early examples of own brand wines bottled at source from 1973.*

Free-flow produce, which was introduced from 1976, proved extremely popular with customers.

new stores so that the fresh fruit and vegetables formed a colourful and welcoming display. This technique, which was already used in America, was even more effective after the adoption of 'free-flow' produce displays from 1976. These allowed customers to select their own produce and have it weighed and priced at a service point nearby. Better choice, improved quality and 'free-flow' display methods led to a dramatic increase in sales. By 1980 Sainsbury's was the nation's largest retailer of fresh fruit and vegetables.

One product Sainsbury's refused to sell after 1972 was the Pentland Crown potato. This was despite its being Britain's most widely cultivated variety. Its popularity with growers was encouraged by the Potato Marketing Board's pricing structure, which rewarded growers for quantity rather than quality. Sainsbury's considered Pentland Crown potatoes to be inferior to other varieties. An advertisement the company published in a number of women's magazines in November 1979 pulled no punches: 'They turn grey and crumble when you boil them. They go soggy when you mash them. And they make very poor chips. Indeed we think they're not much good for anything.' This advertisement – which is the only recorded example of Sainsbury's using 'knocking copy' – caused a storm of protest from the National Farmers Union. However, the national press came down resoundingly on Sainsbury's side. As the *Sun* told its readers, 'Sainsbury's have done us all a service by pointing out what a bad deal we are getting from this potato. No wonder the National Farmers Union are up in arms. Their anger only emphasises how right Sainsbury's are.'

Display features introduced in the 1970s included taller gondolas and overhead signs.

Expanding the trading area

The company continued to expand its trading area in the 1970s. Branches were opened in the West Country at Bridgwater and Taunton (both 1973) and at Exeter (1976). The latter store was located in the newly built Guildhall Centre and was, at 200 miles from Blackfriars, the most distant from the company's headquarters. The store proved so popular that, soon after it opened, an enterprising coach company ran a Christmas shopping trip for customers all the way from Torbay. Sainsbury's first Welsh branch, at Cwmbran, opened a week after the Exeter store. The manager of the store,

Elwyn Davies, and three of his staff were bilingual. He described his branch as 'Bendigedig' which he translated for non Welsh-speakers as 'Wonderful, great, excellent all rolled into one'.

Sites were sought in the North. The first two Yorkshire branches opened in Doncaster (1974) and Sheffield (1975). In 1977 the company placed a number of advertisements in Northern papers for suitable sites for new stores. This provoked an overwhelming response, with some people even offering their back yards for development. After carefully studying the offers, planning applications were lodged for sites at Prestwich (opened 1981) and Prenton, near Birkenhead (1982).

Opportunities for staff

Investment in new stores, their greater productivity, savings in overhead costs and steadily improving buying and marketing techniques made the second half of the 1970s a period of sustained growth for Sainsbury's. Although the government's prices and incomes policy placed limits on pay increases, this growth enabled Sainsbury's to offer excellent career opportunities to its staff. Employees were also encouraged to take a stake in the company. In 1974 every employee who had worked full-time for three or more years became eligible to acquire Sainsbury's ordinary shares under a savings related share option scheme. Five years later Sainsbury's was one of the first companies to introduce a profit-sharing scheme under the terms of the 1978 Profit Share Act. Employees could take their portion of the company's profits in either cash or shares. Those who elected to take shares enjoyed attractive tax benefits. By the end of the first financial year of its operation, 5,200 of the 17,000 employees eligible for profit-sharing had become shareholders in the company. Within three years a quarter of the company's shareholders were employees. Staff saw their investments rise spectacularly as a result both of the rising share price and of capitalisation and scrip issues. The fifty shares which were the minimum an employee could purchase at the time of the company flotation in 1973 had an issue value of £72.50. Any employee who retained these shares found that in 1994 they had increased sixteenfold in number and their value had risen to about £2,850.

Since the introduction of self-service the composition of the company's workforce changed as women began to replace men at the branches. By the early 1970s more than half Sainsbury's employees were women. The company ensured they enjoyed equal opportunity. Equal pay for equal work was phased in gradually over the period 1970 to 1975 and had been completed before it became compulsory as a result of the Sex Discrimination and Equal Opportunities Acts of 1975. Nevertheless the question 'why isn't there a woman on the board?' became a regular feature

As the stores grew larger, displays became more imaginative. At the Bretton branch the wine department was arranged as a self-contained 'shop within a shop'.

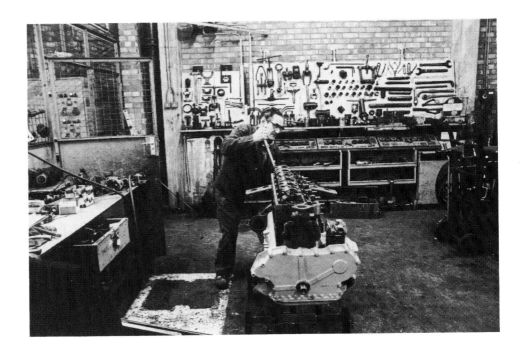

Each Sainsbury's depot was equipped with facilities for the maintenance of its lorry fleet. This photograph shows motor engineer Les Holding in the workshop at the Charlton depot in 1977.

of annual general meetings from 1973 until 1981, when Jennifer Jenkins (later Dame Jennifer) became one of the company's first non-executive directors. There was still room for improvement, however: well into the 1980s the *JS Journal* featured a 'cover girl' each month nominated by male colleagues!

Price-cutting and industrial strife

Although Sainsbury's prices rose less rapidly than the Retail Price Index for food, spiralling inflation, unpredictable costs and uncertain supplies prevented the company from launching a major long-term price campaign during the first half of the 1970s. It was not until inflation began to decline that experimental discount schemes were launched in the large stores at Bretton and Telford. These formed the basis of Sainsbury's 'SuperShopper' scheme of 1976.

The price-cutting campaign entered a new phase in June 1977 when Tesco's was finally forced to abandon Green Shield stamps. As Sainsbury's had always predicted, the public had become more and more reluctant to pay the higher prices which resulted from the administrative costs of the scheme. The stamps had also become devalued by inflation. The money saved by abandoning trading stamps allowed Tesco's to launch its 'Checkout' programme. A publicity campaign over the weekend of the Queen Silver Jubilee prepared the way for a programme of spectacular price cuts. It was an excellent publicity coup which led to an increase in Tesco's market share, although there were some commentators who believed that prices had been pitched so low that Tesco's profits were adversely affected.

While Tesco's had been putting the final touches to the launch of 'Checkout', Sainsbury's had become embroiled in the most serious industrial dispute in its history. The 'Jubilee Strike', as it became know, began on 2nd June 1977, the Thursday before the bank holiday. Staff at the Hoddesdon and Buntingford depots went on unofficial strike after management had rejected a claim, made by representatives of the warehouse and distribution staff, for payment for meal breaks. Workers at the Basingstoke depot came out on strike after the bank holiday. The pay claim was referred to ACAS (the conciliation and arbitration service set up by the 1975 Employment Protection Act) which ruled that the pay demand fell outside the agreed procedure. It was not until the pay claim was modified to come within the terms of Phase II of the government's pay policy that it was possible to negotiate a settlement. The staff of the Hoddesdon depot returned to work on 16th June followed by those at Buntingford and Basingstoke a few days later.

During the strike the distribution of goods to the branches became a battle of wits between the strikers and the rest. Secondary pickets at many suppliers' premises meant that it was difficult to circumvent the depots. Ingenious schemes were devised which included the collection of fresh fruit and vegetables direct from the fields and the 'smuggling' of goods out in branch managers' cars. One district manager, D W Smith, rented space at a farm just outside Bury St Edmunds. This was given the code name 'Glasgow' to prevent pickets from finding the warehouse. Anyone who asked where the goods had come from was given the impression that Sainsbury's had become so desperate to obtain supplies for its East Anglian stores that they were being delivered from Scotland! The Coldham's Lane branch was partly supplied by means of a regular rendezvous which involved transferring goods off a juggernaut in a layby two miles away. Managers were also allowed to fix some of their own prices after haggling for goods at cash and carry wholesalers. This was the reverse of Sainsbury's traditional disciplined and centralised approach.

Buyers, suppliers and branch staff all rose to the challenge. Their ingenuity meant that despite the strike Sainsbury's was able to continue trading at 88 per cent of its normal level. Over the whole financial year the trade lost amounted to just 0.6 per cent of turnover. Sainsbury's staff were so successful in minimising the impact on shoppers that market research carried out at the end of the strike found that less than half its customers knew that it had even taken place.

Soft margarine gained in popularity during the 1970s. By 1974 it accounted for 64 per cent of Sainsbury's margarine sales. This pack design dates from 1978.

The Queen's Silver Jubilee

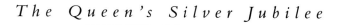

Industrial strife did not entirely overshadow the celebrations for the Queen's Silver Jubilee. Branch staff organised street parties and fancy dress dances to mark the event. The *JS Journal* ran a competition for the most imaginative Jubilee souvenir. Entries included a doorbell which chimed 'God Save The Queen', a talking bust

of the Queen giving her Christmas message, and 'jubiletti spaghetti' made of tinned pasta crowns and other regal symbols. The most bizarre entry was that of Alan Myers, an engineer at the Basingstoke depot. Alan's design was for a solid silver model of Windsor Castle which could be used as a decorative roof-rack or a hot water bottle!

During the summer of 1977 the Queen made a tour of the nation to celebrate her Jubilee. Her visit to Walsall included a luncheon at the town hall next door to the local Sainsbury store. Just before her arrival a harassed middle-aged man arrived at the checkout with ten packets of watercress. 'On a diet, sir?' asked the cashier. 'No, my dear,' replied the customer, 'it's for the Queen's lunch!' Sainsbury's should, perhaps, have applied for a royal warrant.

These glass tankards were one of several products sold to mark the Queen's Silver Jubilee in 1977.

Discount '78

After the 'Jubilee Strike' Sainsbury's was able to reassert its price competitiveness. On 10th January 1978 it launched a new price initiative called 'Discount '78'. Under cover of a massive stocktaking exercise the previous day, staff worked through the night redressing shelves and repricing goods. When the stores opened the next morning customers found around 100 items had been reduced in price by as much as 15 per cent. Typical reductions included 8p off selected cuts of bacon, 4p off own brand cornflakes and 20p off a 4 ounce pack of instant coffee. The *Daily Mail* predicted that the 'price war' would sound the death knell of statutory price

Sainsbury's 'Discount' programme launched in January 1978 offered long-term price reductions on a wide variety of products.

regulation: '. . . such vigorous competition between supermarkets must be good news for the housewife. How irrelevant and ineffective this renders the whole bureaucratic flummery of price controls and monitoring.'

The 'Discount' scheme proved immensely successful and by December 1978 had led to a 25 per cent increase in sales over the previous half year's trading. It also increased Sainsbury's market share from 8.7 per cent to 10.8 per cent according to

AGB figures. Mr JD described the 'Discount' scheme in 1978 as 'without doubt the most important new marketing strategy since we established our unique range of own brand products many years ago'.

Continuing growth

The 1979 *Report and Accounts* summarised the company's achievements during the 1970s: 'Since 1969 when we celebrated our centenary our profits have grown seven-fold. Allowing for the fact that 1969's pound is only worth 33p today, we have increased profitability by 2.4 times while over the ten years our earnings per share have risen in real terms no less than 10 per cent a year. Today we serve about two million more customers every week and sell nearly twice the volume of goods than we did ten years ago.'

The late 1970s had seen important changes at board level. Chief among these were the retirements of Mr Simon and Mr Timothy. Mr Simon had decided to retire early, and passed his responsibilities as deputy chairman to Roy Griffiths in a phased handover which lasted from 1975 until 1979. Mr Timothy, who was elected as MP for Hove in 1973, relinquished his executive duties in 1978 in order to pursue a full-time career in politics, although he retained a non-executive seat on the board until 1983. Mr Timothy's responsibilities for store development were passed to Gurth Hoyer Millar. Peter Snow, who had played a key role in the modernisation of the branches, also left the company.

These changes coincided with the serious illness of three of Sainsbury's most experienced directors. This was particularly unfortunate at a time of acute economic instability. In September 1979 the board was reorganised in order to reflect the continuing growth of the business. Roy Griffiths was appointed managing director in addition to his existing responsibilities as deputy chairman. This allowed more time for Mr JD to exercise his responsibilities as chairman and chief executive, in particular in the direction of the company's marketing and retailing activities. Peter Davis, who had been marketing director since 1977, now became assistant managing director. Derek Henson became director and financial controller. Bob Ingham and Tom Vyner, appointed to the board in 1977 and 1978 respectively, brought new strength to the trading side of the business, and Angus Clark took on Roy Griffiths's former responsibilities as personnel director.

Mr JD's pre-eminent status in the trade was recognised in January 1980 when he received a knighthood in the New Year's Honours List. He generously commented that the award was 'as much a tribute to the company as to me personally and that makes me very happy'. Subsequent events were to confirm the stature of both.

A passion to innovate

The 1970s had been an unpredictable decade for retailers owing to high inflation, uncertain world commodity markets and industrial action at home. Nevertheless Sainsbury's emerged from these diffi-cult years in excellent shape. The sustained investment in new stores meant that most of the company's shops were less than ten years old, while efficient training schemes and the introduction of new technology had greatly increased productivity. These factors enabled Sainsbury's to maintain its lead in strategic and techno-logical innovation during the 1980s and early 1990s while retaining its reputation for quality and value. Mr JD described the company's style and nature as 'traditionalist with a passion to innovate'.

It was during the 1980s that Sainsbury's established itself as a truly national retailer. A steady expansion of the company's trading area in the North-west saw branches opened at Birkenhead (1982), Liverpool (1982 and 1983), Blackpool (1984) and Lancaster (1985). In Yorkshire no less than ten stores were opened during the decade. A presence in the North-east was established when the Middlesbrough branch opened in 1989. The company's position in South Wales was con-

An architectural elevation showing the front of the former Green Park station at Bath after its restoration by Sainsbury's.

solidated when branches were opened in Cardiff, Newport and Swansea. A fur-ther expansion of the trading area took place in the early 1990s when the first Scottish branch opened at Darnley, near Glasgow, in 1992, and branches were opened in North Wales at Wrexham (1991) and Rhyl (1993).

Inner city sites

Many new stores were built on sites made available as a result of changes in Britain's economic infrastructure. The changing methods and nature of Britain's manufacturing industry had led to the closure of many old factories in inner city areas which were no longer appropriate locations for modern industrial produc-tion. The buildings that were left behind were unsuitable for the new light indus-tries which tended to locate their operations on modern edge-of-town business parks that had better access to the expanding motorway system. Many inner city areas began to experience high unemployment and social deprivation.

The government recognised this problem in June 1977 when it published a white paper entitled *A Policy for the Inner Cities*. This outlined a series of measures to improve the inner city environment and to attract commerce and industry back

This aerial view of Sainsbury's branch at Bath was taken in 1982 during its construction. The photograph shows how a disused railway station provided an ideal site for a large supermarket close to a historic city centre.

to deprived areas. Sainsbury's had welcomed the white paper. In the *Report and Accounts* for 1978 the company stated that it shared 'the concern expressed in planning circles and the government about the decay of some inner city areas'. The company recognised that old industrial sites were ideal for retail development as they were close to centres of population yet were large enough to accommodate a modern store with ample car-parking. Other inner city sites later became available when the government put pressure on the public utilities to sell redundant real estate.

The Nine Elms branch, which opened in London in February 1982, showed what could be achieved in these locations. The store was built on land surplus to the requirements of the New Covent Garden Market. As the site had previously been occupied by derelict railway sidings, it was unattractive for most commercial purposes and the company acquired it at a very competitive price. The site was so large that Sainsbury's was able to build a modern store of 25,300 square feet and provide ample surface-level parking. The new store stocked 7,500 lines – the widest range of products at any Sainsbury's branch – which included 60 different varieties of bread, 170 delicatessen lines, over 50 types of fresh fish and a full range of kosher foods. The interest among politicians and the media was so great that no

When the Crystal Palace branch opened in April 1983 it was Sainsbury's largest store, with a sales area of 37,700 square feet. This photograph, taken from above the off-licence department, gives an impression of its scale.

fewer than four previews were held to show off the store. As Mr JD recalled, 'half the cabinet came to look at Nine Elms. Of course most of them lived – and all of them worked – nearby!'

More than half the new stores Sainsbury's opened during the 1980s were built on derelict land. Sometimes the company was able to rebuild historic buildings as part of the development of a site. The branch at Wolverhampton, opened in January 1988, incorporated a disused Victorian church which was painstakingly restored and converted into a coffee shop. At Streatham, in South London, a store was built within the walls of a renovated listed building which had previously been a silk mill. The adjacent listed building, the former Beehive Coffee Tavern, was restored and used as a children's day nursery. Edge-of-town stores were also built on redundant industrial land. These included Canley, near Coventry, which was built on the site of an old Rover car factory; Apsley Mills, near Hemel Hempstead, which formed part of a retail park on the former DRG paper mill site; and Black-hall, Edinburgh, which was built on land reclaimed from the Craigleith Quarry.

Nevertheless, Sainsbury's still found it difficult to obtain planning permission for large stores in the South, where planning restrictions had the effect of protecting existing retailers from new competition. Sainsbury's considered this to be contrary to the consumer's interest as it prevented outdated supermarkets from being replaced by more efficient stores. As the chairman's statement in the company's 1985 *Report and Accounts* made clear: 'the real losers from new, large stores are the typical supermarkets which opened 20 years ago. Should we really be using the planning system to try to protect these from the winds of change?' It was not until July 1985 that the Secretary of State for the Environment ruled in a Development Control Policy Note that 'since commercial competition as

BELOW LEFT The Wolverhampton branch, which opened in January 1988, incorporated a disused church. BELOW RIGHT AND BOTTOM RIGHT *The Streatham branch before and after redevelopment. This store opened in November 1989.*

such is not a planning consideration, the possible effects of proposed major retail development on existing retailers is not a relevant factor in deciding planning applications and appeals'.

This change of emphasis in planning policy was motivated by economic and political considerations. The persistence of unemployment, even in the most prosperous areas of the South-east, meant that local authorities could no longer ignore the fact that the arrival of a large supermarket would create over three hundred new jobs and give a stimulus to the local economy. Central government pressure on local authorities to reduce their spending also encouraged the sale of unwanted land. By 1986 the company was able to report to shareholders that 'we now have more sites awaiting development than ever before'.

The branch at 61/3 Rye Lane, Peckham, was the last of Sainsbury's counter service shops to close. Here the manager, David Sedgewick, and his staff are pictured on closing day, 27th November 1982.

The availability of a greater number of suitable sites, together with the company's growing profitability, enabled Sainsbury's to step up its programme of new store development in the late 1980s. In 1987 it was announced that the average number of stores opening each year would rise from fifteen to twenty. The sales area of new stores grew from an average of just under 18,000 square feet in the early 1980s to about 32,000 square feet a decade later.

These figures disguised considerable variation in store size. The Hedge End branch, near Southampton, which opened in 1991, had a sales area of 48,000 square feet. However, stores in market towns like Alton, Ripley and Whitstable had sales areas of only 23,000 square feet. New display methods and better stock control procedures enabled even these small stores to offer a product range of some 13,250 lines. Older high street branches continued to provide an important service in many towns. A good example of this was the store in Guildford High Street which had opened as a counter service shop in 1906 and was converted to

self-service in 1962/3. Despite the opening of the large Burpham store on the edge of the town in 1985, the High Street shop continued to trade profitably. This confirmed Sainsbury's belief that modern edge-of-town facilities complemented high street shopping. In 1990 the High Street branch was completely refitted with new checkouts and chilled counters and the addition of a small delicatessen counter. A new frontage was also built imitating the shop's original Edwardian facade, which had been removed during refurbishment in the early 1960s.

Innovative architecture

The architectural style of Sainsbury's new stores became more sophisticated during the 1980s. The Canterbury store, which opened in September 1984, was designed by the architects Ahrend, Burton & Koralek and was the winning entry in a competition organised by Sainsbury's. Their innovative design involved the use of exposed structural beams and masts as decorative features and was compared to an insect's exoskeleton. Although highly acclaimed by the architectural profession, it was viewed with mixed feelings by some members of the public.

One of Sainsbury's most architecturally adventurous branches was at Camden (1988), where the local authority was particularly keen to have a 'high-tech' building for a site formerly occupied by the Aerated Bread Company's bakery. Sainsbury's therefore engaged Nicholas Grimshaw, whose design made use of impressive webbed-steel cantilevers and steel hawsers to support the huge arc of the roof – over 40 yards across – without the use of interior columns. This created a sales area of over 30,000 square feet free from obstructions. Martin Pawley described the store in the *Guardian* as 'the most extraordinary piece of take-no-prisoners architecture since the Lloyds building'. Gillian Darley of the *Financial Times* praised the store as 'an unremittingly sophisticated structure . . . as grey as a battleship and as structurally expressive as an oil platform'. Not everyone agreed. Even within the company there were sharply divided views about this uncompromising building. As Mr JD remarked, 'Here was an example of how when we received the most favourable comments from the architectural press, we also had the most adverse

This architectural perspective for the Plymouth branch, which opened in August 1994, shows the distinctive 'sail-shaped' roof details recalling the city's seafaring history.

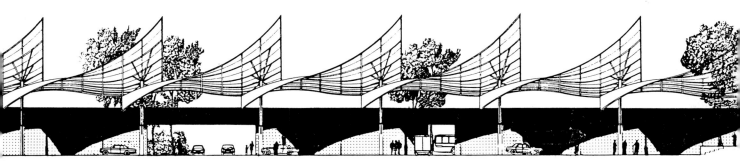

These architectural roof details are from (LEFT) Burpham, 1985, and (RIGHT) Grimsby, 1988.

comments from the general public, many of whom disliked the exterior of this building. I can understand why!'

Under the supervision of Colin Amery, the architectural critic of the *Financial Times,* and Ian Coull, who was appointed as the company's development director in 1988, Sainsbury's took steps to ensure that, as far as possible, the architecture of its stores responded to the environment. A policy document published in 1993 stated that the company's architectural objectives were to 'reflect local circumstances, [and to] respond to the character and context of the site, its immediate locality and the community it serves whilst also taking account of the impact of each new store on the local ecology and landscape'. Traditional materials were used whenever appropriate. The branches at Macclesfield and Rhyl were both built from reclaimed local stone while the Thetford store was clad in Norfolk flint.

The rigorous specifications to which Sainsbury's constructed its new stores meant that it rarely considered trading in buildings designed for other retailers. The only exceptions to this were at Locksbottom, near Orpington, where a store was purchased from Keymarkets in 1981 shortly before it was due to open, and at Mere Green, Sutton Coldfield, where an Asda store was acquired in October 1992. In both cases the buildings were completely gutted and refitted before they began trading as Sainsbury's branches. By the time the conversion at Mere Green was completed, the only recognisable features of the Asda store were the floor and the 235 members of staff who had chosen to transfer to Sainsbury's!

Distribution: flexible solutions

As store numbers grew and the trading area expanded, the distribution system became more complex. The Jubilee Strike of 1977 had convinced the board that the company could no longer afford to remain entirely reliant on its own depots. As Angus Clark put it, 'it was a case of four times bitten, twice shy.' As it was now possible to employ specialist haulage firms, it was decided not to open any more Sainsbury's depots but to use contractors to complement the existing facilities. Often the contractor built depot facilities specially to handle Sainsbury's business. These were some of the first supermarket contract distribution systems to be set up in Britain. From Sainsbury's point of view they offered a flexible solution to the company's growing scale and geographical expansion. By 1994 Sainsbury's was using seventeen contractor depots, each of which was fully integrated into the company's computer system.

The 1980s and 1990s saw changes in Sainsbury's transport fleet. Improvements in lorry design made it possible for a single vehicle to carry goods requiring

ABOVE *A view of the loading area of the Basingstoke depot in 1986 showing goods laid out ready for transfer onto Sainsbury's lorries.* RIGHT *This computerised high-bay warehouse for non-perishable goods was opened at the Buntingford depot in 1989.*

A Leyland truck in the livery used for new lorries from 1980 until the early 1990s.

different storage temperatures. This enabled one lorry to carry a load which had previously needed two or more vehicles. Between 1981 and 1990 the size of Sainsbury's lorry fleet was reduced from 425 to 386 while the number of pallet loads carried increased from 11,961 to 16,707. The fleet played a crucial role in maintaining an unbroken 'cold chain' between suppliers' factories and the chilled and freezer cabinets in the stores. 'High risk' products like cooked meats, chilled ready meals and soft cheese were marked with a red band on their outer packaging which gave them priority in transit and ensured the correct procedures were followed when they were moved from branch cold stores to refrigerated display cabinets.

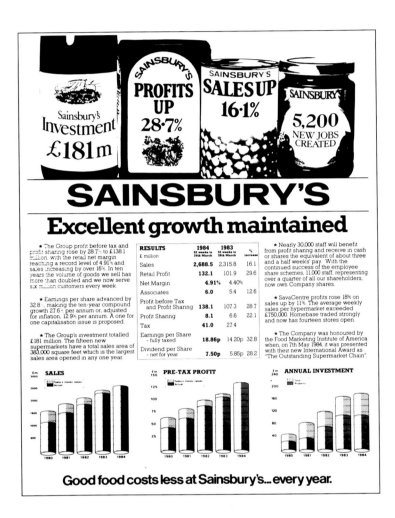

The 1980s was a period of remarkable growth for Sainsbury's. This advertisement dates from 1984.

Energy efficiency

The company also began to experiment with computerised energy management systems. This was pioneering work which was followed with great interest by the Department of Energy. The initial experiment, launched in 1980, was awarded a 25 per cent grant as part of the government's newly established energy demonstration project. This was the first grant made to a retailer for an experiment of this kind. The initial results, however, were disappointing. A further trial was therefore launched using equipment designed to Sainsbury's specifications by a group of graduates from Southampton University who had formed a company called Trend. Peter Ibbotson recalled:

> We tried this new system in one store and it worked very well. We saved about 12 per cent of the energy normally consumed. I wrote a report to the board asking if we could do a limited trial at five new stores. The chairman sent for me to attend the meeting. He said, 'This is very good. If it's as good as you make it out to be why do you want to do another trial? Why shouldn't we just adopt it at every new store? If it's that good we must do it!' The three guys that ran this little company were over the moon!

In June 1984 the Hull branch was the first to open with the new system. It was so efficient that it was no longer necessary to fit boilers to provide hot water for the staff canteen, washrooms and cleaning. The result was that branches built in the mid-1980s used only 60 per cent of the energy required by those built ten years earlier. Sainsbury's energy efficiency continued to receive widespread recognition. In October 1984 Mr JD was able to describe to nearly 2,000 businessmen at a Department of Energy breakfast briefing how Sainsbury's had reduced its energy costs from nearly 1 per cent of turnover in 1980 to about 0.5 per cent in 1984. In February 1989 the Burpham branch – which was typical of all new

190

In 1984, Sainsbury's gained international recognition when it received the Food Marketing Institute of America's first award for 'The Outstanding Supermarket Chain'. The picture shows Mr JD accepting the award.

A standard 13-digit bar-code. The light and dark bars are a machine-readable number which describes the product. The first two digits identify the country in which the code was issued (50 is the code for the UK); the next five digits identify the product's manufacturer; the following five identify the product. The final number is a 'check digit' to ensure that the code has been calculated correctly.

Sainsbury's stores – was awarded the Electricity Council's prestigious Beta award for the most energy-efficient large building in Britain.

Sainsbury's also pioneered the use of 'ozone-friendly' refrigerants. Peter Cooper, the company's chief refrigeration engineer, was the retail industry's expert spokesman on the subject. He worked closely with manufacturers to develop chemicals which were totally benign and to arrange an international timetable for their installation. The first CFC-free refrigeration system was installed at Sainsbury's Swadlincote branch, in Derbyshire, in February 1994. Peter Cooper was awarded a CBE in the 1993 Queen's birthday honours, and a Citation of Excellence from the United Nations Environment Programme, for his work in this area.

Conversion to scanning

Great strides were made in the development of other forms of instore technology. As early as 1967 Mr JD had made a prediction about shopping in the future:

> . . . the checkout would be automatic; the customer would place her purchases on a moving belt and, as the products went along the belt, a code would be read from the label by the mini-computer at each checkout, which would be sufficient for this to be able to total the customer's purchases and pass the information automatically to the customer's bank, initiating the necessary transfer of funds. At the same time, it would be able to pass the information to the depot computer to calculate the order to our supplier.

This remarkable prediction was not, in fact, supernatural prescience. Work had already begun in America to develop numbered bar-codes which could be used to improve stock control and ordering. This resulted in the introduction in the United States of a standardised 12-digit Universal Product Code System that could be scanned by low-intensity lasers. This code was later superseded by a 13-digit European Article Numbering System.

The first experiments with scanning were carried out in the early 1970s by companies such as Migros and Albert Heijn in Europe and Shaw's in America (a company subsequently acquired by Sainsbury's). Although Sainsbury's monitored the trials closely it was felt that the cost of investing in these systems was not at the time justifiable in terms of improved customer service, as in 1980 only 3 per cent of products carried bar-codes. Sainsbury's estimated that this figure needed to increase to around 85 per cent before scanning systems became viable. As Jeremy Grindle, the company's departmental director for branch services and chairman of

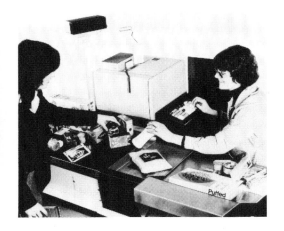

the UK Article Numbering Association, told the *JS Journal*: 'Sainsbury's is happy to be waiting – the systems are becoming more flexible . . . and getting cheaper.'

In June 1979 Sainsbury's began to experiment with computer checkouts at Broadfield, Crawley. The absence of bar-coding was overcome by marking each item with a conventional number which was laboriously punched into the till by the checkout operator. The experiment was beset by difficulties. Oliver Randall, who supervised the Broadfield installation, recorded the progress of the system in his diary. Its pages were filled with descriptions of frustrating hold-ups and equipment failures. A typical entry, for 20th June 1979, read: 'Whole system went out about 11.00am because of peculiarity in testing generator. It came back in about 5 mins after frightening the life out of all concerned.' As the equipment was American it often took several days for help to arrive.

Further trials were carried out with laser scanning systems supplied by IBM and Sweda. However, it was not until 1984 that equipment provided by the British firm ICL proved sufficiently reliable to convince Sainsbury's that full-scale conversion to scanning was worthwhile. ICL was invited to develop a scanning system that was tailored to Sainsbury's special requirements. As Mr JD recalled, 'It was crucial to judge when to jump in and adopt this new technology. It was a huge decision, but one which we got absolutely right. The fact that we were able to

The development of the computer checkout. TOP *The 'Price Look Up System' at Broadfield, Crawley, 1979.* ABOVE *An early scanner at Broadfield, 1980.* RIGHT *A checkout at Camberley, 1993, linked to a computer screen at the customer services desk. This allows checkout operators to specify what kind of assistance they require from supervisory staff.*

adopt the right system for us, and then to push ahead very fast was of tremendous benefit to us.'

On 1st October 1985 the Burpham branch was the first to open equipped with the modified system. Thereafter the new technology was rapidly introduced at all Sainsbury's stores. By 1988 more than half the branches had scanning equipment and almost 75 per cent of all the food scanned in UK supermarkets passed over Sainsbury's checkouts. All the stores had been converted to scanning by 1990. Sainsbury's early lead in scanning brought huge competitive advantage because it gave the company access to accurate information about the sales of each product. It was estimated that Sainsbury's was two and a half to three years ahead of its competitors in introducing the new technology.

Scanning allowed Sainsbury's to offer other services to its customers. In October 1983 it was the first retailer in Britain to link weighing scales to its scanning terminals. Customers were able to have their fruit and vegetables weighed and priced at the checkout, thus avoiding the inconvenience of queuing at pricing points. 'Multibuys', a form of special offer which gave customers a reduction on several similar purchases, were introduced in 1988.

Debit and credit cards

Another important customer service was the introduction of Electronic Funds Transfer at the Point of Sale (EFTPOS), which allowed customers to pay for goods by using a debit card authorising the correct sum to be paid from their current

The Queen Mother, who had never previously visited a supermarket, was given a personal guided tour of the Cromwell Road store by Mr JD on 5th March 1985. Her shopping included Easter eggs, nail polish and petit Suisse cheese.

account. This method of payment was particularly attractive to retailers as it eliminated cheque fraud while avoiding problems caused by the £50 limit on most cheque guarantee cards. In October 1988 Sainsbury's became the first important supermarket chain to commit itself to EFTPOS when it signed an agreement with the Midland Bank to accept Switch. By October 1989 Switch was accepted as a

Unit pricing was introduced on shelf-edge labelling in 1989. This 'barker card' for Beaujolais Nouveau *dates from 1993.*

debit card at all 243 Sainsbury stores which operated scanning, as well as at its 40 petrol stations. Similar agreements were subsequently made to accept all the major banks' debit cards. By 1991 EFTPOS accounted for over 25 per cent of Sainsbury's supermarket sales and had exceeded payment by cheque in popularity.

Sainsbury's was the last of the major supermarket companies to accept credit cards. This was principally because the low profit margins on food made it uneconomic to pay the handling fees charged by the credit companies. Access and Visa were, however, accepted by the company's petrol stations from April 1988. In 1991 a reduction in handling charges, and the success of EFTPOS, led Sainsbury's to reconsider its position. Since November 1991 Access and Visa have been accepted in all its stores.

New ordering systems

Advances in computer technology transformed the branch ordering systems. During the 1980s ICL System 25 mini-computers were installed at each branch and linked to the mainframe computers at head office. These enabled an integrated ordering procedure to be developed which established a link between the branches, head office and the depots. Orders were sent to head office direct from the stores and then sent on to the depots to be assembled, thus enabling the branches and depots to keep the lowest possible stock levels. From 1992 this was superseded by a new ordering system known as SABRE (SAles Based

REplenishment) which made more effective use of the point-of-sale information provided by scanning. SABRE used sales figures to create a computer calculation of the level of branch stock and to anticipate future demand. According to Joe Barnes this system enabled 'each branch to know almost hourly what its stock is, what it has ordered, when it is to be delivered and how it is selling'.

Reduced-fat products and premium meats

Technological improvements such as scanning and sales-based ordering allowed Sainsbury's to continue to respond to customer demand despite the increasing scale of the business and the ever greater range of products. The company was also able to monitor the spectacular changes in demand for some products that resulted from a combination of health concerns and changing fashions.

A good example was the decline in the consumption of milk. A generation who had believed in the health benefits of free school milk was shocked to discover that animal fats were implicated in heart disease and that milk intolerance

was one of many allergies which could affect children. Between 1982 and 1992 the nation's demand for milk fell by no less than 56 per cent. Sainsbury's milk sales, however, remained remarkably stable, as the company had anticipated the change in demand. As early as 1981 it had developed Vitapint, a reduced-fat, vitamin-enriched milk. This was the first product of its kind in Britain and a significant advance on the UHT low-fat milks prevalent at the time. Peter Davis, the company's marketing director, noted how ironic it was that 'four or five major manufacturers . . . spend millions of pounds on developing versions of pot snacks or pot noodles, [but] it takes a retailer to develop different kinds of milk'. Vitapint was the first of several different kinds of milk introduced by Sainsbury's

A group of 'healthy eating' products dating from 1986. Innovations such as low-fat milks and extra-lean meats ensured that Sainsbury's sales of these lines increased against a background of declining national consumption of products containing saturated fats.

in the early 1980s. Other healthy products included reduced-fat sausages, extra-lean mince, virtually fat-free yogurts and fruit canned in juice rather than syrup.

The movement away from animal fats also brought about profound changes in the market for fresh meats. Between 1975 and 1985 the nation's consumption of beef and veal fell by 15 per cent and that of lamb and mutton by 19 per cent. This was due to health concerns, more varied diets, fewer family meals and a growing interest in animal welfare. Consumers had also become more discerning about the quality of the meat they purchased. Sainsbury's responded to this by introducing a

Sainsbury's head beef buyer, John Cleland (on the left) and Larry Kavanagh, of Anglo Beef Processors, with Robert Wilson of Fermor Farm, Northamptonshire, a participant in the Partnership in Livestock scheme, 1993.

range of premium meats. 'Traditional' beef and 'tenderlean' lamb and pork were launched in the late 1980s. These meats were hung to improve their flavour using traditional methods. In 1991 Sainsbury's launched a 'Partnership in Livestock' scheme in which it co-operated with suppliers in improving animal husbandry and applying new technology to the production of these premium meats. This proved so successful that by 1993 over 1,500 producers were participating and traditional meats were stocked at all Sainsbury's branches. The introduction of premium meats enabled Sainsbury's to increase its sales of fresh meat against a background of declining sales nationwide.

New packaging methods contributed to the popularity of Sainsbury's meats. Sales of veal increased by almost 40 per cent in the first fortnight following the introduction of a packaging technique known as Controlled Atmosphere Packaging (CAP) in 1984. CAP was developed jointly by Sainsbury's meat buyers and Quantock Veal of Dorset. Harmless gases were used to arrest the discolouration of the meat and to prevent the formation of bacteria. This gave it a longer shelf life, not only instore but also in the customer's home. The packaging was more appealing to the customer as the meat was clearly visible in a transparent pouch. As CAP enabled accurate assessments to be made of the shelf life of a product, more information about its use could be passed on to the customer.

Supporting British suppliers

The use of integrated crop management systems by the company's suppliers allowed reductions in the use of pesticides. Here purple phacelia is planted between two grain crops to attract beneficial insects.

Whenever possible Sainsbury's attempted to support the home market by establishing relationships with British suppliers in an attempt to reduce food imports. 'We believe it our duty,' wrote Mr JD, 'to do what we can to help those at home, particularly in the light of the assistance that is given by some overseas governments to exporters in this market.' The company's commitment to British suppliers was recognised by the government in 1979 when Mr JD was appointed marketing adviser to the Minister of Agriculture, Peter Walker.

As part of its contribution to the campaign, Sainsbury's ran an annual 'Best of British' promotion each September from 1980 to 1983 and also supported the marketing organisation, Food From Britain, which had been set up by the Ministry of Agriculture, Fisheries and Food in 1982. The company was particularly proud of its support for the British pig industry through its associate company Haverhill Meat Products (renamed NewMarket Foods in 1993). By the early 1980s 75 per cent of the bacon sold by Sainsbury's was British compared with a national average of only 40 per cent.

Despite these efforts the food 'trade gap' – the amount by which the value of food imports exceeded food exports – remained a matter of concern. When

An award-winning advertisement devised for Sainsbury's by Abbott Mead Vickers in 1989.

Sainsbury's gave evidence to a House of Commons select committee on agriculture in 1992, it expressed the opinion that although the recession had led to a reduction in the food trade gap from £6 billion in 1990 to £5.4 billion in 1991, this could be reduced by a further £2.4 billion. As Mr David pointed out, the

An oil change will make your salads go even faster.

To improve your performance in the kitchen, Sainsbury's present their range of speciality oils.

Walnut, hazelnut, sesame and grapeseed.

(The days of the bland salad are definitely over.)

Our walnut oil comes from the Dordogne region of France, where it is made from the first pressing of specially selected walnuts.

Try it in a dressing for Waldorf salad, or in a vegetarian nut roast, or walnut cookies.

Our hazelnut oil, also from France, has a more delicate flavour.

As well as being ideal for sauces and vinaigrettes, it also enhances the flavour of cakes and desserts.

The sesame oil comes from the Far East and you can stir it into salad dressings but it is equally at home in

stir-frys. (Don't use too much, its flavour is full and heady.)

Grapeseed oil is just the opposite. A light, gentle oil made from the seeds of selected Italian grapes.

It is wonderful for salad dressings, baking and shallow-frying.

Sainsbury's speciality oils, although special, are very keenly priced.

Your salads may go faster, but they won't be super-charged.

Good food costs less at Sainsbury's.

A detail from a 1981 'Best of British' shelf-edge 'barker card'.

purchase of British goods made sound economic sense as 'it is in our interests to have the shortest possible supply chain'. Sainsbury's achievements in this area were impressive. By 1993, 90 per cent of the food and drink products that could be purchased at home were provided by UK suppliers.

Customers' changing tastes

There were, of course, some products that could not be purchased in Britain. Between 1971 and 1992 the number of people taking holidays abroad almost trebled, and this led to a significant increase in demand for foreign foods. Among the hundreds of lines introduced by Sainsbury's to cater for its customers' growing interest in food were pizzas and fresh pastas, German bio yogurt, extra virgin olive oil and American ice cream. French bread was also imported part-baked from France and cooked in the company's instore bakeries.

Over the years customers became increasingly willing to experiment with exotic foods. Few holidaymakers could have sampled fruits like carambolas from Malaysia, pawpaws from Brazil or horned melons from Kenya. These exotic fruits were soon forming colourful displays at the entrance to Sainsbury's stores. Primary school teachers even used the range of Sainsbury's fruit and vegetables as a practical geography lesson for their pupils.

Changes in eating habits, rising living standards and an increase in the number of working women all encouraged the development of new convenience foods. By 1992 more than half of all women aged over sixteen had jobs outside the home. Among those in the thirty-five to forty-four age group the proportion was 77 per cent. Increasingly, the preparation of foods was delegated to producers and retailers, as women followed Shirley Conran's maxim in her book *Superwoman* that 'life is too short to stuff a mushroom'!

Kathryn Cleverly won the first Sainsbury's Young Cook of Britain (later Futurecooks) competition in 1989. Her recipe for celery and orange chicken was added to the company's range of ready meals.

Many of these convenience foods were less heavily processed than those of the 1970s. Products like prepared salads and fresh sandwiches were often developed by retailers in conjunction with small specialist suppliers. These own brand products were ideal for Sainsbury's, whose integrated distribution system ensured that the cold chain remained unbroken and that highly perishable products reached the stores in perfect condition. A range of chilled ready meals launched by Sainsbury's in 1986 was highly successful. It included beef and vegetable stew, barbecue spare ribs, vegetarian chilli and lasagne verdi.

Books and other non-food lines

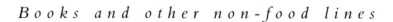

The rate of new product introductions accelerated rapidly during the 1980s. Whereas in 1985 300 lines were introduced each year, this had risen to 1,500 in 1993. Between 1980 and 1993 the total product range rose from approximately 7,000 to 17,000 while the number of own brand lines more than doubled.

Some of the most important new lines were in the area of non-foods. In November 1978 Sainsbury's launched a series of cookery books designed to encourage customers to be more adventurous in their choice of foods. The first of these was *Cooking for Christmas* by Josceline Dimbleby. Other titles included Jane Grigson's *Dishes from the Mediterranean*, Lourdes Nichols's *Cooking the Mexican Way* and Rosamond Richardson's *Vegetarian Meals*. A series of 'food guides' offered advice on the storing, cooking and serving of foods and wines. From the late 1980s encyclopaedic titles such as Oz Clark's *Book of Wine* (1987) and Josceline Dimbleby's *Cook's Companion* (1991) were added to the range.

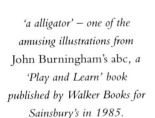

Sainsbury's controversial decision to issue a series of twenty-six children's books in 1985 raised a storm of protest from the book trade, who regarded their highly competitive prices as unfair competition. This opposition was hardly surprising as these quality books were by some of the foremost children's authors and illustrators, like John Burningham, Helen Oxenbury and Nicola Bayley. Educationalists, however, praised their addition to the Sainsbury's range as they encouraged parents to make book buying a part of their normal household shopping. Other important additions to the range of non-foods in larger branches were pot plants, cut flowers, newspapers and magazines. The latter included the own brand title *Sainsbury's The Magazine*, which was launched in 1993. Selective items of clothing from Savacentre's popular Lifestyle range were stocked in Sainsbury's stores from 1993.

'a alligator' – one of the amusing illustrations from John Burningham's abc, a 'Play and Learn' book published by Walker Books for Sainsbury's in 1985.

The most spectacular non-food success – and arguably the most ambitious – was the launch in November 1992 of a range of laundry detergents under the sub-brand of Novon. Although Sainsbury's had sold own brand detergents for nearly thirty years these had never posed a serious challenge to Proctor & Gamble's and Lever Brother's domination of the market. This was due to the huge sums spent by these companies on advertising their products and the difficulty of establishing a distinct own brand identity. As Michael Rosen, departmental director responsible for non-foods, put it, 'to say that a product was "Sainsbury's Wash and Care non-biological non-automatic powder" was too confusing and had very little relevance in the modern market place'. Novon was designed to compete directly with the established proprietary brands.

Careful consideration was given to the packaging of the new range. Stephen Gravelle, the company's chief designer, explained:

The 'J' range of own brand cosmetics was launched in 1981.

Our research found that the two main brands, Persil and Ariel, had polarised demand into two different camps. If you were to try to identify Sainsbury's image it would be much more 'Persil' than 'Ariel' – all about family values, softness and caring, rather than about getting your clothes clean through science. As our designers put together these images they became clichéd. And so, against what the research was telling us, we decided that there was more imagery in the 'Ariel' route. I like to think of Novon as the BMW of washing powders. The logo could be a washing machine tumbling or it could just be a symbol like the BMW symbol.

Novon was highly successful. An advertising campaign linked the range to the traditional qualities of Sainsbury's own brand goods: 'When you hang out your clothes, it's not just your washing on the line, it's our reputation.' By January 1994 Sainsbury's detergents had doubled their market share and were established as the fifth largest brand in the UK.

Novon laundry detergents were launched in 1992 and became the first range of own brand detergents successfully to challenge the major proprietary brands.

Service counters

The most significant change in the internal design of Sainsbury's stores in the 1980s and 1990s was in the growth of service counters. Instore bakeries and delicatessen counters became standard features of all new branches. After successful experiments with fresh fish counters at the Washington Savacentre and at Sainsbury's Lordshill branch near Southampton, they were included in many of the new stores from 1981 onwards. Cheese, loose bacon, pizzas and fresh meats were all added to the range of products sold from service counters during the late 1980s and early 1990s. Although service counters were highly labour-intensive they added to the attractiveness of the store. As Eddie Ricketts pointed out: 'There is nothing more impressive than a good bacon or cheese counter. My gut feeling as a trader tells me that's going to put money on the trade in other departments.'

The movement away from additives

The growing demand for fresh foods was linked to concern about the excessive use of additives like colourings, preservatives and flavour enhancers. The press was full of reports of alleged allergic reactions to artificial additives like monosodium glutamate and the yellow colouring tartrazine.

Both retailers and manufacturers found themselves under increasing pressure to reduce the use of additives in their products. Maurice Hanssen in his influential book, *E for Additives*, listed seventy-nine additives which he regarded as unnecessary or undesirable. He noted approvingly that supermarket companies had been more responsive than food manufacturers to demands for 'the sort of food required by the selective and well-informed customer'. From 1983 onwards Sainsbury's buyers were instructed to remove

Monastère, a naturally carbonated mineral water from the Belgian Ardennes, was launched in 1987.

201

additives wherever possible from own brand goods. Early efforts concentrated on children's food. Sainsbury's introduced colour-free ice cream, additive-free 'Mr Men' yogurts and 'High Juice' fruit squashes.

One consequence of this movement away from additives was a significant increase in the incidence of food poisoning among the population. In May 1988 scientists at the Leatherhead Food Research Association and at Bradford University discovered that the removal of preservatives had led to an increase in the level of bacteria in some products. A particularly worrying development was the appearance of new strains of listeria which could multiply on food even under refrigerated conditions. Fresh convenience foods like chilled ready meals and prepared salads were among those considered to be most at risk.

These findings were soon picked up by the media. One Sainsbury's director remarked wryly that 'reports bred faster than bacteria'. Despite reassurances that simple measures like washing salads and carefully following the instructions on ready meals would ensure their safety, the country was soon in the grip of 'listeria hysteria'. Further concern followed revelations about the widespread occurrence of salmonella in poultry products. It was even suggested that most British eggs were contaminated. Customer confidence in eggs was so badly shaken that the government had to take out advertisements in the national press reassuring the public that eggs were 'a valuable and nutritious part of a balanced diet'.

Sainsbury's responded positively to these food scares. Its team of hygiene officers carried out a meticulous inspection of the refrigerated cabinets in every store to check that foods were being kept at the correct temperature. New technology, including automatic monitoring of refrigeration equipment, was introduced to ensure the efficiency of the cold chain. To make staff more aware of their responsibilities in handling food safely, the company launched 'Operation Foodsafe', a campaign which included 40,000 employees completing a demanding training course. This was the first programme ever to be accredited by the Institution of Environmental Health Officers. The 1990 Food Safety Act imposed on all retailers standards for the handling of foodstuffs similar to those used by Sainsbury's.

An infra-red 'gun' which was developed to measure the temperature of goods displayed in Sainsbury's refrigerator cabinets, 1991.

Contributing to the public good

Sainsbury's lead in promoting improved hygiene standards in the retail trade reflected its long-standing desire to contribute to the well-being of the nation. This was an underlying theme of the company's 'objectives' published in 1986, which were headed by a pledge to 'discharge the responsibility as leaders in our

Sainsbury's has participated in many projects to improve the local environment such as this reclamation scheme in Sheffield.

trade by acting with complete integrity, by carrying out our work to the highest standards, and by contributing to the public good and to the quality of life in the community.' Other objectives laid out the company's responsibilities to customers, staff and shareholders. Behind them was a genuine sense of pride in Sainsbury's status as the nation's leading food retailer.

As a practical example of this community spirit Sainsbury's encouraged the long-term protection of the environment. A board level committee was set up to co-ordinate the company's environmental policies. A wide range of 'Environment Friendlier' products was introduced, including CFC-free aerosols, the first own brand phosphate-free detergents, and paper products made from recycled materials.

Greencare own brand cleaning products were introduced in 1989.

The 'produce' department at the West Green, Crawley, branch. When this store opened in March 1991 it was Sainsbury's 300th supermarket.

A comprehensive audit was carried out of the packaging of all own brand products in order to minimise the use of resources while ensuring that each item was adequately protected. This exercise achieved savings of over 4,000 tonnes of packaging per year.

One of the most spectacular successes was the 'Penny Back' scheme for carrier bags which was introduced in 1990. This was based on a similar programme

operated by Shaw's, Sainsbury's American subsidiary. Customers received a refund of a penny for every carrier bag they returned for re-use. Collection boxes were provided to encourage shoppers to donate the money refunded to charity. The scheme proved extremely popular with customers, who re-used over sixty million bags each year. This saved the equivalent of a thousand tonnes of plastic or over a million gallons of oil per annum.

Outstanding staff opportunities

Another of Sainsbury's company objectives was to offer staff 'outstanding opportunities in terms of personal career development and in remuneration relative to other companies in the same market'. The company's expansion depended on its ability to recruit and retain large numbers of staff and invest considerable sums in their training.

Recruitment was complicated by changes in the nation's demographic structure. The birth rate had fallen steadily between 1964 and 1977 and there were gloomy predictions of a 'demographic time bomb' with fewer young people entering the job market at a time when the number of elderly people continued to increase. The effects of this demographic change had been masked during the early 1980s by high unemployment. However, the country's economic recovery during the second half of the decade made it increasingly difficult to recruit staff. A series of measures was therefore introduced to attract more young people into the business and to appeal to other potential employees like older people.

Steps were taken to make a retail career more attractive to women. It had long been recognised that fewer women were progressing in store management than their male counterparts. In 1981, for example, women filled only a quarter of management posts although they constituted two-thirds of staff. Changes to the branch management structure in 1988 made it easier for women with family commitments to make a career with the company. It also became company policy not to expect members of management to transfer between branches more than twenty-five miles apart in order to gain promotion. A 'career bridge' scheme was introduced in 1989 which enabled employees to take a break of up to five years from work without losing status or benefits. In April 1989 all part-time staff – most of

Kellie Browne, of the Dulwich branch, examining exotic fruits as part of a product knowledge training programme in 1993.

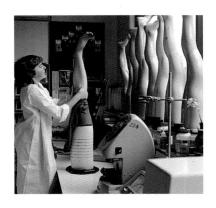

whom were women – became eligible to join the company's pension scheme.

The job of shop assistant also gained in status. Sainsbury's was keen that its staff should become 'multi-skilled' by learning to work in several different departments in the store and also to demonstrate their potential for promotion. As David Clarke, manager of the Canley branch in Coventry, put it: 'We want members of staff to take responsibility, for example by supervising a department during quieter periods. This helps them to develop and also to take a pride in their store.' In addition, members of staff were taught how to use the new instore technology. By 1993 Sainsbury's was spending £30 million a year on its training schemes. It was recognised that the changing nature of shop floor work had put new demands on

Examples of the company's rigorous quality control procedures. LEFT *Testing the strength and elasticity of stockings in Sainsbury's laboratories, c1980.* RIGHT *Measuring peppers at the Basingstoke depot, 1990.*

Late-night trading at the Cromwell Road store, London SW7. This branch, which opened in November 1983, is located on the ground floor of the former West London Air Terminal.

staff, and in 1990 a comprehensive job evaluation programme was carried out which led to average pay rises of 11 per cent for supermarket assistants.

Changes were also made to shift working. In the 1970s it had become usual for an evening shift to be employed to refill the shelves outside trading hours so as not to inconvenience customers. Until 1980 late-night opening was usually confined to Friday evening. During the 1980s it was gradually extended to other days, depending on local demand, and this made it necessary for the evening shift to begin work much later. At some of the larger branches all-night shifts were introduced. This reduced the need to replenish most departments during trading hours and meant that staff no longer needed to travel home late at night.

Extended hours and Sunday trading

One of the most important changes in the 1980s and early 1990s was the extension of trading hours. In October 1979 it had been announced that all Sainsbury's branches would open on Monday afternoons from 12 noon. Trading hours were further extended in May 1981 when it was decided that all stores would also open on Monday mornings and that closing time on Saturday was to be changed from 4pm to 6pm.

Children from the Central School at Chichester, who in 1990 became the youngest-ever winners of the youth section of Sainsbury's biennial Choir of the Year award.

A more controversial issue was Sunday trading, as over time the law had become anachronistic and open to differing interpretations. Under the terms of the 1950 Shops Act the sale of some goods – for example, fresh fruits and instant coffee – was legal. Other products, including canned fruits and fresh coffee, were prohibited. However, many of the goods sold in supermarkets in the early 1990s had simply not been available when the 1950 Shops Act was passed and were not covered by its terms. EEC regulations had made the interpretation of the law even more complex.

Sunday trading was an emotive subject. There were concerns about the protection of the rights of workers who decided not to work on Sunday and fears that small shopkeepers would be squeezed out of the market. A vigorous 'Keep Sunday Special' campaign opposed Sunday opening on religious grounds.

Sainsbury's did not at first favour Sunday trading. This was partly because of

In 1989 Lord Sainsbury of Preston Candover (Mr JD) was awarded the Albert Medal of the Royal Society of Arts, Manufactures and Commerce, in recognition of his outstanding contribution in the fields of business and the arts.

the confused state of the law, but also because the company was not convinced that there was sufficient demand to justify the expense of Sunday opening. However, the announcement by Asda and later Tesco's that their stores would be opening in the run-up to Christmas 1991 led the company to reconsider its position and open its larger branches for the remaining Sundays before Christmas. The response was overwhelming. Soon over a million customers were shopping at Sainsbury's each Sunday. George Robertson, the company's senior legal officer, recalled that 'it became apparent that the vast majority of councils were not enforcing the law, and we also knew that the government was committed to reform. In the light of this we would have been very foolish to ignore the clear demand expressed by our customers.'

Sainsbury's paid higher rates of pay for staff who worked on Sunday. It also preserved their right to decline to work on the sabbath. Along with other members of the Shopping Hours Reform Council, Sainsbury's pledged its support for Sunday opening with unlimited hours for small shops and for larger stores to open between designated hours. It was this option – one of five set out in the government's Sunday Trading Bill – that Parliament approved on 8th December 1993. On 19th January 1994 the government also committed itself to the deregulation of late-night opening.

Cherishing the family traditions

An important change at the top of the company occurred in November 1992 when Mr JD retired as chairman on his sixty-fifth birthday. He was succeeded by his cousin, Mr David. Mr JD had presided over Sainsbury's during the most spectacular period of growth in its history. In 1969 it had been a medium sized regional grocery chain with a 2.5 per cent share of the market and profits of £4.3 million. By 1992 it was a national retailer serving over 10 per cent of the British market and earning profits of £628 million. Mr David, in the company's *Report and Accounts* for 1993, wrote that Mr JD's 'greatest achievement . . . was to anticipate unerringly the rapidly changing needs of customers and to set new standards of quality and efficiency both for the company and for the whole food retailing industry'.

Mr JD had motivated and inspired an entire generation of Sainsbury's employees. His energy and vitality were admired both within Sainsbury's and throughout the country, and had been recognised by numerous accolades. The most important of these were his elevation to the peerage in 1989 and his creation as a Knight of the Garter in 1992.

"Hello, Sainsbury's? Do you sell dog food for naughty puppies? No? Well, I certainly don't blame you. Thankyou Sainsbury's, and goodbye."

Many could recall how his enthusiasm had been expressed with passion. Yet, as Sir Roy Griffiths explained in his speech at a dinner in 1991 to mark Mr JD's forty years of service, 'the dominant impression which one has in any work with him is of the driving, obsessive commitment to ensuring that the customer is well served . . . He has always taken the view that the prerequisite of any corporate greatness is quality – quality of product, quality of service. Nothing, but nothing must get in the way . . . No senior member of a family ever cherished the family traditions more closely. No Roman ever guarded the household gods more zealously and no chairman has ever looked after the corporate values so committedly, and nothing has been too much, no generosity too great for people who serve the customer, and by definition the company well.'

Long-term strength

Mr David, in an interview for the *JS Journal*, made it clear that there would be no 'cabinet reshuffle' as a result of the change in chairmanship: 'We share very similar views on the direction of the business and very similar values. We have a clear strategy and I have been involved in developing that strategy . . . I believe very strongly in the traditional values of the business, but I think you have to innovate all the time to keep up to date.' In his address to the shareholders at the 1993 annual general meeting Mr David outlined Sainsbury's future business strategy:

The Calais off-licence, which opened in 1994. This store enables cross-Channel shoppers to take advantage of the lower rates of duty payable on alcoholic drinks in France.

> Firstly, the greatest strength of our business is the value for money provided by the Sainsbury brand. We will ensure that we enhance this value by improving both our price competitiveness and quality, and broadening our appeal. Secondly, we will continue to pursue further improvements in customer service and operating efficiency. We seek to achieve a virtuous circle of higher productivity leading in turn to lower prices, leading in turn to higher sales. Thirdly, we will continue to invest substantial sums in new stores, new systems and new skills for our staff. We will maintain a consistent opening programme for new Sainsbury stores. We will invest wisely. We are as concerned to achieve efficiency in our use of capital as in any other resource. Finally, we are intent on successfully expanding the activities of our subsidiaries and raising their financial performance to the levels achieved by the main Sainsbury business.

Sainsbury's continued to be optimistic about its role in the future of British retailing. This was despite the pessimism of many analysts – and other retailers – who believed that the food market was becoming saturated. Sainsbury's confidence was based on its policy of store development. Whereas many of its competitors still relied on numerous older small and inefficient shops, Sainsbury's had pursued a rigorous policy of store replacement and modernisation. This meant that

Mr David behind the newly redesigned delicatessen counter at the Cromwell Road branch in 1994.

although it had fewer branches than its competitors – the 300th supermarket milestone was only passed with the opening of the store at West Green, Crawley, in March 1991 – they were newer and more profitable. As Mr David explained to shareholders at the company's 1993 annual general meeting: 'Saturation is not about whether there are enough stores or not. Saturation equals an end to innovation and improved service.'

The following year Mr David told senior managers, when announcing profits before accounting changes of £732 million and an increase in Sainsbury's market share to 11.4 per cent, that as 'the leaders of our industry, we are highly profitable and we are investing heavily in excellent opportunities. There is every reason for us to be enthusiastic about the future and confident about progress.'

Sainsbury's retained the traditional values that had served it so well throughout its history. The same pragmatic approach to short-term challenges – which before its public flotation had enabled it to 'take the long view' – still remained. 'We must never,' said Mr David, 'place short-term profitability ahead of the long-term strength of the business.' These are sentiments John James and Mary Ann would have appreciated when they founded their little dairy shop 125 years ago.

The new businesses

During the 1970s Sainsbury's made a strategic decision to broaden the company's base by diversifying into other retail sectors. This decision was taken at a time when a combination of economic instability and the government's discriminatory attitude to food retailing threatened to curb the growth of the core business. These retail subsidiaries were to become far more than an 'insurance policy' as each business drew upon the skills and strengths of other members of the Group, while also developing a distinctive character of its own.

In 1994 the Merton Savacentre won praise from the Landscape Foundation for its 'harmony with nature'.

Savacentre

In 1970 Mr JD, who had been impressed by the trading methods and huge success of French hypermarkets, floated the idea of creating Britain's first specialist hypermarket chain with the chairman of British Home Stores (BhS). These talks came to fruition when the two companies formed Savacentre on 25th April 1975. Their combined expertise was described by the *Financial Times* as 'formidable', with BhS's experience in non-foods and clothing complementing Sainsbury's traditional strengths in fresh foods.

The term hypermarket described any retail outlet of over 50,000 square feet which offered a complete range of food, hardware, clothing and electrical goods. At the time Savacentre was formed, there were only three stores of this type in the whole of Britain, all of which were operated by Carrefour, a British company in which the French chain of the same name had a minority interest. The first of these had opened in Caerphilly in September 1972. The slow development of hypermarkets in Britain was due to strict planning regulations whereby all stores over 50,000 square feet had to be approved by the Department of the Environment even if the local planning authority supported the application.

Savacentre was more than a marriage of two of Britain's most successful retailers. It was decided that the new hypermarkets should offer not only the complete range of lines sold by Sainsbury's and BhS but also electrical goods like refrigerators, washing machines, freezers, audio equipment and televisions.

The first Savacentre opened at Washington, Tyne and Wear, on 15th November 1977. The store featured counters for fresh fish and delicatessen, an instore bakery, a 380-seat self-service restaurant and 35,000 square feet devoted to textiles, electrical goods and hardware. There were several concessions, including a

Some of the 36 checkouts at the first Savacentre hypermarket at Washington, Tyne and Wear, which opened on 15th November 1977.

tobacconist, an ice cream parlour and a newsagent. The Washington Savacentre was the first British retail store to rely on a computer for all its management information. Each of the thirty-six checkouts was linked to an NCR mini-computer which in turn was connected to a larger central computer. By March 1980 two further Savacentres had opened, at Hempstead in Kent and at Basildon in Essex. Mr JD was able to report enthusiastically to shareholders in that year's *Report and Accounts*: 'These [stores] have outstripped our most optimistic forecasts. The volume of trade being achieved by the first two hypermarkets has caused us to review the systems necessary to handle an intensity of sales per square foot that is rarely achieved in hypermarkets anywhere in the world.'

The number of Savacentres grew slowly during the 1980s as it was recognised that there was much to learn in the development of such an important new venture. Moreover, both parent companies saw plenty of investment opportunities for expanding their core businesses. It was not until October 1993 that the tenth Savacentre opened at Beckton in East London.

In March 1989 Sainsbury's bought out BhS's 50 per cent share of the partnership and Savacentre became a wholly owned subsidiary. This was a logical step as food accounted for about 75 per cent of Savacentre's turnover. In order to ensure continuity while the company built up expertise in buying clothing, a five-year agreement was made with BhS to supply Savacentre with textiles and other non-food lines. BhS's products were gradually phased out following the launch of the Sainsbury's 'Lifestyle' range of own brand clothing in 1991. The latter proved so successful that fast-selling lines like leggings and polonecks were added to the range of the largest Sainsbury's supermarkets.

Talks with Iran

While setting up Savacentre in the early 1970s Sainsbury's was also involved in talks with the Iranian government. These were initiated at the suggestion of the company's merchant bankers. Iran was keen to use some of its massive oil revenues to purchase British equipment and know-how in order to modernise its underdeveloped economy. A four man team from the company led by Gurth Hoyer Millar was sent out to Iran to assess the feasibility of setting up a supermarket chain with centralised distribution and meat packing units. However, after careful evaluation Sainsbury's eventually rejected the proposal to set up a joint

British/Iranian company. 'It became apparent,' recalled Mr JD, 'that not only were the trading circumstances in Iran very different from our own, but that success would depend upon the Iranian government's goodwill and assistance. This was an authoritarian regime which could change its mind about its will-

In the 1980s Sainsbury's operated a small export business. Arabic labels, such as the one above, were used for goods destined for the Middle East.

ingness to grant import licences at any moment. We realised that such an arrangement was not for us.' This turned out to be a fortuitous decision, as the Shah's regime was overthrown by Islamic fundamentalists in 1979. As Mr JD remarked: 'In retrospect the consequences could have been far worse than we anticipated. In the light of what happened subsequently, we were wiser than we realised!'

Homebase

In October 1979 Sainsbury's announced that it had formed a joint company with the Belgian retailer GB–Inno–BM (GIB) to set up a chain of house and garden DIY stores; Sainsbury's held a 75 per cent controlling interest and GIB the other 25 per cent. GIB had sixty 'Brico' stores in Belgium as well as interests in the DIY trade in Germany, Holland and America. The new company, which was given the name 'Homebase', was therefore able to combine this international expertise with Sainsbury's experience of British retailing. The setting up of Homebase represented Sainsbury's first venture – apart from John James's Lewisham drapery shop in 1902 – into a retail business totally unrelated to food.

An interior view of the first Homebase store at Purley Way, Croydon, in 1981.

The first Homebase store opened at Purley Way, Croydon, on 3rd April 1981. It was advertised as offering 'everything needed to build and fit out a modern house from a spade with which to dig the foundations through to cement, bricks, doors, washbasins, . . . paint and curtain rails to a lampshade to hang in the completed room'. A special demonstration house was erected in the centre of the store to illustrate how many of the products sold were used in house construction and building. The store received a fantastic response from the public. On the first Saturday the police had to temporarily close the store as the crowds flocking to visit it had caused traffic jams on the surrounding roads! In the first two weeks of trading, over 60,000 people passed through its doors.

Sainsbury's influence was apparent in the trading policy of Homebase, which drew heavily on the company's traditional strengths in providing information and

The Hull Homebase, which opened in June 1984, was one of many to be located adjacent to a Sainsbury's supermarket.

a high standard of service for its customers. These were not characteristics for which other DIY companies were well known. Among the facilities provided at Homebase stores were free leaflets, instore display panels and a series of simple but informative books. The staff were also trained to offer advice to customers on the use of products and on how to deal with simple DIY enquiries.

The launch of Homebase was viewed with scepticism by some city analysts who believed that the market for DIY was already saturated. In the event the DIY market proved to be one of the major growth sectors of the 1980s as it benefited from the government's policy of encouraging home ownership. By the time Homebase opened its 50th store in Norwich, in April 1989, it was the nation's fourth largest DIY retailer in terms of sales, although it was still some way behind

Texas, Do-It-All and B&Q. Homebase's particular strength was its high sales per square foot, which were equal to those of the market leader, B&Q. Homebase continued to perform well despite the recession in the DIY market caused by the slump in house prices in the early 1990s. 'Homebase has an exciting future,' said Dino Adriano, who succeeded Gurth Hoyer Millar as chairman in December 1991. 'We shall be expanding the business at a faster rate in the future and expect our portfolio to have increased from over 80 stores at the end of 1994 to between 150 and 200 within ten years.'

Shaw's: the New England subsidiary

It was also during the 1980s that Sainsbury's established a presence in the American food retail sector. In 1977 the company had made a strategic decision to move into the United States market as it was felt that Sainsbury's trading style was better suited to American conditions than to those prevailing in Europe. It was decided to acquire a minority interest in a US company in order to learn more about American food retailing before purchasing a controlling interest. Consultants were employed to help in the search for a suitable supermarket company.

Shaw's was founded in 1860 by George C Shaw of Portland, Maine. This photograph shows an early branch at Congress Street, Portland, in c1900.

One company that had already caught Sainsbury's eye was the New England supermarket chain of Shaw's. Shaw's had played a pioneering role in the application of retailing technology and had begun experiments with scanning as early as 1974. In 1978, Jeremy Grindle, in a report to Sainsbury's board on the use of scanning in the United States, had described a trip to Shaw's as 'the most convincing retailer visit of all we made'. In November 1983 Sainsbury's obtained a 21.2 per cent share in Shaw's. This stake was increased by a further 7.3 per cent in 1986 and 20.9 per cent in 1987, by which time Sainsbury's had a controlling interest in the company. On 1st July 1987 full control was gained when a tender of $184.4m was accepted for the remaining equity.

Sainsbury's was attracted to Shaw's because its background and culture were similar to its own. At the time of acquisition the company had been run for almost a century by the Davis family in a regional trading area centred on the three New England states of Massachusetts, New Hampshire and Maine. Shaw's long-established advertising slogan 'Everyday Low Price' emphasised quality and value for money in opposition to gimmicks like stamps, coupons and short-term

The Shaw's supermarket at Carver, Massachusetts, 1991.

An example of a Shaw's own brand product dating from 1990.

promotions. It also had an excellent reputation for fresh foods, backed by an efficient central distribution and ordering system. When Sainsbury's first invested in Shaw's in 1983 the company had forty-one stores. By 1994 this had increased to eighty-six stores. During the same period both sales and profits doubled.

Sainsbury's worked closely with Shaw's management in the development of the company. A good example of this was the introduction of the Shaw's brand. Although own brands had been used by American supermarkets in the past, most consumers regarded them as cheap and inferior substitutes for proprietary products. In September 1990, a new Shaw's brand was launched which drew jointly on Sainsbury's quality control and buying methods and upon Shaw's reputation. The Shaw's 'quality seal', displayed on all its own brand products, together with the adoption of the slogan 'good food costs less' closely mirrored Sainsbury's own marketing policies. By 1994 Shaw's own brand range had grown to around 1,400 lines.

Shaw's potential for future expansion, like those of the two other retail subsidiaries, was particularly important at a time of increased competitiveness in the core business. As Mr David explained in early 1994: 'The figures suggest that no one initiative will provide us with all the expansion opportunities we require. We will need a package of development opportunities, and the obvious place to start is with the subsidiaries . . . Savacentre, Homebase and Shaw's are all important and exciting businesses. In future we will be looking to them to provide a greater proportion of our growth.'

217

Acknowledgements

A book of this kind is dependent upon the support of many people, and it would be invidious to name the individual employees of the Sainsbury Group who have provided advice and information: I hope that they will feel that the finished product adequately reflects their help. Similarly, over the years dozens of Sainsbury's Veterans have added to my knowledge of the company's history; the names listed below include many people who have been repeatedly 'tapped' for their knowledge. Particular thanks are due to the following customers, former Sainsbury's employees and other advisors.

Lord Sainsbury of Drury Lane (Mr Alan); Sir Robert Sainsbury (Mr RJ); Mr Simon Sainsbury; The Hon Mr Timothy Sainsbury MP; the late Sir Roy Griffiths; Mr J H G Barnes; Mr I Barratt; Mr H P Bell; Mr C Blow; Miss M Blow; Mr K Boston; Major W R H Browne; Mrs D Challis; Mr S Cody; Mr A M Cole; Mr K Curtis; Mrs M Farrell; Mr and Mrs A Gorham; Mr J Green; Mr F Hall; Mr G Harrison; Mr L Holmes; Mr J Jones; Mr and Mrs G Lambert; Mr F McManus; Mr J Maunder; Mr D Maunder; Mr F Nash; Mr E Nicholls; Mr A Rickman; Mr and Mrs G Ridgway; Mr C Roberts; Mr J Russell; Mr D Salisbury; Mr R Topp; Mr A Waller; Mr J L Woods.

I am particularly indebted to two people. Lord Sainsbury of Preston Candover (Mr JD), whose support and encouragement have been invaluable. It has been a rare privilege to work with Mr JD, to draw upon over forty years of experience of the company and of the trade, and to benefit from his knowledge and enthusiasm. The other debt is to Nick Salmon. Only he knows how much I owe to him.

PICTURE CREDITS

p17 Camden Local Studies and Archives Centre; p19 Mrs Sophie Jones; p22 Mr H Goshawk; p34 Lloyd Maunder Ltd; p45 (top right) Museum of London; p38 Mrs L Lumber; p52 Mr Alan Stevens; p57 Miss G Harrison; p64 (top) Mrs R A Stemp; p67 British Pathé News Ltd; p71 Mrs J Swift; p83 Mr K Boston; p86 (bottom right) Robert Opie; p103 South London Industrial Mission, Christchurch, Blackfriars; p118 Mrs J Wallace; p147 Nesta Macdonald; pp153, 209 *Punch*; p155 David Steen; p160 *Evening Standard*; p186 *Sunday Times*/Michael Ward; p197 Holt Studios/Nigel Cattlin; p200 John Burningham; p211 *Independent*/Edward Webb. All other images are from Sainsbury's Archives.

Some Key Statistics

The Group since Sainsbury's flotation

Date	Sainsbury's sales[1] £m	store nos	Savacentre sales[2] £m	store nos	Homebase sales[3] £m	store nos	Shaw's sales[4] $bn	stores nos	Group sales £m	pre-tax profits	Market share[5]
1974	362	198	–	–	–	–	–	–	362	13.6	3.0%
1979	1,007	224	26	2	–	–	–	–	1,007	32.6	5.0%
1984	2,647	262	201	5	40	14	812	–	2,689	130.0	7.1%
1989	4,903	292	299	7	180	48	1463	61	5,915	375.1	9.0%
1994	8,865	341	659	10	328	76	1970	87	11,224	777.0[6]	11.4%

1. Sales figures, except those for Shaw's for 1984, are VAT and sales tax inclusive.
2. 50% associate from December 1975 with BhS, until March 1989 when Sainsbury's gained 100% ownership. Sales figures excluded from group sales in 1979, 1984 and 1989.
3. 75% subsidiary since 1979.
4. Sainsbury's acquired 20.02% interest in 1983 and the balance in 1987–8. Sales figures for 1984 are excluded from group sales and are exclusive of sales taxes.
5. Share of UK trade in food and drink shops, chemists, confectioners, tobacconists and newsagents. Figures include Savacentre food sales.
6. Before accounting changes and exceptional costs.

Sainsbury's Portfolio 1869–1994

Figures marked ★ are estimates

Date[1]	No of branches	Turnover £m	New stores' average sales area sq ft	approx no products sold	no of employees	no of customer visits ,000s
1870	1	–	★500	5[2]	2[3]	–
1880	3	–	★500	★10	★9	–
1890	16	–	★1,000	★50	★180	–
1900	47	–	★1,000	130	★950	–
1910	109	2.4[4]	★1,000	200	★2,000	–
1920	124	5.0	★1,500	400	2,800	25[5]
1930	189	9.9	★1,750	500	6,500	–
1940	249	12.0	★2,000	600	8,500	2,50[6]
1950	244	15.8	★2,000	550	8,500	–
1955	255	38.0	3,300	700	10,000	–
1960	256	68.0	5,800	2,000	15,000	★1,000
1965	254	101.1	6,700	2,500	18,000	★1,250
1970	225	187.5	10,200	4,000	32,000	★2,000
1975	201	452.8	17,700	5,000	31,100	★3,000
1980	231	1,226.6	14,800	7,000	37,300	4,000
1985	271	3,070.5	26,000	9,000	60,400	6,000
1990	291	5,644.8	32,300	14,000	75,500	6,750
1994	341	8,864.6	30,200	19,000	93,500	8,000

1. All figures relate to Sainsbury's financial year, exclusive of subsidiaries.
2. Based on 3 products: butter, milk and eggs.
3. ie John James and Mary Ann Sainsbury.
4. Figure relates to 1912, which is the earliest year for which records are available.
5. Based on a 1915 reference to serving '10,000 customers daily'.
6. Number of customers holding accounts with Sainsbury's in 1939.

John James
b1844 d1928
Founder of Sainsbury's 1869
Company service 1869–1928
Chairman and Governing Director 1922

Mary Ann
b1849 (née Staples) d1927
Founder of Sainsbury's 1869
Company service 1869–1870's

John Benjamin
b1871 d1956
Company service 1885–1956
Partner 1915
Director 1922
Chairman 1928

George
b1872 d1964
Company service c1886–c1915
Responsible for accounts and some provision buying

Frank
b1877 d1955
Company service mid 1890s–1898
(From 1902 a major supplier of pig meat, poultry and eggs to Sainsbury's)

Arthur
b1880 d1962
Company service late 1890s–1929
Director 1922
Responsible for provision buying and supervision of factory

Alfred
b1884 d1965
Company service 1906–1941
Director 1922
Responsible for grocery and canned goods buying

Paul
b1890 d1982
Company service 1921–1938
Responsible for building development

Alan
b 1902
Company service 1921–
Director 1933
Joint General Manager, Trading 1938
Chairman 1956
President 1967
Created Baron Sainsbury of Drury Lane 1962

Robert
b1906
Company service 1930–
Driector 1934
Joint General Manager, Personnel and Administration 1938
Chairman 1967
President 1969
Knighted 1967

James
b1909 d1984
Company service 1926–1974
Director 1941
Awarded CBE 1960
Responsible for establishment of 1936 factory, and for setting up Haverhill Meat Products 1958

John D
b1927
Company service 1950–
Director 1958
Vice-chairman 1967
Chairman and Chief Executive 1969
Knighted 1980
Created Baron Sainsbury of Preston Candover 1989
Created Knight of the Garter 1992
President 1992

Simon
b1930
Company service 1956–1979
Director, Financial Policy and Personnel 1959
Deputy Chairman 1969

Timothy
b1932
Company service 1956–1983
Director, Estates, Architects and Engineers 1962
Elected MP for Hove 1973
Held various government posts 1983–94, including Minister for Trade and Minister for Industry

David
b1940
Company service 1963–
Director 1966
Director and Financial Controller 1971
Finance Director 1973–1990
Deputy Chairman 1988
Chairman and Chief Executive 1992

Sainsbury's Directors

The following is a list of directors from the firm's incorporation in 1922 until 1994.

John James Sainsbury joint founder, with his wife, of Sainsbury's in 1869; chairman and governing director on the firm's incorporation in 1922; died in office 1928.

John Benjamin Sainsbury (Mr John) joined the firm in 1885; partner 1915; director 1922; chairman and governing director 1928; died in office 1956.

Arthur Sainsbury (Mr Arthur) joined the firm in the late 1890s; director 1922; retired 1929.

Alfred Sainsbury (Mr Alfred) joined the firm in 1906; director 1922; retired 1941.

Alan Sainsbury (Mr Alan) joined the firm in 1921; director 1933; joint general manager, trading 1938–62; chairman 1956–67; created a life peer as Baron Sainsbury of Drury Lane in 1962; became a life president of the company on his retirement in 1967.

Robert Sainsbury (Mr RJ) joined the company in 1930; company secretary 1931–38; director 1934; joint general manager, personnel and administration 1938–62; deputy chairman 1956; chairman 1967–69; knighted for services to the arts 1967; became a life president of the company on his retirement in 1969.

James Sainsbury (Mr James) joined the company in 1926; responsible for the company's production of cooked meats and for bacon and cheese buying; supervised the Blackfriars factory from its construction in 1934–6 to its closure in 1972; director 1941; first chairman of Haverhill Meat Products 1969–74; awarded CBE for services to the pig industry 1960; retired 1974.

F W Salisbury joined the company in 1914 as a junior clerk; personal assistant to Mr John 1928; assistant general manager 1938; director, 1941, responsible for estates and building development, poultry and fresh meat buying, also for Sainsbury's farms from 1944; retired in 1962 but continued as an 'advisory director' until 1965.

N C Turner joined the company in 1935 as an actuary; company secretary 1938–67; director, 1945, with responsibility to Mr RJ Sainsbury for branch and head office administration, also for distribution; retired in 1967 but continued as an 'advisory director' until 1969.

John D Sainsbury (Mr JD) joined the company in 1950; director 1958; vice-chairman and head of trading 1967; chairman 1969–92; knighted for services to the food industry 1980; created a life peer as Baron Sainsbury of Preston Candover 1989; created Knight of the Garter 1992; became a life president of the company on his retirement in 1992.

Simon Sainsbury (Mr Simon) joined the company in 1956; director, 1959, responsible for financial policy and personnel; deputy chairman 1969–79; chairman, Haverhill Meat Products, 1975–79; retired 1979.

W J Justice joined the company in 1930 as a junior clerk; assumed responsibility for meat trading from 1952; director, 1959, responsible for poultry, meat and egg departments; retired 1973.

Timothy Sainsbury (Mr Timothy) joined the company in 1956; director, 1962, responsible for estates, architects and engineers; elected MP for Hove 1973; retired from executive duties in 1974 but continued as a non-executive director until 1983; between 1983 and 1994 held a number of posts in the Government, resigning from the position of Minister for Industry in 1994.

B T Ramm joined the company in 1949 as chief statistician; director, 1962, responsible for the statistical and data processing departments; retired 1979.

A S Trask joined the company in 1942 as a clerk in the sales office; assumed responsibility for the bacon department 1958; director, 1965, responsible for provisions, off-licence and frozen foods; retired from executive duties in 1973 but continued as a consultant until 1974.

David J Sainsbury (Mr David) joined the company in 1963; director 1966; financial controller 1971; finance director 1973–90; chairman, Savacentre, 1984–93; deputy chairman of Sainsbury's 1988; chairman 1992; deputy chairman, Shaw's, 1987–91, chairman, Shaw's 1993.

G C Hoyer Millar joined the company in 1964; director, 1967, responsible for distribution; development director 1974–88; chairman, Homebase, 1979–91; retired in 1988 but continued as an non-executive director until 1991.

E R Griffiths joined the company in 1968; director of personnel and administration 1969; deputy chairman 1975–88; managing director 1978–88; knighted for services to the National Health Service, 1985; chairman of Haverhill Meat Products 1979–90; retired from executive duties in 1988 but continued as a non-executive director until 1991.

J H G Barnes joined the company in 1956 as an accountant; director, 1969, buying and marketing; director responsible for the retail division 1977–90; assistant managing director, retail, 1986; joint managing director, trading, 1988–1990; deputy chairman, Homebase, 1990–93; retired as an executive director in 1990 but continued as a non-executive director until 1993.

P A Snow joined the company in 1939 as a junior salesman; director, store operations, 1969; retired 1977.

L S Payne joined the company in 1974 as distribution director; assumed responsibility for company systems 1979; retired 1986.

C Roberts joined the company in 1958; departmental director of the grocery division 1973; joint marketing director 1975–77; trading director 1977; subsequently responsible for buying in most product areas, including meat, dairy, produce, frozen foods, bakery and off-licence; retired 1993.

P J Davis joined the company in 1976; director of marketing and non-foods 1977; assistant managing director, buying and marketing, 1979; resigned 1986.

R A Ingham joined the company in 1952 on one of its first graduate training programmes; departmental director, dairy department, with additional responsibilities for the bakery and off-licence departments, 1971; director of dairy, wines and spirit departments, 1977; retired 1988.

R T Vyner joined the company in 1978 as director responsible for grocery and non-foods buying; assistant managing director, buying and marketing, 1986; joint managing director 1990; deputy chairman 1992; chairman, Savacentre, 1993.

R A Clark joined the company in 1966; director for personnel and data processing 1979–88; subsequently responsible for distribution, data processing and information systems; chairman, Haverhill Meat Products, 1990 (renamed NewMarket Foods in 1993).

D E Henson joined the company in 1979 as director responsible for financial control; finance director 1990; retired 1992.

Sir James Spooner was appointed as the company's first external non-executive director in 1981; inter alia a director of John Swire & Sons, Barclays Bank and Morgan Crucible (chairman); retired 1994.

Dame Jennifer Jenkins was appointed a non-executive director in 1981; chairman of the Consumers' Association 1965–79; chairman of the Historic Buildings Council for England 1975–85; retired 1986.

D A Quarmby joined the company in 1984 as director of distribution; joint managing director with responsibility for non-trading functions 1988; assumed overall responsibility for operations in 1990; deputy chairman, Shaw's 1991–3.

The Rt Hon Lord Prior PC was appointed a non-executive director in 1985; Privy Counsellor since 1970; Minister of Agriculture 1970–72; Lord President of the Council and Leader of the House of Commons 1972–4; Secretary of State for Employment 1979–81; Secretary of State for Northern Ireland 1981–84; created a life peer as Lord Prior of Brampton 1987; chairman of GEC plc and a director of a number of other companies; retired 1992.

K C Worrall joined the company in 1953; departmental director, frozen foods and dairy buying, 1981–83; departmental director, meat and poultry buying, 1983–86; director for grocery and non-foods buying 1986; non-executive director 1994.

Lady Eccles of Moulton was appointed a non-executive director in 1986; chairman of Ealing Health Authority; vice-chairman of Durham University Council and of the National Council for Voluntary Organisations; director of Tyne-Tees Television and a number of other companies.

I D Coull joined the company in 1988 as director of the development division; deputy chairman, Homebase, 1993; has lead responsibility for environmental issues.

R Cooper joined the company in 1975; departmental director, poultry and meat buying, 1986; director for meat, pork products, bakery and delicatessen and scientific services 1988; director for meat, fresh fish, off-licence, dairy and frozen foods buying 1992.

C I Harvey joined the company in 1958 as a tradesman; area director 1983; director responsible for the retail division 1989.

J E Adshead joined the company in 1989 as personnel director; also responsible for group secretary's department and from 1994 for information technology.

D B Adriano joined the company in 1964 as an accountant; general manager, Homebase, 1981; area director 1986; managing director, Homebase, 1989; appointed to Sainsbury's board 1990; chairman and managing director, Homebase, 1991; deputy chairman, Shaw's, 1993.

R P Whitbread joined the company in 1969 as a retail management trainee; departmental director, marketing, 1983; departmental director, produce buying, 1985; area director 1989; marketing director 1990; director for grocery and non-foods buying 1994.

R P Thorne joined the company as finance director in 1992.

Sir Terence Heiser was appointed a non-executive director in 1992; permanent secretary, Department of the Environment, 1985–92; also a non-executive director of Abbey National, Smith New Court and Wessex Water.

D J Clapham joined the company in 1964; area director 1982; departmental director, branch operations, 1987; managing director, Savacentre, 1989–93; appointed to the board as director for produce, bakery, pork and delicatessen buying 1992.

Dr J M Ashworth was appointed a non-executive director in 1993; also director of the London School of Economics.

I J Hunt joined the company in 1971 as head of statistical services; departmental director for marketing services 1987; marketing director 1994.

Index